AMERICAN
NATURE
WRITING
1996

AMERICAN
NATURE
WRITING
1996

Selected by John A. Murray

SIERRA CLUB BOOKS
San Francisco

The Sierra Club, founded in 1892 by John Muir, has devoted itself to the study and protection of the earth's scenic and ecological resources—mountains, wetlands, woodlands, wild shores and rivers, deserts and plains. The publishing program of the Sierra Club offers books to the public as a nonprofit educational service in the hope that they may enlarge the public's understanding of the Club's basic concerns. The point of view expressed in each book, however, does not necessarily represent that of the Club. The Sierra Club has some sixty chapters coast to coast, in Canada, Hawaii, and Alaska. For information about how you may participate in its programs to preserve wilderness and the quality of life, please address inquiries to Sierra Club, 730 Polk Street, San Francisco, CA 94109.

ISBN: 0-87156-389-4
ISSN: 1072-4723

Production by Robin Rockey
Cover and book design by Amy Evans
Composition by Wilsted & Taylor

Printed in the United States of America on acid-free paper containing a minimum of 50% recovered waste paper, of which at least 10% of the fiber content is post-consumer waste.

10   9   8   7   6   5   4   3   2   1

For Al Gore

Who is making a difference

Familiarity with the natural world informed great writing of the past, as any sample from Dante, Chaucer, and Shakespeare can demonstrate. If attention to the world—in the ants and the sparrows, to the stone and the dust at our feet—can return us to the human predicament with renewed insight, then so much the better. But let us insist on veracity, or real knowledge, on truth, as it can only be discovered by men and women as they go about their lives from hour to hour, from day to day, and from season to season. John Haines

Nature writing, too, at its best, is not the news about condors hatched in captivity or numbers of endangered species. Like any other literature, its job is to question what we're doing in this world. Certainly, at a time when the health and very survival of the Earth are in jeopardy, it makes sense for writers to be asking, What are our relationships to the land, to our particular places? What are our responsibilities to Nature, other creatures, other cultures? Today in America, some of the most thoughtful and creative literature comes to us as nature writing. Nancy Lord

When the human condition changes, art must change. Indeed, art should lead a change in perception that will help people to recognize and confront the new condition. To a degree, art has done this with the present shift. As far back as the late eighteenth century, early romantic poetry and painting brought the living Earth forward from its traditional Western role as a backdrop for the human drama and made it an actor, an ethical being worthy of consideration in its own right. Later, romanticism obscured this perception, but it continued in the prose tradition of nature writing (for a lack of a better term), which synthesized early romantic feeling about the living Earth with scientific knowledge and philosophical thinking. Nature writing as practiced by William Bartram, Thoreau, Muir, Eiseley, Leopold, and Carson has inaugurated a change in perception. David Rains Wallace

———

These three quotations come from a symposium on nature writing edited by John A. Murray that appeared in *Manoa: A Pacific Journal of International Writing,* Fall, 1992.

Contents

Preface

> *There is a pleasure in the pathless woods,*
> *There is a rapture on the lonely shore,*
> *There is society where none intrudes,*
> *By the deep sea, and music in its roar:*
> *I love not Man the less, but Nature more,*
> *From these our interviews, in which I steal*
> *From all I may be, or have been before,*
> *To mingle with the Universe, and feel*
> *What I can ne'er express, yet can not all conceal.*
>
> Byron

For the third year, Sierra Club Books is providing readers with a collection that celebrates some of the finest nature writing of the previous twelve months. To those who helped ensure the success of the first two volumes—readers, reviewers, booksellers, nature aficionados—I give heartfelt thanks. As always, I have endeavored to bring a diversity of styles, voices, themes, and points of view into the fold, to create a literary ecosystem, as it were, with all the beauty and wildness of nature. The standard for inclusion has been a strong natural content and singular literary achievement. As in earlier volumes, selections by women are alternated evenly with those by men, to create a natural rhythm that will hopefully add to your reading pleasure.

The call for contributions made in the 1994 and 1995 volumes has also been successful. In this volume, the following authors, previously unknown to me, submitted their work for consideration: James Kilgo ("Open House"), Jan Grover ("Cutover"), Adrienne Ross ("Return of the Falcons"), Judith Larner Lowry ("Gardening at the Seam"), Rosalie Sanara Petrouske ("The Root of the Universe"), Jennifer Ackerman ("The Great Salt Marsh"), Marcia Bonta ("October"), Marybeth S. Holleman ("Awakening"), Kate Boyes ("Confluence"), and Deborah Tall ("Dwelling"). To all others—over one hundred—who sent submissions, I extend my deepest appreciation for your willingness to participate in this annual. Please keep sending materials to me for consideration, care of Sierra Club Books, 100 Bush Street, 13th Floor, San Francisco, California 94104.

We all benefit from hearing new voices, and I am particularly interested in nature writing (that is, writings of any genre with a strong natural content) from the following groups: (1) writers known only locally or regionally but with national potential, (2) writers from the Midwest, Northeast, and Deep South, (3) writers with experiences in nature abroad, (4) writers from ethnic groups offering alternative perspectives on nature (such as African American, Asian American, Hispanic American, and Native American). Working together— readers and editor—we can build anthologies in the future that, like this one, hold both literary excellence and thematic and stylistic diversity as the standard.

I have many thanks to give. First, the writers, their agents, and publishers have been extrmely cooperative in securing permissions and I thank them all; no anthology is possible without such quick and enthusiastic assistance. My editor, Jim Cohee, has been a joy to work with—the ultimate professional and someone I can always turn to for expert advice as we guide a book toward publication. The dedication acknowledges the respect I have for the incumbent vice president, an individual who has displayed consistent leadership on environmental issues and who has persevered for those causes during a time of many changes and challenges in Washington. Finally I must give thanks to the Murray family for their love and constant good cheer, and especially to my six-year-old son, who joined me for his first extended hike this spring, and who, in the course of it, nearly caught his first garter snake.

J.A.M.

Introduction

Wild Palms

I

To him who in the love of nature holds
Communion with her visible forms, she speaks
A various language.

William Cullen Bryant, "Thanatopsis"

The heat was gathering. The air was still. It was that time of day in the desert when shadows disappear and the local star reveals its legendary strength. Life goes underground. Hops, crawls, slithers, or burrows down a familiar tunnel and finds a dark, somewhat humid chamber in which to sleep. The quiet above ground becomes as immense as the emptiness of the sky. Nothing moves, except a solitary turkey vulture, idly circling on a thermal. The sensitive skin on the top of the ears, the tip of the nose, and other regions left uncovered begins to redden. Somewhere in the inscrutable recesses of the brain these sensations, and others, are duly registered as developments not to be ignored.

My feet on the hot sand made a steady crunching, and when I stopped walking the silence was enough to hasten the general pace of the journey. Where was I headed? An oasis in the Mojave. I had started the hike late in the morning and was about halfway to my destination. The oasis was reported to have a fine grove of native fan palms, one of the loveliest in southern California.

After climbing the third rise, I stood on a level divide between two broad drainages. To the south was the northern edge of the Colorado Desert, a much lower and drier desert. If James Polk had not made a diplomatic blunder, what lay beyond—the Mexican Baja— would now be part of the United States. There would be a state capitol the size of San Diego, a well-financed public university system, three or four popular national parks, environmental laws and the courts to enforce them, peaceful retirement communities. Not to mention cyclopean shopping centers, unscrupulous resort developers, irregular platoons of off-roaders. To the west were ancient stone hills. If you looked at them long enough, in the vibrating shimmer of heat, they became enormous desert tortoises. You could see the wrinkled necks, the antiquarian-like eyes, the bulky weathered shells, the clawed reptilian feet straining to break free of the earth. You blinked and the mirage lost its effect. Somewhere to the east, in a wilderness of rocks, was my destination, a meandering granitic canyon. At the bottom of the canyon flowed that most rare of desert commodities: a steady trickle of water.

As I hiked along I considered many things: the trail before me, the spring flowers beside the trail, the amount of water in the pack, the number of hours remaining in the day, the possibility of meeting Jim Morrison in these precincts. Every half mile or so I turned and surveyed the desiccated country behind me, noting the position of what were becoming increasingly familiar landforms. A small but distinct knob of rocks topped a faraway ridge. If I aimed for that, even if I lost the trail, I would find my way back to the end of the road. Maps are excellent aids for the backcountry traveler, but sometimes, in the rush to get under way, they are forgotten.

I took particular note of the wildflowers beside the trail, because it had been a wet winter. The only counties in California not yet designated federal disaster areas would, with the melting snows and valley flooding, soon be. In the Mojave, if nowhere else, the record-breaking precipitation was a blessing. The desert wore a light chemise of green. Where the slopes faced south and the seeds had been generously watered the flower displays were spectacular: watermelon-red beavertail cactus, alpenglow-purple hedgehog cactus, sulphur-yellow barrel cactus, and many others. All year long the desert plants saved for this. Absorbed miserly rains. Hoarded moisture in tightly packed cells. Guarded precious buds with barbed spines. This was their Mardi Gras, their Fiesta, their Carnival. Their rite of spring. Van Gogh would have loved it, splashed vibrant colors all over the canvas, probably gotten a really bad sunburn with that red hair and freckled skin of his, madly searched his case of oils for a blood-red pigment to paint the scarlet blossoms of the claret cup cactus.

The cactus blossoms were nice, but the most striking wildflowers favored the Mojave yuccas. Beneath nearly every yucca—picture a plant designed during the Inquisition—was a thick bed of golden Mexican poppies and lavender-blue lupine. From the mixed blossoms subtle fragrances lured all manner of butterflies. There were tiger swallowtails and wayward orange and black monarchs and some sort of local checkerspot I had never seen before. When they sank their antennaed heads into the centers of the petals the gaudily painted wings stopped moving for one brief, delicious moment. The ultimate sugar junkies. The yuccas were also heavily flowered. Each stalk bore a cluster of blossoms with petals the color of white candle wax. I puzzled a long time over the close association and finally concluded that visiting songbirds must disperse wildflower seeds around the yuccas. Either that or mischievous ranger-naturalists sow seeds during the slow winter months.

As I hiked through the rugged rocky uplands there were scattered Joshua trees. Not as many as in Queen Valley or on Cima Dome, but still a good number. These trees are either grotesque or exquisite, depending on your point of view. In 1844 Western explorer John C. Fremont called the Joshua tree "the most repulsive tree in the vegetable Kingdom." A few years later the Mormons passed through. They thought the uplifted branches were like the arms of Joshua beckoning them to the promised land, hence the name. People have been arguing ever since. I stopped in front of a two- or three-hundred-year-old tree. It was an odd-looking plant, no doubt about that. The first impression was of top-heaviness. Imagine the muscular arms of a heavyweight boxer like Joe Frazier set on the compact body of a marathon runner like Frank Shorter. The trunk was small, only about twenty inches in diameter, and the numerous branches were stout and forking. At the end of each branch were heavy daggerlike leaves. Because this was spring, there were also ivory blossom clusters similar to those on their cousins, the yucca. These caused the ponderous branches to droop. As far as I'm concerned, the Joshua tree is a masterpiece of concision and adaptation. Without them, the Mojave would be like the Colorado Rockies without aspen, the streets of New York without Italian ice vendors, the halls of Congress without lobbyists. In a sense, Joshua trees are the Mojave.

An hour later, standing at the prow of a hill, I was afforded a view of the country ahead. The landscape was, in a word, bleak. Here was the Earth before the Cambrian explosion assembled fish and ferns from amoebas and blue-green algae, or, ages hence, after the sun has gone supernova and deep-fried the first three planets. Rocks, rocks, and more rocks. Hulking mountains partially buried in their own rubble, deep canyons with fossil streams, massive boulders the size of ten-story buildings, wind-blasted plateaus, weird basaltic labyrinths, huge eroded buttresses, shattered rock plains. It was as if a race of giants had waged a titanic battle and destroyed everything at their feet, or a prodigious death ray had been brought to bear as the mother ship sought to demonstrate her power to disbelieving earthlings. Or, more accurately, the scene was what remained after ancient volcanoes had violently extruded pumice and lava and then been forced by plate tectonics into retirement as ancient salt waters came and went, depositing coral reefs and fish bones that quietly suffered the ultimate sea change.

Plants were so hard-pressed for soil in this region they squeezed from rock fissures, somehow finding nourishment in the dust and decayed matter at the bottom of the gap. Some were beautiful, such as the skinny ocotillo, with tiny bursts of red flowers like exploding Roman candles. Others were not, like the spiny cholla, which is what a porcupine would be if it were a plant. Taking the scene in, I recalled the lines from the Book of Revelations after the cracking of the seventh seal:

> And he opened the bottomless pit; and there arose a smoke out of the pit, as the smoke of a great furnace . . . and there came out of the smoke locusts upon the earth, and unto them was given power, as the scorpions of the earth have power.

The scene evoked another desolate image—the Valley of the Dead in Egypt. Walk in the Mojave for a day and you can understand why the pharaohs worshipped the sun. The sun was the controlling reality of their desert world, just as it is in the deserts of southern California. The reverence they showed the sun was in keeping with their whole philosophy of nature. Consider this: when Howard Carter opened Tutankhamen's tomb in 1925, what most impressed him was not the 900-pound golden coffin inlaid with lapis lazuli and electrum but the tiny homemade wreath of desert wildflowers—woody nightingale, mandrake, and blue cornflower—placed beside the king's head as "the last offering of the widowed girl queen to her husband." The archaeologist wrote:

> Among all that regal splendour, that royal magnificence—everywhere the glint of gold—there was nothing so beautiful as those few withered flowers, still retaining their tinge of colour. They told us what a short period three thousand three hundred years really was— but Yesterday and the Morrow. In fact, that little touch of *nature* [emphasis added] made that ancient and our modern civilization kin.

What made the Egyptians the only people yet to successfully sustain a long-term civilization in the desert was just that: their respect for nature. The twentieth-century approach? Dam the Nile and destroy fifty centuries of sustained agriculture, and the once robust fisheries of the eastern Mediterranean, in less than two generations.

The trail switchbacked into the abyss and several hundred feet later brought me to the edge of what would elsewhere be a stream. Here there was only sand. In the sand you could see where the current had previously flowed, for the water had sculpted channels and braids and riffles, and you could almost imagine the sand flowing along as a liquid. In fact, if you stared at it long enough, in the heat, the sand began to move. Turn away, look back, and the illusion vanished. Where the sand was heavy and coarse it formed dark edges and some of the patterns were beautiful, radiating concentrically around a sculpted stone or delicately paralleling a cut bank. Where the sand was fine and lighter colored, it spread out thickly, as on a beach. When examined closely the sand was diverse—bits of clear quartz and shiny mica and reddish feldspar and darker volcanic minerals I could not identify. A prospector would know how to read the sand. So would a horned toad hunting for scarab beetles. There were little worlds in the streambed. Ant hills that would become busy under the stars. Dark holes housing reclusive tarantulas. Inch-high flower beds of white fleabane that would require a thick hand lens to peruse.

I widened my search, struck out upstream for a wide stretch where a side trail crossed the dry watercourse. Here tracks—black-tail deer and coyotes and kangaroo rats—were all mingled together in evidence of the local night life. Just how the indigents managed their affairs in such a landscape I do not know. But their tracks indeed confirmed their existence. It occurred to me that a whole book could be written on sand. Not just sand, but the stretch of sand in this dry watercourse. The sand was a book on which was written the story of the desert. I followed the sand upstream, thinking I was on the trail, intently reading the tracks, trying to acquire some sense of the neighborhood. A quarter mile farther on, a ten-foot wall of quartz monzonite blocked the way. There was a smooth lip over which flash floods had poured for about half a million years. Below it was a splash basin where the periodic thundering water had hollowed out the bedrock. Clearly this was not the trail. I retraced my steps.

The trail to the oasis angled up the other side of the canyon, crossed another tedious pile of rocks, descended another canyon, angled its way through sandy subterranean corridors, climbed a second canyon wall, and then repeated the whole process again. This happened two more times. I didn't mind, even if I was half-lost in the middle of the Mojave. I'd known worse. In my old home of northern Alaska the ice on the Yukon River was still five feet thick. Blizzards were drifting through the Brooks Range and wolves were enjoying the best hunting of the year. Car batteries left unplugged overnight would need jumping. Yorkshire terriers forgotten for an evening in the backyard would need burying. In the Mojave, even at the bottom of a nameless canyon, it was a nice summer day.

Nature writers have flocked to the desert in numbers out of all proportion to the size of the region. The current list runs into the dozens. Elsewhere, the literary situation is not nearly so robust, especially in the Old South and the Midwest. Why is that? What is it about the desert provinces that most attracts nature writers? The vastness? The life forms? The mild winters? The public lands? The peace and quiet? The aesthetic clarity? I would guess the last—the desert is, for any artist, pure inspiration.

On and on I trudged, through a maze of narrow passageways with perpendicular walls. On and on, through canyons measureless to man. Finally I began to encounter foot-long black-collared lizards. Not just one or two lizards, but five or six lizards, and this, I surmised, was a good sign. Where animals have the energy to hold a mini-convention at midday, there must be water. If only they could talk and tell me how near I was. Perhaps Jim Morrison, the "Lizard King" himself, would now appear to lead the way. Perhaps not. My pace quickened. Finally the trail took me up the side of another canyon wall. I sensed this was the last, or had to be the last, and I was right.

At the top I caught my breath, stood fully upright and saw a colony of ten or eleven California fan palms perched high in the rocks of an opposing canyon wall. A few quick steps through some

medicinal-smelling creosote brought me to the rim of the famous secret barranca. It was filled a quarter of the way with a fertile oasis of
California fan palms. The sight of palm trees, not mirages but real
palm trees, after walking half the day in a half-baked desert, is as restorative as a good book—Homer, Dante, Shakespeare, Turgenev,
Twain—after a day of reading airline travel magazines and concourse
shop novels.

There was a gentle breeze in the bright green canyon and the palm
fronds swayed slightly, making a pleasant peaceful rustling sound,
and from the shadows underneath the palms came the welcome
sound of moving water and the cheerful song of the canyon wren:
zzzzeeeep, zzzzeeeep, tee-tee-tee-tee-tee-tee-teer-teer.

I listened for a moment, absorbing the music and the scene, realizing I had indeed come to a special place. There was life here. Lots
of it. Hundreds of square miles of desert and here was a piece of
something different. Greater biodiversity, some would say. More poetry, I would say.

Four switchbacks brought me to the canyon floor. Bighorn sheep
tracks prominently marked the sand. They were squarish, blocky
tracks, several sizes larger than the slender cloven tracks of deer. A
good-sized herd called this place home, and some of the rams were
big. Down their ancient trail, a trail wide enough for sheep, I walked.
Beside the trail ran a stream. At times it was three inches deep, flowing over a cool bed of sparkling sand. At other times it hurried over
a ledge and filled a clear pool two feet deep. No pup fish, though. Too
alkaline and isolated for that. The splashing water sparkled on the
trunks of the palms, and there were whiptail lizards scampering up
and down the trunks. Farther back in places I could not see were
scorpions and centipedes, Gila monsters and pit vipers. The well-
armed creatures of the night.

All the while the canyon wrens sang: *zzzzeeeep, zzzzeeeep, tee-tee-
tee-tee-tee-tee-teer-teer.* Occasionally I would see one, slender and
rust-colored, darting among the palms. Just when I fixed on the long

pointed beak, the white throat, the backswept wings, the bird would disappear into the shadows. The canyon wrens were shy and kept to themselves. Only once, exploring the network of sheep trails, did I spot a nest. It was high in the rocks and was constructed of mud and twigs. The parents, like all parents, were preoccupied with the incessant demands of their offspring. What I loved most about the canyon wren was its song, which descended quickly through a series of notes like water falling from ledge to ledge in a little oasis stream. As I listened to the birds I thought of Robert Frost and his oven-bird, or Thomas Hardy and his darkling thrush, or Wang Wei and his Chinese oriole, or Basho and his Japanese skylark, or Keats and his English nightingale. Poets love birds because they learn to sing by listening to them. What was it Keats wrote? "Thou was not born for death, immortal Bird! No hungry generations tread thee down." Something like that. Still true.

My reconnaissance of the oasis was complete in an hour. The oasis was about the size of a forty- or fifty-acre arboretum. It extended only so far as the water ran. At the upper end, among a cluster of palms, the water poured from an underground spring. The stream ran through the grove for a third of a mile and then sank into the rocks as abruptly as it had appeared. A career as short as a hundred-and-fifty-pound wide receiver in the NFL, a pro-wolf politician in Wyoming, a peace treaty in Sarajevo. All along the banks, in a narrow band, grew a dense subtropical jungle of grass, rushes, mesquite, jojoba, creosote, milkweed, willow, palo verde, and California fan palm.

The most interesting plant in the oasis was the palm, the only palm native to the western United States. Mature palms stood sixty feet tall, with a crown of five-foot palm fronds. The sturdy trunks were deeply weathered, with vertical cracks and fissures, and if you looked closely you could see horizontal growth lines. As the palm fronds died they collapsed downward on the trunk. On a few of the trees these dead brown leaves formed a thick "skirt" that reached nearly to the ground. On most trees, for whatever reasons (fire?), the skirts were practically nonexistent, and an energetic twelve-year-old could have climbed the trunk all the way to the top.

There were many nice views of the palms, but the best was on your back, looking upward. This was the view of the desert tortoise, or the coyote. From that perspective you could fully appreciate the pillarlike stature of the tree, the exotic richness of the crown, the symmetry of the split fronds against the sky. The fronds were really quite amazing. Each leaf was long and sharp and deeply channeled. The surface was slightly varnished. The result was that they partially reflected light, a shimmering mirrorlike effect that was multiplied whenever a breeze stirred.

After the reconnaissance was complete and my field and sketch notebooks were put away, I found a flat piece of 700-million-year-old gneiss above a pool and stripped off my sweaty shirt and lay down to sunbathe. Another nature writer hard at work.

Ten minutes later I concluded I was working a bit too hard and found a rock with some shade and took a nap. I fell asleep with a folded-over cotton shirt for a mattress and a rolled up bandana for a pillow. I guess I felt at home in the oasis. And why not? The human race has been living in oases ever since Olduvai Gorge, where we chipped obsidian edges and made palm-leaf shelters and subsisted on wild roots and palm fruit. When the siesta was over I took out my microcassette recorder, small and inconspicuous and useful for interviews, and taped a canyon wren. I let it run for a quarter of an hour, and the bird sang almost constantly in that time. Whenever I turn the recording on now, and I often do before bed, it goes *zzzzeeeep, zzzzeeeep, tee-tee-tee-tee-tee-tee-teer-teer.* Over and over. Trickling water in the background. Light breezes in the palm fronds. The sound carries me back to a lovely canyon in the midst of the Mojave, a cool green place where a thousand years pass and nothing changes. A nation marches to war. A Great Depression ravages the land. A nation marches to war again. A generation of babies is born.

Lives are lived. Cemeteries are slowly filled. Still the canyon wren sings, cheerfully, in a place the human race calls, for lack of a better word, the desert.

II

None other than this long brown land lays such a hold on the affections.
Mary Austin, *Land of Little Rain*

In 1994 the United States Congress did a good thing. It set aside that lovely palm oasis, and 792,000 acres around it, as Joshua Tree National Park. At the same time Death Valley National Park and East Mojave National Preserve were established, as well as more than seventy new wilderness areas. At 3.3 million acres, Death Valley is now the largest national park outside Alaska. All of this was achieved under the aegis of the California Desert Protection Act. Much is written about the shortcomings of this nation and its institutions, and some of it is true, but I can tell you, having spent several weeks this spring exploring those new parks, that you can't help but feel a little more proud of your country when you visit these places. Here is the best of America—generosity, optimism, reverence for life. Here, too, posterity will forever be able to experience the hardship, adversity, and danger that helped to create the unique American spirit. It is instructive to remember that without the work of many desert nature writers—from Mary Austin to Joseph Wood Krutch to Edward Abbey—it is doubtful that the constituency would have been there to vigorously support passage of this legislation.

This year's collection begins with an essay from the president who accomplished more for nature conservation than any other leader in our history. In one stroke of the pen—the 1980 Alaska Lands Bill— Jimmy Carter doubled the national park system. At the same instant he tripled the wilderness system. Having lived in Alaska for half a dozen years, and visited many of the new parks and preserves, I can attest to the fact that the American people do not yet realize how great the treasures are in the forty-ninth state. But they will, in time, and those parks—Lake Clark, Gates of the Arctic, Kenai Fiords (to name just three)—will become as beloved as Yosemite and Yellowstone. Jimmy Carter stands with Thomas Jefferson and Theodore Roosevelt as an accomplished naturalist who was also president. He never gave up in his battle for these lands, steadfastly refused to compromise on core issues like oil development in the Arctic Refuge, and ultimately achieved what was in the best interest of the American people he was elected to represent.

The 1996 annual also includes a number of selections on deserts. Greg McNamee, a member of the "Tucson Group" of nature writers, writes of desert wind, a force of nature not often evident in desert landscape photographs but always clear in the recollection of anyone who has ever hiked in cactus country. McNamee humorously recalls a night outside a Motel Six in Palm Springs when he was "careened off dumpsters and fire hydrants" by a particularly energetic San Gorgonio blow. Gary Nabhan, also of Tucson, approaches the desert from the perspective of ethnobotany, or the native uses of plants, a subject in which he holds a doctoral degree. In his essay "Finding the Hidden Garden" Nabhan chronicles his search for *Agave murpheyi,* a scientific quest that brings him face to face with five Uzi machine guns in Old Mexico. Less intrepidly, Terry Tempest Williams, who lives in the Great Basin desert of Utah, focuses on the canyon frog, and offers a symbolic meditation upon the importance of water in the arid lands of the West.

Water is a theme evident in several works. Brenda Peterson, a novelist and nonfiction writer from Seattle, relates her experiences with whales, which range from a dead humpback on Venice Beach to very live humpbacks at a nursery off the coast of Kauai. Her wish is "that we might remember our balance between species and apprentice ourselves to the vision of birth and rebirth. Because the whole world is a nursery for what comes next." From his summer cottage on the Atlantic coast, naturalist Robert Finch chronicles a mass stranding of pilot whales near Provincetown, Massachusetts. After a herculean rescue effort by Finch and others, six of the original sixteen are saved. In Delaware, just down the coast, Jennifer Ackerman's concerns are not with leviathans of the deep but with the smaller life forms that inhabit the margins of the sea, particularly the fragile salt marshes. "I've learned," she writes, "that the way into a new landscape is to pull at a single thread. Nearly always it will lead to the heart of the tangle." Surfer Dan Duane of Santa Cruz, California, is also concerned with the margins of the sea—the offshore surf zone—and chronicles his experiences with waves large and small in his to-be-published book, *Caught Inside*. Some of the most exciting chapters in the book concern sharks, the surfer's nemesis: "Sharks are the world's only known *intra-uterine cannibals:* eggs hatching within a uterus, the unborn young fight and devour each other until one well-adapted predator emerges. If the womb is a battleground, what then the sea?"

Much of the writing in this year's annual is concerned with place. Not place in the abstract sense, but home residence: how best to meet obligations, confer respect, share values. Alaskan cultural anthropologist Richard Nelson writes in "The Embrace of Names" about the words we use to signify the features of the earth, and how much has been lost by replacing the original place names with those of European origin. One of the most notable examples is Mount McKinley, which was named by officials in Washington, D.C., for a lawyer from Canton, Ohio, whose greatest accomplishment was to select Theodore Roosevelt as his vice president. How much better—more poetical, more powerful, more appropriate—is the original Athabaskan name of Denali, "The Great One." The dispute is not trivial, as Nelson convincingly argues, but is intimately connected with how we view the land, ourselves, and our homes.

Louise Wagenknecht was born and raised in an Idaho logging town and has spent twenty years in the Forest Service as a firefighter. She has seen the complex environmental issues of her home region from both sides, as the daughter of a dying logging town and as an environmentalist working for more enlightened policies in the federal government. Wagenknecht writes poignantly of the "Greek tragedy" of her home town, which is representative of so many home towns in the Pacific Northwest. Although locals were promised robust annual cuts by the Forest Service in the sixties, today the annual cuts are a fraction of what they were a generation ago. Some clearcuts have been "replanted six or seven times, and [are] still not regenerated sufficiently to meet Forest Service standards." Wagenknecht finds it "impossible to listen with a straight face to anyone who tells me that enough old-growth remains on this district to support a cut of 55 million board-feet a year in perpetuity, or indeed for more than a decade at the outside." The problem of the local residents, plainly stated by one of their own, is this: "We allowed our options to be curtailed and forcibly channeled because we could not conceive of any other reality than the one the Forest Service placed before us."

One of the most compelling books on the subject of place to be published in 1995 is Deborah Tall's *From Where We Stand: Recovering a Sense of Place*. Tall believes that one of the chief problems in contemporary America is our mobility, which has resulted in mass rootlessness. She believes that when people fail to attach themselves to the land they also fail to attach themselves to any significant ethical structure. The result is what we see in the headlines every day: a shattering of the spirit, a nation in some ways adrift, an epidemic of violence. "Frequent dislocation," Tall observes, "or the sudden destruction of a known environment, can be fundamentally deranging. It means the loss of personal landmarks—which embody the past—and the disintegration of a communal pattern of identity."

Some of the writers take a different approach to the theme and look at home place as metaphor. Minnesota writer Jan Grover, for example, compares the ravages of a cutover stand of Wisconsin timber to the devastation inflicted on the body of a friend by AIDS:

I've learned to find beauty in places where I never would have searched for or found it before—in an edematous face, a lesioned and smelly body, a mind rubbed numb by pain. Pain. A burned over district. Mortal lessons: the beauty of a ravished landscape.

In a similar analogical mode Georgian James Kilgo casually notices that a queen hornet is building a nest against the window pane of his living room. Over the next few weeks, the queen fills the colony with eggs, from which hatch workers. Soon the nest is "as big as a man's fist." The story ends with Kilgo's wife calling him over to watch as a summer tanager violently attacks the nest, eating the larvae while the workers and queen are away. The narrative of "Open House," to some readers, will also be the story of a marriage to which only oblique references are made.

Barry Lopez writes of a place he knows intimately: his 35-acre homesite on the banks of the McKenzie River in Oregon. For 24 years he and his wife Sandra, an artist, have lived there, keeping careful watch of the Roosevelt elk and old-growth Douglas-fir, spawning chinook salmon and orange salmonberries. Their affection for the land, and understanding of the complex web of life it fosters, have deepened over time:

> Sandra and I know we do not own these 35 acres. The Oregon ash trees by the river, in whose limbs I have seen flocks of 100 Audubon's warblers, belong also to the families in Guatemala in whose forests these birds winter. . . . I'm moved to forgive whoever does not find in these acres what I do. I glance into the moving picket of trees and shadow, alert for what I've never noticed before, in a woods I'm trying to take care of—as in its very complicated way it is taking care of me.

In the last sentence Lopez has articulated an important truth: that we preserve nature—especially areas around our homes—out of self-interest as well as altruism. We need them, individually and collectively in order to endure.

Finally, on this score (would that we had room to mention all) John Haines, distinguished poet laureate of Alaska, writes movingly of his beloved frontier homestead in "Days in the Field." Haines built the cabins, outbuildings, writing studio, and greenhouse on his 160 acres in 1947 and lived a sort of Robinson Crusoe existence there through the summer of 1994. For Haines, the most beautiful time of the year in his part of the world—the northern lights country—was the autumn, when from the valley fields he would harvest potatoes, onions, and turnips and from the spruce woods he would bring in cranberries, blueberries, mushrooms, and the winter meat. Fall was the season in which Haines felt closest to the land:

> It is good to remember . . . what it was to stoop down and lift something from the earth, dry tuber or damp mushroom; to close one's hand on the brown, crumbling soil, to sink one's fingers deep into the moss and feel the night and the frost that are waiting there; if only for a moment, to feel oneself once more at home on the earth.

For him the memories of those bountiful days are bittersweet, contrasting as they do with an era in which such allegiances are fast being lost. At some level all the writers in this year's annual are concerned, like Haines, with a world that is changing at an accelerating rate. They each seem acutely aware of the fact that they are in a sense historians, bearing witness to an age in which whole landscapes, and entire plant and animal nations, are perishing in unprecedented fashion. Each would probably agree that the major cause is uncontrolled human population growth, and that current measures to address the issue fall short. It may be that present political systems are inadequate to the challenge, and that world governments will fail in their efforts to solve the problem. The editor of this book, however, is too much an optimist to believe that. A few years ago, Barry Lopez wrote that he believes nature writing "will not only one day produce a major and lasting body of American literature, but that it might also provide the foundation for a reorganization of American political thought."

In many ways, that process has already begun: the 1964 Wilderness Act, the 1978 Endangered Species Act, the 1980 Alaska Lands Bill, the 1994 California Desert Protection Act. The chief virtue of democracy, in this respect, is that it can undergo tremendous growth with relative ease. It can, like an organism encountering new challenges in the environment, adapt as conditions change. No other political system yet invented can move so swiftly when necessary. Natural history writers, like others in the guild, function as the nerves, transmitting information to the darkly radiant center in which far-reaching decisions are made.

III

There is a relation between the hours of our life and the centuries of time. . . . The hours should be instructed by the ages, and the ages explained by the hours. Ralph Waldo Emerson, *Journals*

A few days after leaving Joshua Tree I visited the Kelso Dunes in the East Mojave National Preserve. Here, at the end of a gravel road on the far side of the Old Dad Mountains, I came face to face with what the national debt would look like if every grain of sand was one dollar. Forty-five square miles of sand. To the south and west were jagged volcanic peaks the likes of which prospectors dream. To the north, though not wholly in view, was a landscape of uneroded lava flows known as the Devil's Playground. To the east were the Providence Mountains, a heavy solid range with timber on top and dusted with snow. Rumor had it desert bighorn sheep lived there.

In the center was a sea of sand. And sea is a carefully chosen noun, for the sand was sculpted in massive waves. It was a sea that moved with refined slowness, the wind-driven waves forever about to crest and crash. If I listened carefully I could hear the sand blowing, a soft pleasant murmur. The dunes were all that remained, a BLM ranger had told me that morning, of previous desert mountains eroded by the elements. Such would be the fate, she assured me, of the Rockies, the Sierra, the Himalayas. As I climbed the tallest one—which was the height of a seventy-story building—the sand underfoot made a peculiar hollow sound, presumably caused by the rubbing together of the polished grains of rose quartz. It was a low rumble, a distant thunder, the dead mountain remembering the stature and power it once had. This venerable patriarch—ground to its essentials by the ages—had presided over a vast span of North American history. The coming and going of the dinosaurs, epic migrations, dramatic conflicts, spectacular events we will never know about.

Much to think about, climbing seventy stories in the shifting sands. At the top of the dune I sat down, something Sisyphus was never permitted to do. It was hot in the heights but still slightly cooler than at the base. All along the crest, amazingly, grew the yellow upright flowers of desert primrose and clustered purple mats of desert sand verbana. Most people would give such plants little heed, but each one was a miracle, the culmination of a billion years of evolution, the triumph of persistence over adversity. Here, in a square yard, was more life than on all the sand dunes of Mars. We could spend eternity exploring this universe, and, likely, find nothing so fantastic as a yellow primrose on a Mojave sand dune, a colony of sulphuric-acid-eating bacteria on a deep sea vent, a child eagerly raising his or her hand to answer a question in a first-grade classroom.

I looked around, took my bearings. Twenty miles to the south, over a wide pass in the Old Dad Mountains, was Route 66. I had driven over the road earlier on my way to the Kelso Dunes, stopped and taken a photograph of the now forgotten thoroughfare. A considerable amount of twentieth-century American history journeyed down that highway. The refugees of the Dust Bowl in the 1930s knew Route 66 well. They had little choice when the Great Plains were turned into a desert as a result of human greed, grotesque agricultural practices and egregious drought. Forty million unemployed, one in four farms foreclosed, the California valleys beckoning like

Arcady. In *The Grapes of Wrath* John Steinbeck described the Mojave of the Joads' era as "the terrible desert, where the distance shimmers and the black cinder mountains hang unbearably in the distance."

Terrible?

Only to those who do not recall the lessons of history, who fail to learn the principles of nature.

Emerson was right. The ages should inform the hours. We need places like Joshua Tree National Park and East Mojave National Preserve, places to go and sit outside time for awhile. Places to remember what is important and what is not. Places, in a world of hatred and violence, to absorb the silence and the tranquility. And we need the naturalists—Austin, Krutch, Abbey, Nabhan, McNamee, Williams—to sing the praises of these sanctuaries, to protect them from those who would, out of avarice or ignorance, destroy them. Words, after all, have power. Books can make a difference. Thoreau, writing in *Walden,* put it this way:

> No wonder that Alexander carried the Iliad with him on his expeditions in a precious casket. A written word is the choicest of relics. It is something at once more intimate with us and more universal than any other work of art. It is the work of art nearest to life itself. It may be translated into every language, and not only be read but actually breathed from all human lips . . . Books are the treasured wealth of the world and the fit inheritance of generations and nations . . . Their authors are a natural and irresistible aristocracy in every society, and, more than kings and emperors, exert an influence on mankind . . . How many a man has dated a new era in his life from the reading of a book.

Jimmy Carter

The Forty-ninth State, but First in Fishing

from *Outdoor Journal*

One of my major legislative battles as President was over the reso-
lution of a long-standing controversy concerning the disposition of
tens of millions of acres of Alaska lands. When Alaska became the
forty-ninth state in 1959, a serious question arose as to how much of
the enormous area would be in private hands and how much owned
by the state; retained by the native Eskimos, Indians, and Aleuts;
opened for mining and oil and gas exploration; or set aside for public
use as monuments, parks, scenic and wilderness areas.

For more than twenty years a bitter debate had raged in Alaska
and in the Congress. I was determined to settle the issue. With Secretary of the Interior Cecil Andrus and key members of the House
and Senate, I pored over the detailed maps of the region, trying to
decide how much of Alaska's natural beauty could be preserved
without interfering too much with the state's economic development. Slowly we forged compromises that resulted in a landmark
bill, which I signed into law on December 2, 1980, one of my last legislative decisions as President. We set aside for conservation an area
larger than the state of California, doubled the size of our National

Park and Wildlife Refuge System, designated twenty-five free-flowing Alaskan streams as wild and scenic rivers—and, as a result, instantly tripled our nation's wilderness system. At the same time, we were able to open up all the potentially productive offshore areas and 95 percent of the land areas where exploratory drilling for oil and mineral resources might be fruitful.

It was one of my most gratifying achievements in public life. I knew that for centuries to come, visitors to Alaska would be thrilled by some of the most beautiful scenery on earth, undisturbed by the ugly scars of an advancing industrial civilization. This final victory was especially pleasing because it was also a triumph over a mighty phalanx of greedy special interests who had made a last-minute effort to kill the bill.

In July 1980, when I stopped briefly in Alaska on a return trip from Japan, Governor Jay Hammond, Rupert Andrews, director of Sport Fishing, and Chris Goll, outfitter and hunting and fishing guide, had arranged for me and Secretary of State Edmund Muskie to go fishing for grayling for a few hours. We flew northward from Anchorage, circled Mount McKinley, landed on one of the glaciers to see the slowly flowing ice at first hand, and flew close to some cliffs to observe a number of Dall sheep on the steep mountainsides. I was thrilled by the stark, spectacular beauty. During this summer, passage of the Alaska lands legislation was still in doubt, but this brief trip renewed my determination to succeed, at the same time giving me some new arguments to present to doubtful members of Congress whose votes I would be seeking back in Washington.

We finally landed on a small body of water known as Clarence Lake. Wading out into the extremely cold water for a few yards, we placed our flies as far out as possible, let them sink for twenty or thirty seconds, and then reeled in slowly as the fly conformed to the steep underwater slope. Although I was relatively inexperienced at fly-fishing with sinking tip lines and my casts were shorter than most of the others, I had one small fly I'd created that seemed to be exceptionally attractive to the grayling. It was an imitation of a small yellow caterpillar, tied with a chenille body and peacock herl strips down the back, and it worked when nothing else would. That was a proud moment for me, as a novice fly tier, when I shared my creation with the other more experienced anglers.

We kept enough fish for a noon lunch, which we cooked on the lake bank, and then moved to the narrow but deep stream draining the lake. Since the water was crystal-clear and quite swift, wading was difficult. I spotted fish rising on a curve in the stream, but after wading out chest-deep was barely able to reach the feeding grayling. Unable to see any edible insects on the water, I tried several small Alaska patterns without success. Then I tied on my smallest Irresistible, a fuzzy-looking deer-hair pattern that floated like a tiny cork, and began to catch fish regularly. Again, I could share my flies with the other fishermen.

On the way back to Elmendorf Air Force Base, flying low over small streams, we saw hundreds of Chinook salmon on their spawning run. Their red bodies were packed together in the larger pools, and a number of bald eagles and grizzlies were feeding on them. This scene typified the savage beauty of the region.

Although the entire trip had lasted only about six hours, it was a pleasant respite from the duties of my office, compounded at that time by the Iranian hostage crisis. I resolved to return to Alaska as soon as possible for a more extensive visit, with enough time to see the natural beauty and wildlife and to fish for some of the trophy rainbow trout that dwell in the remote streams.

While I was in the state, opponents of the pending Alaska lands legislation had made their feelings obvious. Led by land developers, professional hunters, and leaders from the mining and oil companies, organized demonstrators expressed their disapproval of my well-known position. There were strong feelings on both sides. On my arrival I had met several hundred of the citizens at an airport reception, and both the supportive and the critical comments were delivered to me with little restraint. Later I heard that at the state fair in Fairbanks the Junior Chamber of Commerce had accumulated a large pile of empty bottles. For a fee the fairgoers could throw them at photographs of me, Secretary Andrus, Congressman Mo Udall (a key sponsor of the legislation), and the Ayatollah Khomeini. I never did know for sure who won this "popularity" contest, but I was told that my pile of broken bottles was a little larger than that of the Ayatollah.

After leaving office, I looked for a chance to go to Alaska again, this time for a visit devoted primarily to fishing. Then, early in 1985, Chris Goll called to invite Rosalynn and me to come to his isolated Rainbow River Lodge on the Copper River, about two hundred miles southwest of Anchorage. We accepted immediately, planning our trip for late June, after the ice melted and before the enormous runs of sockeye salmon began. We wanted to fish for rainbow trout, not Pacific salmon, because we thought the trout would be more elusive and challenging in their permanent habitat than the salmon, who were crowding into the stream of their birth for a final spawning run.

A couple of weeks before our departure, Rosalynn found that business obligations would prevent her going. As I thought about the perfect companion to replace her, I recalled the good times my father and I had had fishing together when I was a child. All my sons were grown men, and so I decided to call Chicago to invite my oldest grandson, Jason, who was nine years old, to join me. He was overjoyed, even after I cross-examined him.

"How about the bears?"

"I'm not afraid," he said.

"Big black moose?"

"They won't attack us."

"Bald eagles? Mammoth ice floes, frozen hands, big mosquitoes, perpetual daylight and no dark hours for sleeping, a long time away from your parents?"

"You can't talk me out of it."

"Can you cast with a fly rod?"

"Not good enough, but I'll practice now and learn more in Alaska."

Although Rosalynn and I had had all our grandchildren with us on several occasions, including fishing at Spruce Creek, this would be the first time I would be off alone with just one of them. I was as excited as Jason, eager to please him and to be a special friend. Before the trip we talked often on the phone, every time either of us could think of a new idea about fishing tackle, books to read, travel arrangements, or just an old subject that was good enough to be revived. Jason had never made a journey so distant or different before, but he didn't seem concerned about being away from home. His dad, Jack, added to the excitement by pretending to be jealous and wanting to replace Jason on the trip.

When we met in the Atlanta airport, Jason was proudly and ostentatiously carrying his oversized hip boots (there were no chest waders available for his small size) and his dad's fly rod. As we waited for our flight, he told me that he and his father had been practicing every day.

"Can you throw a fly to that wall?" I asked him, pointing to a partition about forty feet away.

"No, sir, but I wouldn't have any trouble reaching those chairs."

"Could you hit the one in the middle?"

"I could come close to it on the first cast and hit it on the second."

"That's good enough to catch fish," I informed him, laughing.

During the long flight Jason read a simple book I had brought him on casting and fly-fishing techniques. As I questioned him, I was surprised at how much he remembered from the few times he had fished with me in Pennsylvania.

When we stepped off the plane in Anchorage, Chris was there to meet us. Soon we had loaded our gear into his single-engine float plane and were on our way to the Copper River. Jason and I plied Chris with questions about the camp, fishing, distances, mountains, tackle, boats, wildlife, and other important subjects. It happened to be the first day of summer, and Chris reported that he had observed a large caddis hatch the previous week. He interrupted our questions about fishing long enough to express a hope that we might see some whales as we flew southwestward from Anchorage over the Cook Inlet. Looking down at the shoreline, we noticed that the thirty-two-foot tide seemed to be at maximum ebb; in some places the milky glacier water lapped miles from the nearest bluffs, where the shacks of duck hunters were erected.

Jason, sitting in the back, had his nose pressed against the window. Suddenly, Chris pointed ahead and exclaimed, "There's a whale!" Jason and I finally sighted the white shape maneuvering on and near the surface. Soon we could see several hundred, their rolling white bodies easy to spot. "They're belugas, mostly twelve to fifteen feet long, feeding on king salmon," Chris explained. "We usually find them when the salmon are approaching the streams for their spawning run, but this is the most I've ever seen at one time."

When we reached land we flew at minimum safe altitude, at times just a few hundred feet above the surface, all of us on the lookout for wildlife. We saw nesting trumpeter swans on the small lakes, several bald eagles, an occasional moose along the riverbanks, two grizzlies, and a black bear. Finally we crossed Lake Iliamna. Almost halfway down its ninety-mile length we sighted the Copper River and then landed alongside it on a small lake, just large enough for a heavily loaded float plane to take off safely.

Being in this secluded lake was a special thrill for me as I recalled the political battle we had waged to protect this and other wild regions, many of them equally beautiful. As we taxied to the shore, Chris said to Jason, "This is called Pike Lake; it drains directly into the river. Maybe later this week you can learn firsthand where it got its name. Mostly, though, we're going to be fishing for rainbows. The ice has recently cleared out of the river, and the sockeye salmon haven't yet moved this far inland from the sea, so it's a good time to concentrate on the trout. We'll be seeing some trophy-size fish, whether we catch them or not. Because we would like fishing in the Copper to stay as good as it is, we'll be fly-fishing only—it is an Alaskan policy that in the Lake Iliamna drainage basin we release all the rainbows we catch."

This was exactly what we had planned, but Jason asked if there would be any fish to eat during the week. "You might catch some grayling, Arctic char, and northern pike—if you're lucky," came the wry reply.

After Chris beached the plane we quickly unloaded our gear. Rainbow River Lodge was a beautiful spot, almost completely in its natural state. The man-made structures that made up the camp had been placed with great care to disturb the hillside as little as possible—just a few small cottages along the wooded shore, connected by narrow paths. The only surrounding trails leading up the steep hills and around the lakeside were made by bears and other wild animals, each path only six or eight inches wide and at least a foot deep in the tundra. There were no open or flat places; I would not need my jogging shoes and Frisbee this week.

In the center of the camp was a shallow open pit lined with stones for a campfire and outdoor cooking, surrounded by a few small cabins, a mess hall, two outdoor toilets, a shed within which the diesel generator ran during the necessary hours, and a storage room submerged in the tundra that served as a natural icebox. Aside from the wonderful food, one of the most enjoyable features of the lodge was the shower, which provided unlimited hot water, instantly heated by propane gas when the water was turned on. The June weather was chilly but not uncomfortable.

Tired from the long trip, we went to bed right after supper. In this far north country it was light enough to read a newspaper all night, except for an hour or two after midnight. Although the long hours of dusk and predawn light conjured up eerie feelings for us southerners, I never had any trouble sleeping. But Jason must have been too excited to stay in bed. I heard his voice out by the campfire, asking trivia questions about baseball. An avid Chicago Cubs fan, he easily dominated this and many other conversations during the week with his encyclopedic knowledge of the sport.

The temperature was a little above forty degrees Fahrenheit the next morning as we moved through Pike Lake and entered the Copper River. We had rain gear in the boat, but a light sweater was enough to keep warm. This is a beautiful stream, whose ample flow of water is so powerful as to be frightening. With a gravel or rock bed and little if any runoff from glaciers, the water is almost perfectly clear. Although there are deep holes where very large fish can be seen, wading is quite safe in the tail ends of pools and alongside gravel bars if normal precautions are observed. I warned Jason that he had to be careful when he stepped off the bank, because the water's clarity caused us to underestimate its depth. Jason usually stayed in the boat or quite near the shore. With the help of a wading staff in the deeper water, I had a close call for a bad spill only once during our stay.

The first morning we traveled upstream about five miles. Since no trout were feeding on the surface, we decided to fish each pool as near the bottom as possible, using sinking tip lines. We tried nymphs, streamers of different kinds, and imitation salmon eggs, but neither Jason nor I had any luck for the first few hours. I watched Chris carefully as he took three or four nice trout and finally sought his advice.

"You're waiting for a heavy strike, which will rarely come," he said. "The extremely delicate 'takes' are almost impossible to detect, so you almost have to sense the proper time to tighten your line. If I feel the slightest tug or observe just a fleeting hesitation of the line, I assume it's a fish and respond instantly. This happens several times on almost every long drift downstream. There are a lot of false alarms, but every now and then you land one."

Using his technique, I soon had a heavy fish on my line, but after a few minutes he broke off.

"What tippet are you using?" Chris shouted across the stream.

"Three-X, about five-pound test," I replied.

"Go to two-X or bigger when fishing deep," he instructed. Naturally, I complied.

Jason practiced for a long time, standing in the relatively shallow water or in the boat, and his ability quickly improved. Chris and I taught him a few of the standard knots that are necessary for fishermen. Nevertheless, the length of casts and the patience required were a little more than a nine-year-old could handle. Soon Jason was spending more time with the binoculars and exploration of bear trails than with the rod. Since Chris's daughter, Betsy, who was the same age as Jason, had come along for the day, they had a good time rambling along the shore.

By noon, after four hours of steady fishing, I had not landed a single fish and was somewhat discouraged. My limited skills did not rest in the use of heavy tackle, deep water, long casts, and subtle takes. I'd spent most of my time fishing on the surface with dry flies, or with small wet flies across and downstream. I knew the fishing in farm ponds and small creeks very well, but had been in large rivers like this one for only a few hours.

In the early afternoon came a sign of a possible turn in my future: I was delighted to observe the beginnings of a caddis hatch. Soon a few trout began to rise in one of the deep pools. They were quite distant, under an overhanging cliff, and I could reach them only by fishing downstream. Every now and then I managed a good float, but the fish ignored my best caddis patterns. Finally I tied on a very small Adams and caught a couple of rainbows, the smallest about thirteen inches. Even though the hatch was short-lived, this fisherman's spirits rose.

Chris commented, "The hatches will be much better later this week if we have some warmer days."

In midafternoon, while Jason was playing around the boat with Betsy, she fell in the river. After a great deal of laughter from the two, Jason "accidentally" fell in also, and now both of them had fun splashing around near the boat. Although the water was very cold, they assured everyone that they were all right and would prefer to let the warm sun dry them out rather than go back to camp. I kept quiet, figuring that forty-five years ago my daddy would have let me swim too.

Shortly afterward, Chris and I spotted several large trout feeding in the tail end of a long pool, their heads softly breaking the surface every now and then as a choice morsel drifted overhead. Although the surface riffles made it difficult for me and the fish to see one another, I decided to stay well away from them to avoid detection. While Chris and Jason watched, I waded out waist-deep and tried all my tricks and a wide variety of flies in vain attempts to coax a trout to strike. One of the fish, well over three pounds, attacked a multicolored Sculpin, but after a few seconds of furious rushing he was able to dislodge the hook.

In the aftermath of this encounter, I moved downstream a few yards and took a position on a submerged gravel bar, with the water chest-deep and a deeper channel on either side of me. Now I could cast somewhat upstream, have a better and more natural float, but could not see as well the location of the fish. During this time Jason's teeth began to chatter, and Chris volunteered to take the two children the three miles or so back to the camp for a hot shower and a change into dry clothes.

After the boat's motor sounds faded down the river, I waited about ten more minutes and began to cast again, trying a series of wet and dry flies. I got an occasional rise, and once I was startled to see a huge head come gently out of the water and then sink quietly back. This was truly a monster rainbow! As I looked through my box of flies, I noticed a yellow stonefly nymph that George Harvey had sent me as a gift, one of his skillfully woven patterns on a #10 hook.

I tied it on and placed it far above where the fish seemed to be, stripping in line as the fly slowly sank and drifted back downstream. Suddenly there was a tremendous whirl in the water, and the rod was almost pulled from my hands. At first the trout moved upstream, near the bottom; through the vibrating line I could feel its head shaking. As I carefully shifted my feet around to move toward the fish and into shallower water, he leaped into the air—the biggest trout I had ever seen.

The fish headed resolutely downstream. I put maximum pressure on the tackle, keeping the #8 rod bent as much as it and I could bear. With majestic inexorability, the great trout continued on its course. In a few minutes my fly line was gone and the twenty-pound backing was disappearing at a steady rate. From time to time the fish would pause, and I would attempt to regain some line and turn him my way, but this aggravating pressure always precipitated an additional run downstream. The water was already lapping over the top of my chest waders and, because of the much deeper water on three sides, it was impossible for me to move in any direction except upstream, away from the fish. I could think of no way to shorten the distance between us. I had mixed emotions about being alone; it heightened the drama of an epic struggle between man and fish, but I could have used Chris's advice—and I knew that the distance was rapidly increasing between my adversary and me.

The fish and I struggled for every foot of line as I tried to keep the pressure strong but steady. Once, when I gave the rod an extra tug, way down the river a big fish leaped. I could hardly believe that this was my fish, so far away, almost out of sight. Practically all of my 150 yards of backing was gone and the outcome of this angling saga was becoming quite clear, but my dwindling hopes were revived when I heard the distant sound of a motor and saw Chris and his boat rounding the bend. He instantly saw what was happening and proceeded toward me cautiously, going around the other side of an island just below me and keeping the boat in shallow water, as near the shore as possible.

"He's really a big one," I shouted as he approached. "I've had him on about twenty minutes, but my line is almost gone."

Chris brought the boat close to me. With his help, I managed to hang over the side and then fall in, holding my rod as best I could so it wouldn't break. I didn't let Chris touch it; this had to be my struggle alone. As the boat drifted downstream I reeled in some line. The trout had by then gone around a sharp curve below the island, and the line was running through grass and tree roots against the bank. When it was clear again we moved closer to the fish, into shallower water. I stepped out of the boat, got a firm footing, and managed to bring in enough line to return all the backing to the reel.

Chris was giving me a constant stream of advice. "There's a gravel bar ahead. Maybe you could beach him there. But watch out for that big cluster of submerged roots in the deep water under the bank."

I couldn't stop the fish's progress toward the roots, and soon my heart sank as the vibrant motions of the trout were replaced by the sickening, steady pull of a fouled line. Following a brief expletive, I added, "I've lost him!"

I waded as close to the roots as possible, stuck the rod tip into the water, and the line came clear. Again the rod came alive in my hands.

"He's still on," I told Chris in excitement, "and not ready to give up!"

As I brought the big rainbow closer, Chris beached the boat and walked down the bar to help me land him. Finally, the fish was in shallow water, still wanting to fight but subdued now by the tight line. Chris prepared his camera while I protected the trout from any injury. I supported the fish gently upright as its body eased up on the sandbar. My fish, as I thought of him, was a brilliantly colored male, deep-bodied and heavy, with his lower jaw hooked slightly upward. He measured thirty inches long and nineteen inches around his midsection; Chris estimated his weight at twelve pounds.

I eased the tiny hook out of the corner of his mouth, supported his body with both hands under the stomach, and slowly moved the fish forward into the current as he faced upstream. After a few minutes, the trophy rainbow moved his tail strongly and eased off into the deeper water. As I watched him swim away I knew he was probably the largest trout I would ever catch in a lifetime of fishing.

"How would you like to have him mounted?" Chris asked.

I was a bit surprised by such a foolish question. "I'd rather the fish were alive in the Copper River," I told him.

Chris explained that I could have it both ways. "We've taken a representative number of Alaska rainbows to a superb taxidermist, along with photographs of the fish taken just as they came out of the water. Now we measure and photograph each trophy fish, and the taxidermist then creates a mounted trophy identical in color and size to the fish you caught and released. Along with it you get a plaque certified by an official guide, describing the circumstances of the event."

"Sounds good to me," I said. I certainly wouldn't mind having proof of my catch, as long as it wasn't at the fish's expense.

Inspired, we prepared to resume fishing, but before long I realized I had a chill; I couldn't get warm. Perhaps the excitement plus the long time in the deep and cold water had sapped my strength and taken away my inclination to fish any more just then. Or perhaps I felt that the great fish deserved to be honored in some fashion—if only by an hour or two of quiet contemplation of the event. In any case, we were soon on the way back downriver to Rainbow River Lodge. Our arrival was somewhat anticlimactic; there was just no way to recount to Jason and the others the excitement of my adventure.

That night Chris explained that the sockeye salmon was the foundation for the rainbow-trout life cycle in the Copper River. About five hundred thousand of the salmon enter the river each year to spawn, dying after their eggs are laid and fertilized. The decaying bodies, eggs, spawn, fingerlings, and growing salmon then support the indigenous rainbows. In this particular Alaskan stream, there are good hatches of mayflies, stoneflies, and caddis flies; they and their larvae and nymphs supplement the diet of this native strain of trout and help to explain their large numbers and exceptional size. Furthermore, in less-remote areas, long years of hatchery breeding for fast growth have reduced the life span of trout, but these wild rainbows have not been affected. They live much longer than stocked trout and grow larger when fully mature.

Although Jason and I fished hard, we didn't land a fish the next morning. However, about 2:00 P.M. there was a good caddis hatch, and our dry flies began to pay rich dividends. Since we couldn't reach the rising fish from wadeable water, we anchored the boat near enough to make successful casts. With a little help Jason landed two large rainbows. I caught several larger than seventeen inches and brought a twenty-four-inch fish in close enough to net, if we had been using a net. Demonstrating a final explosion of power, this fish broke my leader and swam off with a Royal Wulff in its mouth.

When not exclusively preoccupied with fishing, we also observed some of the wildlife in the valley and on the hillsides near the Copper. Both mature and immature bald eagles soared overhead or perched on rocky crags or in the tops of the spruce and cedar trees. Brown bear and moose could also be seen every now and then, watching our boat go by or cautiously observing us from a distant vantage point. Once, while eating lunch on a bluff above the river, we thought we glimpsed an otter, underwater, looking for his lunch too. An occasional marten or other small animal scurried up and down the riverbank. Although there were also a lot of beaver dens, one recently destroyed by a grizzly, we never saw a single beaver during our fishing excursions.

One day we flew about seventy miles southwestward to the Brooks River and Nanuktuk Creek, but the drizzling rain and strong winds made fishing difficult. After flying about halfway back home, we landed on Lake Kukaklek to take a look around. As we walked back toward the float plane, we suddenly confronted a large grizzly, less than a hundred yards away. He was proceeding toward us, rising up periodically to feed on the tender leaves growing near the stream. I looked around quickly to find Jason. He was between me and the plane, also watching the bear and wondering what he and the bear were going to do next. We and the grizzly examined each other carefully, our side snapped a few photographs, and we moved quietly out of his way. Unmolested, the bear pretended to ignore our presence and soon disappeared over a small hill.

We then flew over to the Battle River, spotting two more single bears on the way. They seemed to be gathering around the streams in anticipation of the forthcoming salmon runs, when they and the eagles would feed voraciously on the spawning fish. Leaving the planes at the mouth of the river, we began a long hike parallel to the water, visiting the bank every now and then to see if we could find a fordable place or spot any fish rising. A bull moose watched us calmly from just across the stream. I thought its four-foot antler span magnificent, but Chris told me that was about average in these parts.

Walking several miles on this particular tundra was extremely difficult for all of us, especially for Jason and Betsy. Although covered with beautiful tiny flowers of many kinds, the springy surface was pockmocked like a moonscape. Each round hole was from two to six feet in diameter, sometimes three feet deep, and most often filled with water. To make things even more difficult, the holes were too close together to walk between them. In addition, large areas of the terrain were covered with low bushes whose branches were frequently intertwined. A careless step put us in the bottom of a hole, ankle-deep or waist-deep in water. Then again, getting wet was not much of a concern, because after just a few minutes we were all soaked with sweat. Later, when I asked Jason to tell me his greatest achievement of the entire trip, he replied, "Walking up and down the Battle River without crying."

His greatest fishing achievement came two days later, when we flew over to the north side of Lake Iliamna to scout for grayling and Arctic char in some small, unnamed lakes. On the way over we saw our first caribou herd, about a dozen moving eastward through the tundra. We had no luck in the lakes, but the connecting streams were small and wadeable—just right for Jason. He had been at a decided disadvantage in the large Copper River and so far had landed only two or three trout. Here, the water never lapped over his wading boots. I stayed with him and gave him a few pointers while he fished upstream with dry flies in the riffles, using a classical approach and a surprisingly delicate presentation. The strikes were swift and immediate. I was very proud to see him catch more than two dozen trout during the afternoon. Again, we released all the rainbows but kept enough of the larger grayling for our supper that evening.

The abundant wildlife provided almost constant excitement during the trip. Bear, caribou, otter, moose, and eagles were plentiful, and once, while I was fishing under an overhanging bluff, a light-gray wolf came across the tundra, lay down on the cliff above me to watch for a while, and then quietly loped away. I spent several hours watching two common loons who were nesting near the lodge on a small island. While one stayed on the nest, the other was usually on the lake fishing. They are anything but common—among the most beautiful of birds, with their intricate black-and-white summer markings. Only once or twice did we hear their strange cry, like a maniac laughing.

When we arrived back at the lodge that afternoon, some of Chris's neighbors were there as additional guests. While the children played up on the tundra, the rest of us sat on rocks and logs along the shore and discussed how the permanent residents were trying to prevent too many changes in their Alaskan way of life while still welcoming tourists and new jobs. It seemed like a hopeless task, but at least this group agreed that the new Alaska Lands Bill offered the best guidelines for protecting the places that were especially lovely.

Chris thought we might need a few more fish for supper, so he and I decided to try the northern pike just around the bend from our camp. On my first cast with a small silver spoon I landed a twenty-four-inch pike—a ferocious prehistoric-looking monster. Two casts later, a larger one nearly came into the boat with us when he attacked the lure just as I prepared to lift it from the water. It was almost frightening. We moved a hundred yards and began casting again in the gathering dusk. As the lure hit the surface in one small cove, we could see waves from several pike converging on the splash point. Each racing to see which could reach the lure first, they looked like crocodiles in an old Tarzan movie. In anticipation of a strike—or perhaps subconsciously to avoid one—I snatched the spoon out of the water! On the next cast, I took a thirty-four-inch pike, enough for a fine meal. Later, cooked in foil, the pike fillets proved to be the favorite fish of all the diners.

The weather had warmed rapidly since our arrival. The morning temperature was now up about fifty degrees Fahrenheit and the afternoons fifteen degrees warmer. We could tell within the week that much of the snow on the nearby mountaintops had melted. More important for us, the caddis and stonefly hatches multiplied. After lunch on the last few days of the trip it was not hard to spot rising trout. Usually we would catch a few fish during the early morning on wet flies and heavier tackle, and then shift to dry flies, a #5 rod, and fine leaders to fish the hatches. While Jason cast in the shallow pools and around the edges, I braved the deeper waters where we could see the larger rainbows.

Despite the plentiful feeding trout, it wasn't easy to match the tiny caddis flies the trout seemed to be taking. Sometimes, after trying small flies of all sizes, we had success with a #12 Royal Wulff. On only one occasion did the trout rise regularly to a #16 or #18 elk-hair Caddis, but this was to be the preeminent dry fly-fishing of my life. In midafternoon, large fish began feeding near the deeper bank on a wide stretch of the river. Even when I waded out the maximum safe distance, standing on my tiptoes, I could barely reach them with my longest cast using a double haul. The strong center current between me and the trout began dragging the line as soon as it landed; at best I was able to give the fly four or five feet of natural float. However, with almost every "perfect" cast, a big rainbow would take the tiny fly with a determined, rolling strike. Then I would have to keep a tight line and at the same time ease back out of the deep water until I found a firm enough foothold in the loose bottom gravel to let me put tension on the line.

It took me twenty-five minutes to land my first fish, a twenty-one-incher, using a three-pound-test tippet. After that I changed to a stronger leader, so that neither the trout nor I would be too exhausted when the battle was over. Despite careful retrieve I still broke two leaders but landed a dozen rainbows, the smallest one fourteen inches. When the hatch was over I could hardly raise my arm. Fishing from a sandbar farther downstream, Jason had had an equally thrilling time.

He and I were both saddened as our week drew to a close, a feeling tempered only by the prospect of a reunion with my wife and Jason's parents. We knew it would be impossible for us ever to recount our experiences to them. They were truly indescribable: our immersion in the beauty and grandeur of Alaska's mountains, tundra, and waterways; our close encounters with the bears, moose, eagles, and other wildlife; and the testing of our wits and skills against some of the greatest fighting fish on earth. Most important, at least for me, was my companionship with Jason. Repeatedly during these few days I was flooded with memories of outings with my father. Sometimes I watched my grandson react to a thrilling spectacle— or an unexpected challenge—and imagined that I was seeing myself two generations ago.

From Rainbow River Lodge we flew up the Copper River, west across Cook Inlet, and then northward up the Kenai Peninsula back to Anchorage. It had been an exhausting week, but Jason still had his face pressed against the window as we looked down at just a few more of Alaska's wonders. We didn't talk much, except to speculate on when we might return. Jason and I had developed an undying appreciation for our forty-ninth state.

Terry Tempest Williams

Water

from *Desert Quartet*

At first, I think it is a small leather pouch someone has dropped along the trail. I bend down, pick it up and only then recognize it for what it is—a frog, dead and dried. I have a leather thong in my pack which I take out and thread through the frog's mouth and out through its throat. The skin is thin which makes a quick puncture possible. I then slide the frog to the center of the thong, tie a knot with both ends and create a necklace which I wear.

I grew up with frogs. My brothers and cousins hurled them against canyon walls as we hiked the trail to Rainbow Bridge when Lake Powell was rising behind Glen Canyon Dam.

I hated what they did and told them so. But my cries only encouraged them, excited them, until I became the wall they would throw frogs against. I didn't know what to do—stand still and soften their blow by trying to catch each frog in my hands like a cradle or turn and run, hoping they would miss me altogether. I tried to believe that somehow the frogs would sail through the air in safety landing perfectly poised on a bed of moss. But inevitably, the tiny canyon frogs (about the size of a ripe plum) quickly became entombed in the fists of adolescents and would die on impact, hitting my body, the boys' playing field. I would turn and walk down to the creek and wash the splattered remains off of me. I would enter the

water, sit down in the current, and release the frog bodies downstream with my tears.

I never forgave.

Years later, my impulse to bathe with frogs is still the same. Ha-
vasu. It is only an hour or so past dawn. The creek is cold and clear.
I take off my skin of clothes and leave them on the bank. I shiver.
How long has it been since I have allowed myself to lie on my back
and float. The dried frog floats with me. A slight tug around my neck
makes me believe it is still alive swimming in the current. Travertine
terraces spill over with turquoise water and we are held in place by
a liquid hand that cools and calms the desert.

I dissolve. I am water. Only my face is exposed like an apparition
over ripples. Playing with water. Do I dare? My legs open. The rushing water turns my body and touches me with a fast finger that does
not tire. I receive without apology. Time. Nothing to rush, only to
feel. I feel time in me. It is endless pleasure in the current. No control. No thought. Simply, here. My left hand reaches for the frog
dangling from my neck, floating above my belly and I hold it between
my breasts like a withered heart, beating inside me, inside the river.
We are moving downstream. Water. Water music. Blue notes, white
notes, my body mixes with the body of the water like jazz, the current like jazz. I, too, am free to improvise.

I grip the stones in shallow water. There is moss behind my fingernails.

I leave the creek and walk up to my clothes. I am already dry. My
skirt and blouse slip on effortlessly. I twist my hair and secure it with
a stick. The frog is still with me. Do I imagine beads of turquoise have
replaced the sunken and hollow eyes?

We walk. Canyons within canyons. The sun threatens to annihi-
late me. I recall all the oven doors I have opened to a blast of heat
that burned my face. My eyes narrow. Each turn takes us deeper inside the Grand Canyon, my frog companion and I.

We are witness to this opening of time, vertical and horizontal, at
once. Between these crossbars of geology is a silent sermon of how

the world was formed. Seas advanced and retreated. Dunes now stand in stone. Volcanoes erupted and lava was cooled. Garnets shimmer and separate schist from granite. It is sculptured time to be touched, even tasted, our mineral content preserved in the desert.

This is the Rio Colorado.

We are water. Without it nothing is swept away. Desire begins in wetness. My fingers curl around this little frog. Like me, it was born out of longing, wet not dry. We can always return to our place of origin. Water. Water music. We are baptized by immersion, nothing less can replenish or restore our capacity to love. It is endless if we believe in water.

We are approaching a cliff. Red monkeyflowers bloom. White-throated swifts and violet-green swallows crisscross above. My throat is parched. There is a large pool below. My fear of heights is overcome by my desire to merge. I dive into the water, deeper and deeper, my eyes open, and I see a slender passageway. I wonder if I have enough breath to venture down. I take the risk and swim through the limestone corridor where the water is milky and I can barely focus through the shimmering sediments of sand until it opens into a clear, green room. The frog fetish floats to the surface. I rise too and grab a few breaths held in the top story of this strange cavern. The green room turns red, red, my own blood, my own heart beating, my fingers touch the crown of my head and streak the wall.

Down. I sink back into the current which carries me out of the underwater maze to the pool. I rise once again, feeling a scream inside me surfacing as I do scream, breathe, tread water, get my bearings. The outside world is green is blue is red is hot, so hot. I swim to a limestone ledge, climb out and lie on my stomach, breathing. The rock is steaming. The frog is under me. Beating. Heart beating. I am dry. I long to be wet. I am bleeding. Back on my knees, I immerse my head into the pool once more to ease the cut and look below. Half in. Half out. Amphibious. I am drawn to both earth and water. The frog breaks free from the leather thong. I try to grab its body but miss and watch it slowly spiral into the depths.

———

Before leaving, I drink from a nearby spring and hold a mouthful—
I hear frogs, a chorus of frogs, their voices rising like bubbles from
what seems to be the green room. Muddled at first, they become
clear. I run back to the edge of the pool and listen—throwing back
my head, I burst into laughter spraying myself with water.

It is rain.

It is frogs.

It is hearts breaking against the bodies of those we love.

Rick Bass

Thunder & Lightning

from *Sierra*

I am hovering like an outlaw up on the Canada/Montana border, over on the east side of the Divide, the Front Range, where I have just made a fool of myself, have been rude and socially unacceptable. I've come over from the deep woods of the west side—the wet, clearcut-riddled side—to read at a benefit for a nonprofit organization from Hollywood that's trying to raise dollars to purchase critical habitat for the grizzlies and the wolves—the beautiful, glossy creatures that have been so kind to Hollywood in the past. The reading has been advertised to the public as an evening of "bears, wolves, and writers"—implicit is the notion that it will be an evening of fun and celebration. Everyone's all duded up; everyone's eating and drinking and merrymaking. As luck would have it, I'm first up at the mike. They're trapped now, everyone in their seats, smiling and expecting poetry about the muscled hump of the grizzly and the night-howl of the wolfpack.

Instead, I ambush them. Instead of giving them a nice reading, I ask for something. I read them a shrill diatribe about the Yaak Valley—the most northwestern valley in the U.S. Rockies, a vital cornerstone to the health of the entire West. I harangue my tender, sweet-smelling audience with a request for letters to Congress to designate the last few roadless areas in the Yaak as wilderness. I point to the raggedy-ass, ink-smudged mimeographs that will be on the table on their way out.

I don't read any pretty poems that day, but instead tell them the harsh facts—about the low-elevation rainforest of the Yaak, the only one like it in the United States; about how it grows big trees, and about how those trees have been clearcut by corporations that are abandoning the area now that most of the big trees are gone. I tell about the thousands of miles of road that the Forest Service has built for the timber industry throughout the valley, and of the nobility of the animals that are hanging on there. I spell out the names of the senators and representatives to write to; I spell out the addresses. The audience shifts, squirms, yawns, rolls eyes, checks watches. No shit, Sherlock, who's up next? We all know the Rockies are being lost, they're thinking. But what I'm thinking is, if we all know it, then why is it happening?

The good thing about my breach of etiquette is that at the cocktail party afterward I have lots of space to myself. Beware the zealot.

I know I've been behaving badly, passing out my little Yaak-flyers at all social gatherings—weddings and christenings included, everywhere except funerals—but I can't help it. Time is so short, and the land, the entire West, is no longer being cut up into halves or quarters or even eighths, but into sixty-fourths now, and one-hundred-twenty-eighths next year, and then into thousandths, and millionths, while we sit complacently idle, or at best strap on our roller blades and hitch up our sagging Lycra. I see too much play in the Rockies these days, and not enough work. I am damn near frantic over what is being lost.

The four largest national parks in the Rockies—Yellowstone, Waterton/Glacier, Banff, and Jasper—are currently of no real or lasting importance to the region's biological health. They are like the large, showy muscles of a bodybuilder who has ceased to work out. They're not going to last; the cardiovascular system's been ignored. The wild, fresh blood can't get from one big muscle to the next.

We're losing the big animals first. In the Yaak Valley, for instance, the animals that we most think of as defining the American wilderness are now down to single- or at most double-digit populations. That means nine or ten grizzlies. Two or three wolves. A single woodland caribou. Perhaps three or four lynx. A handful of black-hearted, uncompromising wolverines.

Some creatures can adapt and move through, across, or around our exponentially increasing fragmentation. But not wolves. Unlike salamanders and woodpeckers, wolves will be shot by our own species whenever we see them. And certainly the grizzlies need the space that's being lost. Down to less than 2 percent of their former range, they simply will not barter with humans.

Conservation and ecosystem biologists refer to grizzlies and wolves as "umbrella species"—meaning that they are animals whose charisma and habitat requirements can help humans save broad, intact ecosystems. If grizzlies and wolves are present, everything else in a system will be present.

When it is raining, I want an umbrella—and believe me, it is pouring, and there aren't enough to go around. The spirit of the Rockies and its wildness is getting soggy, is tattering, falling apart.

Sixty million years ago, the earth not too far from the Yaak Valley got up and left: it was folded and pressed and thrust about 70 miles eastward, up over the Continental Divide and into what would much later become the Blackfeet Indians' sacred grounds, the Badger–Two Medicine region of northern Montana. A pattern of big things traveling great distances was set in motion. And the pattern only got stronger. With the new mountains in place, the frigid hearts of glaciers began to form, sliding up and down the mountains, cutting and shaping them for the species that existed then, and for the ones that would come later.

With sharp, loving teeth, the glaciers sculpted hideaway cirques, hanging valleys, fast, wild rivers, and then eased, groaning, down

onto the plains, dumping moraines and clacking boulders and cob-
bles, stopping at the edge of what is now called the Front Range of
the Rockies—where the mountains meet the plains.

There was also a great glacier out on the plains, and a narrow band
of open ground between the two ice sheets, a corridor running north
and south along the Front Range. This was a corridor for humans,
bear, bison, and mammoths—big mammals, even giant mammals,
always moving.

Paleontologist Jack Horner (the guy who was advisor to the
movie *Jurassic Park*, but who is not responsible for its fictions) has discovered 75-million-year-old fossils along the Front Range of a previously unknown dinosaur he calls a myosaur, which he believes
traveled in great herds like bison. *Tyrannosaurus rex*, the terrible
16,000-pound "lizard king," followed them, feeding on the bodies of
the drowned, the sick, and the diseased, much as grizzlies move
down low in spring to feed on green-up grasses and the carcasses of
winter-killed deer, elk, and moose.

Once there were hundreds of thousands of individuals, even millions, in the herds of Rocky Mountain megafauna, but due to a lack
of intact systems, and a lack of predators to drive the herds into large
groups and keep them moving, our herds—elk and antelope,
now—are much smaller and more spread out.

Yet the essence of the emerging science of conservation biology,
beyond the recognition that all of nature is interconnected, is that a
habitat must not become fragmented, cut off from other wildlands.
Should it be made into an "island," then it will be able to support
fewer species, and some stranded populations will go extinct.

To avoid such losses, you protect the richest ecosystems first,
along with places strategically located between them, to allow genetic transfer between the systems.

Which—surprise!—brings me back to the Yaak, up on the Canadian border. Like some wild species hiding out in the dense, wet
timber, I seem unable to leave, in my frantic heart, this one relatively
small but cornerstone valley: among the most biologically diverse in

the Rockies, and one that is totally unprotected, with not a single acre of designated wilderness. Not a single protected wildlife refuge, park, nothing. It's just open season.

If the Yaak falls, then the wild creatures in British Columbia will lose an important link to the Bitterroot Range along the Montana/ Idaho border and the Salmon Mountains to the south (where they would have a straight shot into Yellowstone to the southeast, or into Oregon's Blue Mountains to the southwest).

The Yaak similarly connects the Northern Continental Divide ecosystem—Glacier National Park, the Bob Marshall Wilderness, Badger–Two Medicine country, and the Swan Valley—to the Selkirks of northern Idaho, and to the North Cascades, which connect to the Central Cascades and the Coast Range.

Because the Yaak so strategically links north to south and west to east, it has the combined, teeming diversity of all these systems. Not just grizzlies and wolves, but wolverines, woodland caribou, snowy owls, and sculpin.

If the Yaak is not saved, if we allow it to fall, we might as well cut open the body of the Rockies and reach in and grab the hot, bloody, steaming red heart and twist it free, yank it out. Steam will rise from the empty carcass. Blood-flow will stop. The brain and body might function a few more seconds—five or ten years. But then no more.

Am I asking people to flock to see this place? I am not—not until there is some system of preservation, some plan, in place. It frightens the hell out of me to be focusing on it. But the Yaak is so much at the edge—so heavily fragmented—that if we do not draw attention to it, it will surely be lost. The populations of the big creatures are dwindling, and yet the lushness, the biodiversity, is still here. Even as I write these words, in the early fall, the chitter of a kingfisher is mixing with the caws of ravens. Earlier this morning, I heard coyotes; last night, elk. There is still a symphony, still a harmony—but the big guys are in trouble, and when places like the Yaak are in trouble, then so too is the West: Jasper, Banff, Glacier, Yellowstone, and Rocky Mountain National Park. All of it.

On a visit to India last year, a friend explained the Buddhist cere-
monies to me—how the high priest, before each service, would grip
a bell symbolizing thunder, or force, in one hand, and a *dorje,* a rattle,
symbolizing lightning, or direction, in the other. He would ring the
bell and shake the *dorje,* thunder and lightning, the *dorje*'s lightning
giving direction and purpose to the brute power of the bell's thunder, heaven's message to the earth that we need both. For me it all
came back to the symbolism of the disappearing bear and wolf in my
own country, our own form of holiness: the great berry-grazing,
thunderous, brute power of the grizzly, drawing his or her strength
from a single mountain year-round—*sleeping* inside the mountain, in
the winter—and the *dorje* of the wolves, traveling single file sometimes, on the hunt, or on the move, searching—always, it seems—
for a new valley where they might be safe, where they might rest,
even if only for a while. Thunder and lightning.

Never mind that grizzlies once gathered in great numbers on California beaches to feast on the carcasses of washed-ashore whales, or
that they roamed the deserts of Texas and Mexico, the prairies of
Kansas, and the forests of Minnesota. All we are talking about right
now is trying to hold on to what we've got. If grizzlies don't have
cores of pristine wildness, and if they cannot move from core to core,
then they're gone.

One summer day I find myself sitting barefoot in a field up in the
Yaak with local conservationists Chip Clark and Jesse Sedler, and
Evan Frost of the Greater Ecosystems Alliance in Bellingham, Washington. Evan has come all the way over here because he recognizes
the vital location of the Yaak.

We're talking about how absolutely critical it is to have corridors;
we're naming creeks in the Yaak, elk-wintering flats, grizzly-denning
areas, wolf runways. We must sound like modern versions of the old
trappers and mountain men who first came to this country almost
200 years ago. Like them, we're describing routes and passes; special,
shining places that are a long journey away, through wild, rugged

country. Evan is listing the valleys to cross, the rivers to get from here to the Pacific Northwest. It's a short list, and you're there: fresh, new genes. Meanwhile, Jesse and I are diagramming how a wandering wolf could come out of Canada, down through the Yaak, and head all the way to Mexico. *If.*

The Bull River Valley and Trout Creek country, through the Nine-mile, then straight down into the Salmon/Bitteroot. A day's or two-days' journey into Yellowstone, and down to Bear Lake in northern Utah, near the Cache Valley, where a grizzly bear once leapt up out of the marsh and chased Jim Bridger and bit Bridger's horse in the ass. Into the high Uintas, then, where grizzlies and wolves may still be secretly holed up. Down into the Weminuche Wilderness in the San Juan Mountains of Colorado, and into New Mexico. Down the ridge of the Sangre de Cristos toward Mexico.

Except it's not quite like the old mountain men's talk must have been. We're sitting here in the late-summer sun, surrounded by cool, dark trees. Clearcuts have scarred our valley, made it unattractive to humans. Evan and Chip and Jesse are spreading out Mylar sheets on top of maps of the Yaak, computer-generated overlays that show remaining stands of old growth—*stability*—and grizzly–radio-collar telemetry locations, and polygon mapping of elk herd movements. Some of these data, put together by Jesse in his spare time on a borrowed computer, were gathered while he was cruising the valley on his old motorcycle with a busted-out headlight, like Easy Rider dodging deer in the dusk; some are from Chip and Jesse's work measuring trees for the Forest Service.

We have more data, and less hope.

I can barely even talk about woodland caribou. They used to be all through the upper part of this valley, but now we have only one lonely bull that wanders over every few years during breedimg season, sniffing the ancient scent of the soil, old migration corridors, where so many of his kind once lived.

He's sort of an embarrassment, the way he keeps hanging on. (One year he showed up on the golf course at Bonners Ferry, Idaho.)

Neither the state nor the feds will list the woodland caribou as an endangered species, and I get the feeling they're all wishing he'd hurry up and die, and that another two dozen in the Idaho Panhandle would go ahead and kick the bucket too, so that the problem would just go away. The bull trout, a little-known migratory fish found in northern Montana and Idaho, is also vulnerable to habitat fragmentation. It lives in rivers or lakes, and in the fall travels as far as 160 miles upstream to spawn (when anglers and dams will allow it). But it doesn't die after spawning, like a salmon does; it returns to its home. Some live to be as old as ten years, and as large as 25 pounds.

Some bull trout spawn every other year, while others spawn every third year, so that if there is a drought or a fire, a whole lake's population will not be lost; there'll be some survivors back in camp who didn't make the journey that year. Once they've made that great cruise up through the forest, beneath the cool cedars and across the shallows (their huge, humped backs tingling with fear, perhaps, at the knowledge of ospreys and eagles above—traveling up toward the Yaak at night, perhaps, under the moon, past otters, wolves, and bears; past coyotes, lions, lynx, and wolverines)—once they've made it up to the creek's headwaters, each female excavates a redd (spawning ground) roughly the size of a pickup bed and buries her eggs a foot and a half deep.

The eggs are fertilized; and then, beneath gold larches, red maples, and aspen-blaze, with the days growing colder, the bull trout head back downstream, coasting, to their home.

The fry are born around the first of the year, like good thoroughbreds. They don't come out of the gravel after hatching; they'll wait until spring for that. But such is their fury, their lust to enter the system, that even as immature fry they are predators.

They hang out in their river, then, for one to three years before beginning their migration down to the lake or larger river they have never seen or been to, but which is their home. These days there is an introduced species, lake trout, in those lakes, that will eat the young bull trout with a vengeance, but still the trout migrate.

Beyond lake trout, what's hurting the bull trout? Dams. Eroded soil from roadbuilding, overgrazing, and clearcutting that washes straight into the creeks and rivers, preventing fertilization of their eggs. Even though the Yaak River is still clear, there's about a quarter inch of sediment covering the best spawning riffles. What the giant trout need is habitat protection.

There are fewer than 20 bull trout in the Yaak. One creek where they are making a last stand is a place with scabrous, lunar-gray clearcuts perched on steep slopes. Those 20 bull trout—maybe only 10 or so each year—cut off by Libby Dam to the north, and by sedimentation downstream—are still moving back and forth through the autumns, as they have through the millennia—back and forth, back and forth, being big, being wild, in nature—but with the nature around them getting smaller and smaller.

I've got this theory that even though the populations in the Yaak are down, they're maybe a hundred times more important, genetically, than denser populations. For these individuals to have survived, in the face of such heavy development, they must have super-genes, survivors' genes—and should be saved at all costs. I believe their genes can save the other populations. In other words, the fish up in that creek are high-grade ore, as good as gold.

The wolf biologist Mike Jimenez tells of a lone, male wolf he followed in Idaho, the first known wolf in that state in a long damn time. Jimenez refers to that wolf as "a super-individual," one with survivors' genes. Hunting on his own, the wolf was bringing down adult moose, something I had not thought possible and which I don't readily understand, when deer and elk were also available.

A wolf killed in Yellowstone 2 years ago, the first known wolf to make it back to the park in more than 60 years, was DNA-tested and discovered to have come directly from a valley near the Yaak, Ninemile—or, if not, then from that pack's ancestors, which started out in Canada and Montana's Glacier/Pleasant Valley country, up in this dark, wooded part of the state.

The animals are not resting. If they're not resting, why should we, who claim to be bound up with them in the weave? Any good work that is going to be done must happen now, this year, these next few years. We can rest only after we make a good resting spot.

"When despair for the world grows in me," Wendell Berry writes in his poem, "The Peace of Wild Things,"

> and I wake in the night at the least sound
> in fear of what my life and my children's lives may be,
> I go and lie down where the wood drake
> rests in his beauty on the water, and the great heron feeds,
> I come into the peace of wild things
> who do not tax their lives with forethought
> of grief. I come into the presence of still water.
> And I feel above me the day-blind stars
> waiting with their light. For a time
> I rest in the grace of the world, and am free.

I take a hike up a steep, timbered hill to a special spot in the Yaak. It's at the edge of one of the roadless areas that we have to save if any wilderness—any thunder and lightning—is going to survive. It's springtime, and I am in some old-growth cedars at about 5,000 feet, when I hear the sound of frogs. I have been looking for bear sign, but I move quietly toward the sound, toward a little alder-bench on the side of the mountain.

I've just read David Quammen's disturbing essay on amphibians' mysterious, worldwide demise. The cause may not be ultraviolet radiaton or global warming, but something more basic: fragmentation. It's never really occurred to me before, how frogs and salamanders maintain genetic vigor. A grizzly or a wolf can always try, at least, to get up and go. But how far, really, can a frog go, over the dam's spillway, or down the sedimented creek, or across the road? It's a whole new problem to brood about.

I'm tired from hiking all day. I find the little pond where they're calling. It's not even a pond so much as a rain puddle, a snowmelt catchment, about the size of someone's living room. I've been on this mountain a hundred times, but never knew it was here, ephemeral. The frogs grow silent, even at my stealthy approach.

How long will this little high-elevation marsh last? How long do its inhabitants have to find it, lay their eggs, and then hatch? And then where do they go? What kind of frogs *are* these? I don't even know their damn name. They're not leopard frogs, or green frogs; they're kind of funky-looking, tiny, but with big heads, as if for shoveling, burying themselves.

All any wild thing wants is a place to settle, a sanctuary with the freedom to roam if it wants or needs to. I take Berry's poem to heart; I curl up on the hillside and rest, very still, waiting for the frogs to forget about me, and to start up again. I've heard frogs singing so loudly during breeding season in southern Utah that the din made me nauseous. But when this little chorus starts back up, it's nowhere near as thunderous. This pond is not that crowded.

Earlier in the afternoon, farther back into the roadless area, I'd heard a grizzly flipping boulders just above me, looking for ants. It was right up at snowline, and the boulders were immense. I feel certain it was a grizzly. There was no way I could go higher to see, though; I was afraid it might be a sow with cubs. I turned and went back down the mountain, having heard only the music of those boulders.

Now I lie here in the spring grass like a child, listening to the frogs, and thinking about the future: thinking about grizzly music, wolf music, elk music, trout music, and frog music. I try to feel the old earth stretching beneath me, whispering, or singing.

"I listen to a concert in which so many parts are wanting," Thoreau wrote, in the springtime, in 1856. "Many of those animal migrations and other phenomena by which the Indians marked the season are no longer to be observed. . . . I take infinite pains to know all the phenomena of the spring, for instance, thinking that I have here the entire poem, and then, to my chagrin, I hear that it is but an imperfect copy that I possess and have read, that my ancestors have torn out many of the first leaves and grandest passages, and mutilated it in many places. I should not like to think that some demigod had come before me and picked out some of the best of the stars. I wish to know an entire heaven and an entire earth."

The music of predators and their prey: big predators and big prey are heard most easily and clearly. Yet we are learning to hear other, subtler harmonies, too, even as they grow fainter in the Rockies: the beetles and the rotting logs, the mosses and the frogs.

As blue dusk comes sliding in, I'm sitting there curled up like a child on a warm spring night, up on the mountain, a long way from home, listening to frogs. I'm on the side of the mountain that faces civilization. Two miles away, below me, there is a logging road, and someone's been cutting firewood; I just heard his saw shut off. I imagine it's already dark, down there.

I picture the woodcutter, a neighbor, sitting on a stump, resting from his day's work, mopping his brow, and also listening—hearing the silence after his saw is shut off, and then the sound of the night.

After a while I hear his truck start up, and he drives away. I watch the yellow of his headlights wind far down into the valley as he heads home, where he will sleep, and rest, that night, as will I.

We will not hear anything as we sleep, but the frogs will keep singing, the elk will keep bugling, and the wolves will keep howling, until the fire within them goes out. We are still part of their song, too, but we just are not hearing it yet.

We should not rest much longer. We should only take naps. We should listen more closely. We should save a few places, like the Yaak, that have never been saved. It's simple; it's what we've known all along. We need to put the pieces back together.

Louise Wagenknecht

How Two Logging Towns Were Lost

from *High Country News*

I grew up in two lumber towns. The first died, with no fanfare, no parades of logging trucks, and no spotted owl controversy. The second was recently catapulted into a changed world. Each reflects part of the Greek tragedy of the Western lumber industry.

My first home was Hilt, Calif., named after John Hilt, who built a sawmill near the California-Oregon line. In 1883, a railroad was built directly through the future townsite, and the surrounding forest was chopped into a checkerboard ownership pattern. Some of the alternate sections were purchased by John Hilt's successors. When my grandparents arrived in 1929, the place was a thriving company town. "The Company" was Fruit Growers Supply Company, a subsidiary of Sunkist, which had decided years before that it was cheaper to build fruit boxes from its own lumber. For almost 50 years afterwards, the Hilt operation was serious about only one type of lumber: *Pinus lambertiana,* the mighty sugar pine.

Sugar pine does not grow in pure stands, but is scattered among the ponderosa pines and Douglas-firs of the Klamath-Siskiyou Mountains. The loggers did not limit themselves to sugar pine, of course. The entire town of Hilt, its houses, sidewalks, garages, store, and school, were all built of local woods. Everyone in town burned wood for heat. Culverts were hammered together from incense cedar in the company's carpenter shop.

The company practice of high-grading its forests meant that when the post–World II building boom began, a lot of trees were left. In 1954, the company built a new dry kiln and planing mill; lumber prices were up, and Hilt was ready. Fruit Growers became the third largest lumber producer in California in the 1950s. At the same time, the box factory began a phase-out, as sturdy cardboard boxes took over the fruit container market. My grandfather retired as foreman, and the remaining workers were moved to other plant operations.

My grandparents moved away in 1961. Their house on Front Street stood empty for a while. I went there sometimes, to crawl far up into the cherry tree in the back yard and meditate upon the changes rushing upon us all. Change was happening too fast for me. The interstate between California and Oregon was completed. Some of my schoolmates left: their parents purchasing houses in Ashland or Yreka, and commuting to work.

For myself, I could not imagine a better place to live than Hilt. The mill whistles that measured our lives; the unpaved streets where we rode our bicycles with impunity; the board sidewalks which yielded up stray coins (we fished them out with gum on a stick); the fields and streamlets where pop bottles and frogs awaited the enterprising searcher; these were our worlds. So long as we respected certain boundaries, our parents didn't worry about us. "I never knew a child who didn't like Hilt," a younger contemporary said once, and to this day the intimate geography of that small valley on the state line is branded onto my mind and heart as no other place can be. Even the ripe smell of the millpond was pleasant to me. It was part of the peace of summer evenings, when nighthawks wheeled and swooped, and the long-gone sun backlit the far, jagged horizon.

The vacant houses and missing families were tangible, but behind them lurked larger changes. Fruit Growers was running out of timber. The company began to bid on national forest sales, but the price was often higher than it could pay. By 1972, the Hilt operation didn't have enough timber left to keep the mill running. Next year, the company shut down, and began to sell or demolish most of the town.

Although I saw Hilt only infrequently by then, it was a relief when the razing was complete, sparing just a few structures. The community church, the firehouse and two or three houses stayed. Some townsite land was rented out, and alfalfa grew on the Little League diamond. The tall black locust trees on our former lawn went down with the house, but a dozen suckers grew, and remain.

Was this the sustainable reality of Hilt, and all else an illusion? If so, its passing brought regret and nostalgia, but no public outcry, no suggestion that the body politic should keep it going. The company honored its pension commitments. The office workers kept their jobs, in some form. Fruit Growers still owns forest land, sells some timber and maintains an office in Hilt. It is, ironically, operating on a deliberate sustained yield basis for the first time in its history.

Elsewhere, the old-growth controversy was a decade away. The Forest Service was selling its quota, and there were other towns where mills ran three shifts and had plenty of timber.

Happy Camp, Calif., for instance, where four mills ran day and night. Roads were fierce with screaming jake brakes and huge grills in rear-view mirrors. Saturday nights were good for at least two street brawls as loggers staggered from bar to bar. Just as Hilt was fading, Happy Camp was booming. In 1962, my eyes saw it as raw, uncultured and unfinished-looking, the way it probably looked in 1852, when the boom commodity was gold.

Despite its look of impermanence, Happy Camp was far older than Hilt. It was isolated, and although only 75 miles away, it might have been in another country. The winding highway that followed the Klamath River into a darkly forested canyon was long, and my brother always got carsick on it. But where Indian Creek flowed into the river, the country opened up a little, and long before the first white miners stormed in, a large village of Karuks settled there. Then in 1851, a group of miners built some log shacks and stayed the winter. There has been an "American" community there ever since. By the mid-1850s, the early prospectors had moved on, leaving the country to well-financed mining companies.

Digging great ditches to carry water from far up the creeks, miners rigged hoses and blasted terraces out of the mountainsides.

One of these became Happy Camp's airport. Small sawmills mushroomed in the wake of each mine. On the heels of the miners came storekeepers and homesteaders, husbanding the precious meadows near the river to raise hay, fruit and vegetables. In the niches of mines and ranches, the Karuks salvaged remnants of their culture, adopting the implements of white men that seemed useful to them. Small and remote, the town was a place apart during the 90 years or so between boom times.

My mother remembered bits of this world. During the Depression, one of her uncles eked out a living on a mining claim up Indian Creek. Visiting him was a three-day adventure that started on the endless unpaved road. There were no big sawmills in Happy Camp. No large logging companies worked in the vast forests. Yet several hundred people lived there.

Some were miners, a trade taken up with the Depression. Some were subsistence ranchers who worked for wages when they could. Livestock, hay and enormous gardens supplemented their meager cash income. The Forest Service employed a ranger and some temporary help. There were teachers, mail carriers and state and county road department employees. Their paychecks were spent in local stores. Rents and taxes were low, to an extent many of their descendants would find unimaginable. Happy Camp's people did not need the outside world. Consumerism was limited to what Evans Mercantile stocked and what the mail order catalogs described.

Life changed when large-scale logging and milling arrived in the early 1950s. Roads were improved and extended, and suddenly there was full employment, at least in the summer. Hordes of newcomers created an insatiable market for rentals. The old residents still hunted, fished and picked blackberries, but now they bought frozen foods and went to Medford to buy clothes. New cars and pickups arrived. The old ranches began to be purchased as fishing retreats by southern Californians, as their owners fled to town and the wage economy. Locally grown hay all but disappeared as bales arrived on trucks from Scott Valley, 40 miles away. Behind the old barns, their roofs rotting and falling in, dump rakes and mowers rusted in the engulfing blackberry vines.

Good wages and cheap gasoline allowed prosperity to be defined as a new house trailer on a quarter-acre terrace carved into a 40-percent slope with a D-8 Cat. Gradually, wooden appendages grew around the trailer—a porch, a woodshed—until the original metal box virtually vanished from sight. Three or four kids played in the dirt banks behind the trailer. Those kids were my classmates and their younger siblings.

Those children were a shock to me. Compared to Hilt kids, they were loud, profane and rough. They hooted when I naively admitted that my father now worked for the Forest Service. "Piss-fir Willie!" they shrieked delightedly. But I loved their free, go-to-hell attitude, so refreshing after the status-conscious snobbishness of children in Hilt, where everyone knew who your father's boss was.

The kids knew that by the time they got out of high school, there would be a job waiting for them in the woods or the mills. They knew this because their elders told them so. They saw that their parents were more prosperous than their grandparents. They could look out over ridge after ridge of unbroken, unroaded old-growth timber.

The Forest Service assured them that the forest was being managed for something called "sustained yield." Yet these children, grown into thirty-something adults with their own children preparing to enter the labor market (we marry young in Happy Camp), have recently learned, from the lips of the Klamath National Forest supervisor herself, that the annual cut for the forest must and will be revised downward. Drastically downward, to half of what we children of the 1960s were assured it would always be.

News like that affects not only the several hundred primary wage earners employed in logging and milling, but also those who work in supporting services and businesses. Perhaps the unthinkable could really happen. Perhaps the world of car payments and cable TV and take-out pizza is an ephemeral one that cannot be sustained.

The newspaper headlines blame the spotted owl and the environmentalists, and a myth persists that there is still plenty of timber, if only "they" would let the Forest Service do its job of feeding the mills. Yet, if every stick of old-growth timber on the Happy Camp Ranger District not in a designated wilderness area were laid out in timber sales this year, how long would it last?

On a wall in someone's cubbyhole in the Happy Camp Ranger District office, there was (before the devastating 1987 forest fires) an aerial photograph of the entire Happy Camp Ranger District. On it, the huge scar of the Indian Ridge Burn was visible. This 12,000-acre fire occurred in 1966. Large areas of it are now brush fields, having resisted all efforts at reforestation. Also visible are the big clearcuts from the 1960s, some of them replanted six or seven times, and still not regenerated sufficiently to meet Forest Service standards.

This aerial montage, remember, did not show the scars of the 1987 fires, so large they were no longer called "fires," but "complexes." It did not show the salvage logging that took place after the fires were out. When I think about that photographic map, I find it impossible to listen with a straight face to anyone who tells me that enough old-growth remains on this district to support a cut of 55 million board-feet a year in perpetuity, or indeed for more than a decade at the outside.

Yet this was the annual cut in the 1960s.

It is instructive to consider that same aerial view of the district from the point of view of one of the original rationales for the creation of the Forest Service: the protection of watersheds. Compare that view with other aerial photos of watersheds taken before the great Christmas Flood of 1964, and then notice the many hundreds of miles of logging roads, and the thousands of clearcuts that post-date that event. What will the next big flood be like, with so much more ground exposed to the rains, subject to runoff?

Despite its rhetoric about providing for the stability of local communities, the Forest Service has never been able to guarantee that local mills will be the beneficiaries of a particular timber sale. Timber from the Happy Camp area has been milled as far away as Roseburg, Ore. With only one large mill still in Happy Camp, and with that mill's products having to travel a minimum of 70 highway miles to reach even the means of access to a market, the difference between profit and loss can be very small indeed. Transportation costs alone are formidable when a mill is 70 miles from a railhead. This mill is owned by a large corporation with headquarters in Chicago. Its executives do not know Happy Camp, except, perhaps, as a pin on a map in someone's office.

What they do know is the bottom line. Someday someone in the Chicago headquarters will peer at that pin and demand to know why the corporation runs a mill there. With no regrets, without a backward glance, that mill could close.

If the mill closes, will the town die, as Hilt died? If the logging stops, will a community cease to exist? Probably not. Geography favors a town at that spot. But it need not be a large one. Its size would depend on how well its residents adapted to changed conditions and how well they were able to make use of the area's true amenities and capabilities.

We who were in high school in Happy Camp in 1964, for instance, would never have dreamed that the day would come when substantial numbers of our neighbors would make their livings in such bizarre ways as shepherding raft-loads of tourists over the river's rapids, or selling small portable suction dredges to recreational miners, or growing and selling marijuana, or harvesting and selling wild mushrooms and yew bark. The perceived needs that have fueled these small industries did not yet exist.

We were unable to imagine a day when lumber would not be king in Happy Camp, so, like crazed junkyard mechanics, we proceeded to take our own ecosystem apart and toss out the pieces. We allowed ourselves to burn and bulldoze the inoffensive yew because it was not commercially valuable. We allowed the Forest Service, in the name of our future prosperity to fell, burn and poison ancient groves of oaks and madrones. We allowed our opinions to be curtailed and forcibly channeled because we could conceive of no other reality than the one the Forest Service placed before us. We did not think.

We must think now. We must save all the parts and consider how they fit together, and we must not be hurried into sacrificing any of these parts on the altar of short-term gain. If we drive by an eroded field, we sneer at that farmer for not knowing that by losing his soil he is losing his farm. Yet we have watched the natural riches of our home bleed away and have said nothing, except to attack those who try to tell us that what is good for a large corporation is not necessarily good for us.

Louise Wagenknecht

Pride and Glory
of Firefighting
Is Hard to Resist

from *High Country News*

The southwest winds brought waves of red smoke streaming into the valley from the fires near Boise and McCall every day last summer. A helicopter would come in overhead, and I'd hear the almost subsonic whump-whump-whump that meant a *big* craft.

The smoke and the morning air and the noise took me back to a mountainside, to a morning years removed, when that most reassuring of sounds hit my ears: large helicopters, flying again, after our long night of cutting fireline into the dark.

The firepack is on my back and the pulaski in my gloved hands. With a scoop of chew tucked into my lower lip, I see the river, 2,000 feet below, and the faint wisps of September fog trailing up the canyon. And cutting through it all, rising like a dragonfly off the helibase pad, Helitack 1, or 2, or 3. Whump-whump-whump. It sounds very, very good.

That's the part of firefighting that makes you just a bit cocky, just a bit proud. You feel stronger and smarter than you really are. Firefighting is a skill, a craft, a yearly dance in which roles are clearly defined and where certainties abound to compensate for the uncertainties of the enemy. It requires specialized, even arcane knowledge, and those who master some particular part of it are professionals.

Line boss, sector boss, buying unit, camp leader: Titles that often have nothing to do with our usual jobs are ours on a fire. Actual GS-ratings mean very little: GS-4s order GS-13s around.

I started "going out on a fire" because I needed the money. Bit by bit, my firepack acquired the little comforts that make 48-hour shifts more bearable. I kept a few cans of baked beans, fruit cocktail and juice stashed away in case of inadequate sack lunches. Headlamps furnished by the Forest Service were awkward and unreliable; most of us bought better ones from an industrial catalog with our own money. My pockets were full of hard candy, gum, tobacco, paperbacks (as in any military operation, much of firefighting consists of waiting) and toilet paper.

Firefighting changes your ideas about outdoor recreation. Standing on an 80 percent slope at midnight, listening warily for the ominous creaking noises that mean a giant vegetable is about to kill you, then curling up just before dawn to catch a few winks in a ditch filled with ashes and the odd scorpion, erodes the desire to go camping just for the fun of it.

Once, while mopping up in deep ash in a grove of giant, conk-ridden Douglas-firs, we heard the fearful groaning of a dying tree.

Whirling 360 degrees in panic, we tried to see the assailant. Impossible. The sound was everywhere. With a final seismic thump, the tree fell. It missed everyone, but the concussion raised a blinding ash cloud that reduced visibility to zero. The crew boss shouted, and we groped our way uphill, out of the grove, and into an open area. Shaken, we all sat down.

"Lunch!" said the crew boss. We made it last until our shift was over.

In my experience, it is the common sense of crew bosses that saves lives on a fire, but it takes a strong one to refuse a hazardous order. It was a brave crew boss, for example, who refused to continue night mop-up on a nearly vertical slope with rocks the size of clothes dryers hurtling by in the dark. In the face of Al's assertion that this was dangerous and unnecessary on a 12-acre fire already plastered with retardant, the honchos down at fire camp insisted that we continue.

Al stopped arguing, but led us out of the burned area to the fire-lines, where we spent the night improving the trenches, out of range of rocks, while Al lied his head off on the radio.

It took a tough crew boss to categorically refuse to have our crew flown to the top of a 100-acre fire burning in heavy fuels so we could dig line downhill toward the fire.

"No," said Rick to the line boss. "We're not going to do that. We're going to start digging *here,* at the bottom, and you will have *two* crews coming up behind us, and you will have a spotter across the canyon to keep us informed, and you will get some engines down here and start pumping out of the river and putting a hose lay up behind us."

Through a long night of chain-saw work in dense, jackstrawed trees, while squirrelly winds fanned the flames and 80-foot firs crowned out above us, ours was the only line that held. If we had been up on top cutting line downhill, would we have died for the line boss's error in judgment?

Working downhill toward a fire has been a factor in many fire fatalities over the years, yet it continues to be done on uncontained fires, as happened on the fatal fire in Colorado this summer [1994].

I stopped going on fires after the Great California Cookout of '87. I saw the plantations that we had thinned so carefully only a couple of years before go up like A-bombs as the slash ignited, torching so thoroughly that not even stumps remained.

I saw fire fronts come to a dead halt as they hit an area of old growth that had experienced an underburn a few years before. I came off the fires in October with a raging ear infection, bronchitis that swiftly became pneumonia, and the realization that firefighting, like combat, is for 20-year-olds who still believe they're immortal.

Yet, when the chopper came in that morning last summer, just for that moment, I missed the dirt and the smoke and the camaraderie of the fireline. I suddenly mourned the fact that the fire stories I have to tell are the only ones I will ever have.

When I work on fires now, it's in an air-conditioned building, and although I know I've done my bit and don't need to suck any more smoke to prove myself, the smoky winds can still send adrenaline into my blood.

Danger Is the Drug

As the Forest Service struggles—perhaps more than any other wildland agency—to change its attitude toward fire and reject the put-'em-all-out-now shibboleth that has landed us in this fix, Chief Jack Ward Thomas may find an unexpected barrier to true fire management: It's this love of the rush that belongs to firefighting, all the more powerful because no one talks about it.

Any threat to the status accruing to blackened, sleep-deprived, hard-hatted, snoose-dipping smoke warriors will be resisted; any suggestion that those who make a career of firefighting do so because they *enjoy* it will be rejected as somehow immoral.

Ending the war games will be unpalatable to many. But the games will end.

The beginning of the end came last summer when the Payette National Forest in Idaho announced that an all-out effort to extinguish the Blackwell and Corral Complexes would cost $42 million and stand only a 15 percent chance of succeeding before winter did it for free. With that, the government admitted it can no longer afford to indulge career fire managers in their hobby of battling an element which should never have been allowed to become an enemy in the first place.

It is time for the fire gods to admit that they love battle for its own sake, and for what it has brought them in the way of pride, and power, and glory. It is time for them to recognize this, and get over it, and get another life.

Those who have died deserve that from us, at least.

Frank Stewart

A Walk on the Everlasting

First publication

On a recent winter morning, under a haze of volcanic fog and tropic sunlight, my partner Lisa and I unloaded our gear at a trailhead in Volcanoes National Park and began hiking toward the site where Kīlauea is currently venting—a 900-foot-high cinder cone called Puʻu Ōʻō that erupted violently out of the rain forest only about ten years ago.

Ever since the island of Hawaiʻi emerged from the sea—just as Puʻu Ōʻō emerged from the forest—this landscape has been churned by fire. Erupting and roiling lava has poured across the blackened hills and lowlands for half a million years, creating a steaming world of glassy slag, molten scrabble, and scalding flues. Swollen and shattered, melted and remelted, the land has skittered and crumbled in fiery glaciers and been thrust up into sharp, clefted peaks.

Amazingly, over millennia this volatile landscape was colonized by extensive rain forests. The rain forests in their turn were torched and inundated by new lava and the land where they stood became stark again. Then new forests grew once more, only to be inundated repeatedly. And so on, in a wheel of destruction and regrowth.

Nowhere on earth is the geological cycle of devastation and regeneration more observable than in the rift zones around Kīlauea, the most active, and yet most accessible, volcano on the planet.

The two of us planned to spend the night as close to Puʻu Ōʻō as we could get, at one of the smallest and more remote campsites indicated on our trail guide. Volcanoes National Park is a 377-square-mile refuge for native Hawaiian plants, wildlife, and geology. A dotted line on the map threaded among the park's east rift-zone wilderness of old lava flows and forests, recently recolonized lava plains, pit craters, and cinder cones. A tentative "x" seven miles in marked what the park ranger called a "meadow."

"No one will be there," the ranger had told us the day before. "It's too remote, the hike is too hot, and that primitive campsite is just too close to the current eruption." It sounded perfect.

After months in the city, we were hungry for such remoteness and wildness. The dangers, if there really were any, appealed to Lisa in particular. In planning our trips, it seems she's always got her sail up first, ready to rush ahead. I'm the slow one, dragging the sea anchor, making a list of things to be cautious about. By the time we reach our destination, however, we've often reversed roles, only to reverse them again, one rushing ahead unpredictably and the other holding back.

The early part of the trail was faint, consisting of scuff marks and small cairns winding across hard black rock cracked open where sulfuric steam continued to billow out. At 3,000 feet, the tropic sun adds to the internal heat of the ground. Though it made our packs heavy and bulky, we carried plenty of water. There was none where we were going and none along the way.

Some two miles in we saw the first signs of vegetation large enough to provide shade. To our left rose a symmetrical cinder cone 200 feet high, an example of how areas of lava, together with their oases of ancient green life, can remain untouched in the paths of active flows. Bypassed for centuries by lava spilling across the landscape, Puʻu Hululu's forest cover is roughly 500 years old.

We climbed to the top, took off our packs, and peered down inside. Echoing out of the small, ancient rain forest within the collapsed pit were the sharp calls of red-and-black 'apapane—an endemic honey creeper, native only to Hawai'i—and the chittering of small, yellow-green passerines called white-eyes. The steep interior walls of the crater and their dense vegetation made a descent into this enclosed green world all but impossible. After skirting the crater's fragile edges, just to be sure, we concluded that without ropes and gear our chances of climbing out again were no better than our chances of getting in.

Less than 300 yards away, adjacent to Pu'u Huluhulu, is Mauna Ulu, a lava cone equally high. But this cone ceased its violent formation and fountaining fewer than 20 years ago. In recorded history, only Pu'u Ō'ō, our destination, has poured out as much lava from Kīlauea's underground magma reservoir as Mauna Ulu. Having left the trail and clamored up the jagged, vitreous slope, we looked down into the iron-red mouth of Mauna Ulu's gutted volcanic chamber, riven and still hissing. Clouds of steam rolled up from a rift in the shattered throat far below. The cracked overhang on which we lay to peer downward seemed about to collapse into the maw. We crawled back cautiously from the rim and returned to the trail.

Not all of our hike crossed bare ground. As the day wore on we veered off the lava fields and plunged through old, though not ancient, forests composed mostly of native 'ōhi'a, a slow-growing hardwood tree that looks as gnarled as the land it colonizes. Its vivid red blossoms are like splatters of fire. Giant tree ferns are associated with 'ōhi'a in these old groves, since one way 'ōhi'a is able to colonize lava is by germinating on the damp surfaces of such plants. The resulting understory of mature 'ōhi'a-fern forests is gloriously tangled and biologically rich.

Late in the day, having trekked through dark, wooded glens and across sweltering lava, then back again into the forests, we were relieved to see ahead of us a green field of thigh-deep ferns. We assumed this was what the ranger had called a meadow. The ferns appeared to be moist. They looked cool and bright in the declining sunlight, a relief from the harsh conditions of the trail. We were parched and tired, more than ready to throw down our packs and rest.

As we approached, though, we saw that a volcanic meadow is not clover and wildflowers. Rather than being the downy children of loam and moss, the reddish ferns that grow on lava—breaking it down so that larger plants can come after—are the true offspring of the iron-hard ground they flourish on.

The ferns in this meadow are a false staghorn called uluhe in Hawaiian. Unlike the more delicate members of the fern family, uluhe is as prickly as nettles, varying from pale green to rust red. Like its habitat, uluhe is tough and aggressive. As it grows, it creates a thicket of tangled stems that grasp and penetrate the lava, seeking a sliver of soil or a moist fissure. Binding many plants together, uluhe's forking stems and long rootstocks create a dense mesh about three feet high. This coarse net readily tangles around a hiker's legs, making a meadow of established uluhe nearly impassable.

The park service had hacked a square just big enough for two or three tents among these ferns. Barely enough daylight remained for us to set up our camp site, eat quickly over a tiny camp stove, and prepare for the wet weather that had been coming on with sunset.

In the declining light we got our first chance to gaze at Puʻu Ōʻō, looming on the horizon. Clouds had accumulated in a low ceiling over the cone, reflecting a vermilion glow emanating from the peak. As the sky darkened, the red stain on the clouds wavered and flickered.

Puʻu Ōʻō is almost perfectly conical, like the drawing of a volcano a child might make. Though three miles up slope from our camp, it looked considerably closer and, glowing in the night, decidedly dangerous. All day we had seen sulfuric clouds billowing out. The summit's colors alternated from ashen white to orange, from pale reds to bronze. Hot gases rose through the porous surface materials, and tephra and debris blew high into the air.

Finding my flashlight, I set off through a trail in the ferns toward a recent lava flow fifty or sixty yards away. Newly formed ground crackled and shifted underfoot. Filtered through broken clouds, moonlight bathed the meadow and, where the path ended, illuminated the precipice of an enormous crater called Nāpau. Lava from Puʻu Ōʻō had recently poured over the northern wall of the crater and flooded a good part of the floor.

Turning toward Puʻu Ōʻō, I knew that this was precisely what my friend and I had hiked into the rugged backcountry to experience— volcano, forest, rain, lava, and darkness all together, all interlocked in this fiery place.

I know of no substitute for the powerful feeling that rains down on us like grace in certain moments in the wild. Somehow we must find our way toward these direct experiences with the land. Without them we miss that true and complete sense of belonging to the earth which is still ready to embrace us. Our gardens and picturesque scenery are not enough. Now and then we must approach the land as it exists without us, in remote and, occasionally, in volatile places, where we can witness the earth's own will at work. Paradoxically, it's there that we often feel ourselves most genuinely included in nature.

This is what Henry Thoreau meant when he said that in wildness is the preservation of the world. "Every sunset I witness inspires me with the desire to go to a West as distant and as fair as that into which the sun goes down," he wrote. Go west far enough, he added, and you'll find "a wildness whose glance no civilization can endure." Such a place contains not only "the strength, the marrow, of Nature," he asserted, but also the strength and marrow of the human heart.

There is hardly a region farther west for Americans—in metaphor or geography—than these high volcanic plains of Hawaiʻi. But the National Park Service has had its share of troubles preserving even such a wild location as this—from low-flying helicopters and air tours that buzz the land and disrupt the mating sites of endangered birds, from tourists who litter Kīlauea with so-called offerings to the volcano goddess, and from careless hikers. Only as long as green and fiery wildernesses like this one are protected will we be able to experience firsthand the great rhythms that, in their profound ways, preserve us, just as they preserve the very marrow of the living earth.

The next day, as the sun rose over a landscape of glittering black, Lisa and I were already out on the flows. Lava had poured in molten rivers from the higher ground of the northwest and now these rivers lay like enormous, extruded serpents, their roiling currents arrested and petrified by sudden cooling. In places, the tumultuous currents had roped around huge trees that, having caught fire and burned, had left cylindrical molds of their trunks in the hardened black eddies. Through rifts in the ground, we could see the molten red that had once colored these rivers and made them run.

Clearly, fire has been the creator of this landscape. Fire from the center of the earth has joined the fiery heat of sunlight. One radiance drives the engine of photosynthesis, nourishing the trees and understory of plants and the other powers the hydrological and carbon cycles that make all biology possible.

Two thousand years ago, the Roman author Pliny said, "I marvel to think that scarcely anything is brought to a finished state without the involvement of fire . . . but I wonder whether its essence is more destructive than creative."

Pliny knew fire's destructive essence close up. During a cataclysmic eruption of Vesuvius, the old naturalist attempted to save a group of people huddled in their houses at the edge of the sea, trapped on one side by violent waves and on the other by lava and falling debris. With great difficulty, through a downpour of rock from the volcano's peak, Pliny managed to land his rescue craft on the coast. But once he was in the village at the base of Vesuvius, he couldn't resist delaying the rescue mission in order to observe the eruption as near as possible, to satisfy his curiosity about volcanism. Unfortunately, he delayed too long and perished in the landslides and poisonous gases.

Hiking the Kīlauea rift zone, I've thought a lot about Pliny's devotion to nature. His 37-volume *Natural History* is one of the great works of the classical world, filled with 20,000 facts—both true facts and doubtful ones. Such writers can still tell us much about nature and our relation to the natural world, even when their facts are patently wrong. The ancients thought about the natural world more intensely than most of us do any more. They were interested in the whole, in how the world's parts work together—ethical conduct in relation to the flights of birds and the growth of crops, geometry and mathematics in relation to geological events and the birth of children.

I recall as a young student the sleepy lectures in my philosophy classes about Heraclitus of Ephesus, a man who lived about 500 years before Pliny and regarded fire in a different way. His beliefs were simplified for us students into something like "Everything is fire."

The claim sounded especially improbable to us then, on those gentle afternoons, in a quiet classroom that smelled faintly of chalk dust and early spring. What Heraclitus actually said was, of course, more complicated and elegant. "This world is God's consciousness and it is an everlasting incandescence in which all things are becoming their opposites," he wrote. "It is a constant incandescing," he added, "kindled and extinguished by measures of its own design."

It was hard even to begin to understand such a world view. For us, an hour seemed infinitely long, the world was an unchanging place, and the old Earth felt forever solid, cold, and dense beneath the scraping of our desks. We imagined the flickering inside a fireplace and thought to ourselves: How could *everything* be fire?

If we could have been transported to the rift zone of Kīlauea—framed by the sea below, with more volcanoes above, and between them the steaming, luminous rain forests being ignited and intercut by rivers of dark lava—who knows if we might not have made the leap to Heraclitus's conception of the natural world?

In one of his aphorisms, Heraclitus said, "The first metamorphosis of the everlasting fire is to become the sea, and half of the sea becomes the earth, half the volcanic flash." It was decades before I saw sea and volcano together, along with the great diversity of plants and animals of the Hawaiian Islands, all of them a product of fiery geological formations and of a myriad of regenerations out of the volcanic destruction. It was decades before I felt the fire of the world bodily, directly under my boots, and at last got a glimpse of the everlasting.

Brenda Peterson

The Whales of April

from *Seattle Times*

Very early, in the *vog*—that volcanic mist off Hawaii's Big Island where Pele births new land in brilliant, bright-red lava flows—we quietly slipped our three kayaks into warm, turquoise waters. This graceful curve of protected bay on the Kona Coast is one of the world's rare reef waters where spinner dolphins swim so close to shore. Here they rest in small groups during the long tropical days before joining up with larger pods to fish in the Pacific's deep coral canyons. Here, too, the spinners breed, birth and nurture their next generations—in a watery nursery.

Much of the world's warm oceans are nurseries for whales and dolphins. I was in Hawaii to study and observe the humpback whales that, from January through mid-April, also breed and give birth in these mild winter waters before their long migration back up to Alaska's summer feeding grounds.

All winter the Hawaii cetacean nurseries are full of the sonorous bass and ultrasonic singing, the stunning breech and embrace of these gracious sea giants. In two southerly nurseries in Mexican lagoons off Baja, there is more mating and birthing as gray whales engage not only with one another, but with humans, earning them the name "friendly whales."

In these Mexican lagoons, gray whales often approach people ex-

ploring in small rubber Zodiacs; the grays lift their great, barnacle-
encrusted heads, revealing a kindly unblinking eye the size of tennis
balls. They study us with a curiosity and a compassion which shows
no grudge against our species which little over a century ago turned
this birth sanctuary into a slaughter-at-sea. Whalers invaded these
birthing waters, often killing calves to entrap protective mother
whales; the gray whale population fell from 25,000 to near-extinction
levels until 1946, when the gray whales were finally protected.

Today, thanks to the Endangered Species Act, the gray whale population has rebounded to 18,000 and last year it was taken off the endangered list—truly one of the real success stories of cooperation
and restoring balance between our species.

Cooperation, balance and successful interdependence between
species was what my trip to Hawaii was all about. I had recently seen
my first humpback whale—and sadly, she was dead, washed up
ashore in Venice Beach, Calif., after a huge boat propeller chopped
off her belly and tail. Marine biologists, knee deep in bloody foam
dissecting the great humpback, believed her to be a female returning
to Alaska from birthing and breeding waters off Mexico. I had wondered, as I mournfully watched the men saw through purple layers
of whale blubber, if the humpback female were a mother whose
death left a calf somewhere alone out in those rough waters; or if she
were newly pregnant. As I stood on the beach eye-to-eye with this
beautiful, brave creature, I swore I would not let my only contact
with humpbacks be this funeral rite.

So a month later when I was offered a pre-Easter trip to watch the
last of the humpback nursery off the Hawaiian Islands, I leapt (or joy-
fully breeched) at the chance. And the very first day out in a fast catamaran off the Na Pali Coast of Kauai, I scanned the choppy waters,
looking for that mystical spume of air and mist that is a whale's
breath in open seas.

"Dolphins at 12 o' clock!" a 12-year-old girl shouted out and our
boat rocked with us scrambling to the bow to see a pod of lovely

spinner dolphins alongside. Even scientists have to note that the spinner dolphins' gymnastics are not only functional—for fishing, signaling, or defense. Sometimes, suggest marine mammal scientists Bernd and Melany Wursig, "the dolphins seem to be performing, and it is difficult to imagine that they do so for any reason other than 'pure joy.'" Echoing that joy, several of the children on our catamaran pirouetted in perfect sync with the spinners.

Soon someone else shouted, "Thar she blooows! Straight ahead!"

Again a rush to the bow, a 20-foot geyser of air shooting up ahead of us as the skipper stopped the motor. We rocked in two-story-high waves, our stomachs full of flutters like an elevator dropping. But no one made a sound. There was just the whoosh of waves as we waited, watching, eyes on the moving horizon. Then, so close, we were startled at the gliding rise of this behemoth body—a high ridge of spine and fin curving into the deep and the slow-motion grace of tail flukes like a wave goodbye as they rose up and then slapped the water.

"Hear that?" a man next to me exulted. "That slapping sound is what I heard last winter when two mating humpbacks rose up right in front of our little dingy. Their huge pectoral fins clapped one another's bodies just like that with . . . with such affection. It sounded sweet . . . like rumbling thunder!"

So I asked him, this man who'd heard humpbacks' lovemaking, "Have you heard them singing?"

"Oh, yes," he sighed. "It's so complicated, their songs. You know, they sing not only when mating but also to pass along the singing skills to their young . . . like lullabies."

I have heard these humpback whale lullabies, but never live. In the Hawaiian Islands, almost everyone I'd met had heard through underwater microphones these complex songs as they were being sung by the great humpback whales. One man, Danny, a native Hawaiian singer, dives every day and listens in the canyons as those low wails and bass tones reverberate all around him.

"Once about 15 years ago," he told me, "I was very deep down

diving . . . listening. Then suddenly this huge humpback is right before me, his song blasts into my whole body and echoes off every
bone inside me, inside my heart. Whoa," he said and shook his head.
"That song is still inside me."

As Danny told his story I thought of the theory of resonance: Take
two tuning forks. Strike one to a certain high pitch and the other,
without being touched, will soon vibrate at exactly that pitch. If the
humpback whale's song was the first tuning fork, then it was no
wonder Danny's body vibrated in deep resonance. And it is no wonder that he is still listening, still learning the song of the humpback.

Learning this year's song of the humpback—an awesome and
perhaps humanly impossible task—is what my kayak guide, Don E.,
was doing in Hawaii this year. This Easter weekend, as he guided my
companion and me into the spinner dolphin bay nursery, Don E.
softly sang the first phrase of the humpback song he'd learned.
Humpback whale singing is like a combination of Tibetan overton-
ing, Gregorian chant, cello arpeggios, haunting moans and a low lute
that suddenly lilts up into astonishing trills. The sun rose above the
vog and we sang softly, dipping our paddles into the water as the
whole world woke up.

We'd heard that humpbacks had been sighted here even this late
in the birthing season. But it was not the humpbacks who answered
our song. It was the sleek spinners. Suddenly they were right next to
us, 20 feet away, their small, dark dorsal fins rising in synchronized
arcs. First there were only six or so spinners, and then off to our right
swam a group of more than 30. I was so grateful to see this many dolphins all at once and I remembered Don E. telling me that this bay
was nursery to the largest pods of spinners left in the world; as such,
this bay is crucial to their survival. There is a state proposal in the
works to develop a huge visitor's center here which will bring in up
to 300 people a day, deeply threatening this important pod. If we
bring so many people into the whale nurseries, how will they rest
and regenerate a new generation?

When a dolphin or whale gives birth, there are attendant mid-

wives, other dolphin females who, when the newborn enters the watery world tail flukes first, lift the calf up to the surface to breathe.
I thought of these first conscious dolphin breaths as I heard around
me 30 spinner dolphins exhaling—that *twoosh, twoosh* of warm, misty
air exhaled at 100 mph. So enraptured was I by the sound of their
breathing that I tilted my kayak and capsized in a second.

Underwater, I heard that familiar click and bleep and Geiger-
counter racket of dolphin sonar as they scanned me—their sonar so
sensitive that dolphins can hear a teaspoonful of water poured into
an oceanarium pool. The sound pictures of echo-location, like a far-
advanced version of our ultrasound, let them see the tumult of my
stomach gases, my heartbeat, the pulse of my nervous system. We
listened, one to another, and in that underwater reverie I felt the
deep privacy and nurturance of this nursery where another species
births its new generations. I also felt the kind companionship of
these, our fellow creatures. But this is a birthing place and I did not
want to intrude any further, so I eased myself back into my kayak.

For a time, the spinners courteously accompanied us through the
bay, their dorsal fins only 10 feet behind my kayak, their breathing
like a meditative mother's lullaby. And as I paddled I thought how
wonderful it was to be one of only three humans in this nursery bay,
surrounded by more than 30 dolphins. These 300-pound creatures
could deep-six us on the spot; but they chose to offer their affectionate company.

And here again was a kind of balance and interdependence between species. Here on Easter weekend when much of the world
celebrates resurrection, the return of spring and rebirth—here in
these island nurseries of dolphins and whales, I wondered if we've
forgotten what connects us, all species alike—our children, our
young. There is so much dying about our planet that we have forgotten what is being born.

When it comes to imagining a future for our next generations, we
all become visionaries. What do a passionate environmentalist and a
corporate executive considering the cost of oil-spill prevention in

Puget Sound have in common? Both sides give birth and share this Earth, our birthplace. Both sides worry and protect and hope the best for the children of the new century.

In so many ways, animals are as much our children's teachers as we parents. Look in a children's book or movie—animals everywhere telling our children about the world. What children know, adults often forget: We are all animals, human and nonhuman alike. We have much to yet say and listen to and sing together.

If we can save and make safe the nurseries of our seas, from the spinner and humpback birthing waters off Hawaii to the Mexican lagoons of gray whales, we will also be assuring our children that they will have such teachers as humpback whale songs and gray whales' friendship and forgiveness; that they will marvel at spinner dolphins in watery pirouettes alongside their land cousins.

In South America, children are often taught that when they are born an animal is born with them as a guardian and guide. If we could teach our children and ourselves to commit to just one other species, one other animal besides ourselves, what might the next generation of interdependence between species be? It is already a scientific fact that a dolphin fetus looks eerily like a human fetus. If we commit ourselves, as mammalian kin, one to another, might our inner lives also resemble that of the whales and dolphins—unfailingly affectionate, altruistic and devoted to nurturing our young, and to mutual survival?

It is Easter Sunday as I write this and I am back in my home on Puget Sound. But I can still feel the spinner dolphin sonar in my skin and hear the humpback tail slap. As I write this, I'm listening to recordings of humpback songs, haunting and beautiful. Outside on the shores of this beloved Puget Sound it is low tide and there are children scuttling around the tidepools like brightly colored little crabs. They are running back and forth between beach and their parents, showing them wondrous discoveries—seaweed and shells and barnacles.

What they hold in their small hands is the future. And what we hold for them whenever we nurture another species to accompany and guide our children, what we create for the next generations, is the vision and loving connection of our birthplace—our planet, our place of birth. On this Easter Sunday, nearing the 25th anniversary of Earth Day, my wish is that we might remember our balance between species and apprentice ourselves to the vision of birth and rebirth. Because the whole world is a nursery for what comes next.

James Kilgo

Open House

from *An Inheritance of Horses*

For the last two weeks a summer tanager has been pecking at the window in our den. All day he's at it, fluttering, breast to glass, peck, peck, peck. I know, of course, what he's doing. He is mistaking his reflection for a rival tanager. Cardinals and mockingbirds are famous for the same behavior, but I have not known either of those species to sustain its belligerence for so long.

At first I was glad to have the tanager. Wild creatures have always been welcome in our yard. My wife and I put out nest boxes for tit-mice, crested flycatchers, wood ducks, and screech owls; we keep the feeders filled with sunflower seeds and the birdbath with clean water. I let the grass grow high around the edges of the yard for rab-bits, and chipmunks entertain us on the stone wall outside our den. So I was pleased when I noticed that summer tanagers were building on an oak limb within view of our breakfast table. In past years I had heard them calling from the woods below the house, but they had never nested in the yard. And they are beautiful. In contrast to the subdued plumage of most songbirds, theirs is glamorous—the male totally bright red, the female just as completely yellow-green. Now that they had taken up residence on the oak limb, I was looking for-ward to seeing a lot of them. Little did I know.

When the male discovered the intruder in the window, I pulled up a chair. Indifferent to my presence or blinded by the reflection, the bird would launch forth from a stem of ivy that grew alongside, hit the window, and strike with his beak. For the second or two that he was splayed against the glass, light from behind shone through his wings and the spread feathers of his tail. I was glad for the opportunity to observe such a bird at close range, but as it became apparent that he meant to fight to the death, I began to worry that he might be the one to die, that, exhausted, he would flutter to the ground where the cats could get him. Instead, he always retreated to the ivy and after a moment's respite hurled himself again into the fray. I worried about the damage he might be doing to his beak. He was not a woodpecker. Nature had not equipped his kind to peck on glass all day, day after day. I could imagine how sore that beak must be getting. Dribbles of fluid soon flecked his corner of the window. But whether his beak was sore or not, I was getting tired of its constant tattoo. I cut out a silhouette of a hawk and taped it to the glass, but that had no effect at all. Next I covered the window with sheets of newspaper—no small task; it's a big window—but I succeed only in blocking out the light. The obsessed tanager searched for his enemy up and down the narrow alleys of exposed glass, and, finding him at last, renewed his efforts to drive him from the yard.

The female, meanwhile, quietly kept the house. By looking closely I could see her on the nest, her beak motionless among the dappled leaves. When the eggs hatch out, I thought, the instinct to provide food for the babies will override her mate's mindless determination to defend his territory, and we'll all be relieved.

One day about this time I spotted a commotion on the oak limb. The male, of course, was too busy battering the window to notice the trouble at home, but I looked just in time to see a cowbird at the nest.

Cowbirds are the parasites of the avian world. Having missed out somehow on the nesting instinct, the female finds the active nest of another passerine species, and, while the parents are away, she deposits among the host clutch her own fertilized egg. The parents, none the wiser, incubate the alien along with their own, and when the eggs hatch, the baby cowbird, which is usually larger than his stepbrothers and -sisters, gets most of the food, often to the detriment of the legitimate occupants. The size of the cowbird flocks I see in the winter is an impressive sign of their success at this business, but I had never caught one in the act. Now I had, and so had the female tanager. With trumpets blaring *charge,* she swooped in on the interloper and drove her away. Anthropomorphically, I cheered, while her valiant mate, oblivious to her cries of alarm, continued to beat himself silly upon his own reflection. The only way to stop him now, I figured, would be to break the mirror he was using.

That, of course, was out of the question. Though he wasn't trying to get in, he looked like he was, and the window was there to keep things out.

At Walden Pond, Henry Thoreau flung open his door and windows to admit not only light and wind but birds and squirrels as well. Wanting to live intimately with nature, he refused even to begrudge wasps a warm place for the night.

The notion is appealing. Even as I enjoy the comforts of air-conditioning, I grumble about the artificial habitat it creates and fear that it may be costing me more than the hundred and fifty dollars I pay to the power company each month. Surely we could learn to tolerate a wider range of weathers than the narrow comfort zone marked on the thermostat. Then perhaps we might grow gradually more resistant to pollen and other irritants, impervious to mosquitoes, more sensitive to smells.

But the summer tanager, still pecking away at the window, forces me to admit that I'm not as hospitable as Thoreau. It also reminds me of a hornet that built a nest against our window screen several years ago.

Sitting in my living room one afternoon in May, I noticed that one of the panes looked flyspecked. Closer, I saw that the dirtiness was on the screen—disparate flecks of matter clogging the little square holes. Even as I watched, the insect alighted, selected a space, and deposited into it a mouthful of some kind of broth. Whatever it was, hornet or wasp, the creature was boldly marked, white on black, reminding me of an outrageously patterned World War I fighter plane, a Fokker, say, designed to terrify. Its most menacing feature was its all-white face, as baleful as a skull. *Of course,* I thought, *a bald-faced hornet. But aren't they the ones that build those big nests, those heavy globes that hang in the summer woods? What is this one doing on my window screen?*

I called an entomologist I knew.

"Sounds like she's building a nest all right," he said. "But it's really unusual for that species to build against a vertical surface, especially up against a house. We had some captive insects in a lab once that built against the glass wall of the cage, but I don't think I've ever heard of that kind of thing in the wild."

"I've only seen one hornet," I said. "It must take more than one to build an entire nest."

"That's the queen. Among the Vespinae she's the only one that overwinters. About this time of year she comes out from behind the bark or wherever she's been for the last six months and begins to look for a nest site. She'll get it started, but as soon as the first workers hatch out, they'll take over and leave her free to lay eggs."

"So she's already fertilized?"

"Oh yeah. That happened last fall, before the males died. Frankly, I'd be surprised if she completes the nest in a place like that, but if she does, let me know. I'd like to come out and take a look. It would be a great opportunity to observe interior activity."

I always had an irrational fear of insects that fly and sting—the kind of fear some people have of snakes—and I have been a relentless enemy, blasting their nests with Hotshot when I found yellow jackets excavating in the yard or wasps building over the eaves. But this was different. This was an opportunity, as my friend was saying, to observe the hornet's hidden life. I was reminded of the ant colonies I had imprisoned in mason jars when I was a child and how I had watched as they pursued their busy errands along exposed sections of tunnel. But the hornet's nest was better, the activity inside more complicated. From the comfort of my living room, protected by the glass, I would be able to observe their behavior as carefully as a scientist.

"If she does complete it," the entomologist continued, "you're going to have to be careful. Those nests get big in a hurry, and once the new queens start hatching out, the whole colony becomes protective. Along about August they get real mean, especially on days when the barometric pressure falls."

I felt a bit of a chill when he said that, but August was too far away to worry about, so I put a pad and pencil on the table by the window and settled in to watch the progress of the nest.

Typically, *Dolichovespula maculata* suspends its nest from a tree limb, beginning the operation by constructing along the underside a thin sheet that tapers into a triangle. At the bottom the hornet elongates the point into a petiole, and upon that she fashions the first cluster of cells. My hornet, however, continued to clog the holes of the screen with wet paper. After three days, the random flecks assumed a pattern, something like a horseshoe about three inches across, apparently the base against which the nest would be constructed. When I looked again, the hornet had fashioned an eave that extended from the top of the horseshoe, and against the underside of that she went to work on an appendage that turned soon into a cluster of hexagonal cylinders. The comb comprised no more than six or eight of these cells. As the hornet worked on it, the whole structure moved a little from side to side like a bell.

The eave and comb took the hornet more than a week to complete, so I expected the housing, the outer shell that entomologists call the envelope, to take at least that long. Instead, she managed it in just a day or two. When I returned from work one afternoon, there it was, the finished product, small but complete. From the outside it resembled a hemispheric cone, a gray, papery whelk, clamped against the window screen. At the bottom it tapered into a tube, and at the end of the tube was an opening. Even as I watched, the hornet came crawling out and flew away.

Back inside, with a flashlight fixed upon the interior of the nest, I awaited the return of the queen. That did not take long. Suddenly she was at the lip of the tube, and in a moment she was emerging from its hole into the chamber, where she resumed her work upon the comb. I could not see closely enough to tell whether she was building new cells, laying eggs, or feeding larvae, but whatever the task she did it with purpose and deliberation, crawling back and forth across the open ends of the cells, flexing her abdomen upon them, tending them with her legs. Only at night did she rest.

For several days I noticed no further development of the nest, no increase in its size, inside or out, but one day two new hornets appeared, smaller insects and darker than the queen. I turned on the flashlight and saw inside a third, still wet and folded, just emerged from its cell. It crawled down into the tube and a moment later appeared at the lip. There it waited for several minutes, until, dried by light and air, it opened its wings and zoomed away.

By the end of the next day I was able to count four workers. These insects, whose genetic codes prepared them for work on a free-hanging globe, began their labor by increasing the area of the base, daubing the holes of the screen with a mash of chewed wood. Next they papered over the outer shell, layer by layer, until raised latitudinal bands appeared. They were of the subtlest woody pastels—pale gray-green, mauve, faint lavender—colors bearing witness to the kinds of wood chosen by the hornets.

As the outer shell expanded, the size of the chamber increased proportionately, making room for the growing comb. That was the queen's sole business now. Freed from the task of constructing the hive, she devoted herself to the nursery with maternal solicitude, fondling the comb, tamping it, turning it this way and that.

As the days lengthened toward the solstice, the queen became more fervent, and I spent longer stretches at the window. For the first time in years I was ignoring the return of summer birds. Waves of warblers moved through the treetops without my going outside to watch; the songs of wood thrushes came floating up in the late afternoons from the woods below my house, and still I kept my vigil at the window. From time to time I heard the staccato calls of summer tanagers but hardly paused even to wonder where they were nesting. My fascination with the hornets had grown as fervent as the labor of the queen.

"How much longer are you going to let it go on?" my wife asked one day.

"I don't know."

"If you wait much longer, and I really don't see how you can, it could be a real problem to get rid of."

That was truer than she realized but not in the way she meant. By some genetic glitch, I surmise, this queen had built a nest in such a way and such a place that the tender life inside was vulnerable not only to my eye but to a blast of insecticide as well, sprayed through the screen. Apparently indifferent to her unprotected rear, the queen felt secure behind the barrier of tough paper she and her offspring had constructed. Like my own house, hers braved the outside world, the pestiferous environment that always threatens. Hornets or not, I couldn't bring myself to take that kind of advantage of her mistake.

"You're not thinking about letting it go on all summer, are you?"

"Maybe we could put a sign out front," I said. " 'DANGER: HORNETS AT WORK—USE BACK DOOR.' Hand-lettered in red."

My wife did not answer.

By June 22 the nest was as big as a man's fist, sculpted and smooth. The tube had disappeared, and, on the inside, the workers had begun a second tier of cells. From first light to dark, hornets came and went, bringing food to their little larval sisters. By flashlight I could see what appeared to be an interaction between workers and pupae that I took to be feeding. Other workers continued to enlarge the nest, and the queen kept on laying eggs.

One day when the colony had increased to perhaps twelve or fifteen workers, I opened the window. With nothing but screen between the nest and me, I detected an odor, faint but distinctive, a kind of dry organic smell. As I drew nearer, the insects inside began to buzz. Suddenly, the screen seemed a flimsy barrier, and I was reminded of a story I had heard from a friend named Joe. When he was in high school, he and a buddy, riding around in the woods in a four-wheel drive, bumped into a hornet's nest, bashed it with the windshield. They just had time to get the windows up. Though they were protected by the glass, Joe said, the fury of the hornets' attack was unnerving. Before long, the windshield was wet with toxin, but it was the high-pitched hum of the hornets' rage that really undid them. Joe's friend wet his pants. I closed the window on the nest, and firmly resolved to stop this business before August. As things turned out, I was spared that disagreeable task.

A day or two later, just past first light, my wife awakened me with an urgent call: "Come quick," she said. "Something's happening to the hornets!"

I stumbled into the living room, trying to bring the world into focus, and knelt at the window. Rubbing sleep from my eyes, I was confronted by a summer tanager—a red flurry in the dim light, inches from my face, beating the air. The bird was darting at the nest, attacking with its heavy beak—swoop, flutter, and strike—breaking ragged holes in the tough paper shell. I flinched. From where I knelt, daylight opened in the envelope. The comb was exposed. I saw larvae extending from their cells like blind fingers, and the tanager was picking them, one by one. *Where are the workers?* I wondered. *Why aren't they protecting the nest? And where is the queen?* The yellow-green female joined her mate; he flew up onto a branch for a moment but soon returned and completed the pillage. It was all over in a minute or two.

I went outside. The nest was utterly ravaged. Tatters of paper clung to the screen. The comb of cells, so long in construction, was broken off and lay on the ground below, empty of occupants. From the oak above I heard the static calls of the tanagers, *p-tek-a-tek, p-tek-a-tek.*

———————

The tanagers that nested outside the window this year are gone. I never saw the brood hatch out, though I watched. About the time they were due, we had a week of rain. When the skies cleared, the nest was abandoned. Maybe the cool wet weather, the incessant rain and wind, chilled the nestlings even as they were hatching, or it could have been a cowbird, starving out its smaller foster siblings, but I don't think so. I want to believe they all survived, the whole family skulking off into the dripping overstory when no one was looking. In any case, the male left behind a window fouled by specks of hardened fluid—little apostrophes of bird spit, I guess—as strong a reminder as the remains of the hornet nest, which still clogs my screen, of our losing battle against things that want in.

Linda Hasselstrom

The Song of the Turtle

First publication

In the pasture ponds, Painted Turtles make living carbuncles of color on rocks and weeds, basking in the sun until I step out of the pickup. Then the earth quivers with their scramble, and they slide down gumbo chutes into the pool. If I move to the pond's edge either very slowly, or very swiftly, I may snatch a slow-moving turtle and hold it in my open palm, watching the water's surface, pocked with snouts as if fat raindrops were falling. The turtle in my hand pulls her head inside, imitating a warm rock. Or perhaps I've found the carapace of a tiny alien being, a suit of body armor with divisions outlined in green, yellow or red.

Slowly the legs emerge, then the venerable face with unfathomable eyes. Tiny claws dig, tickling my calloused hand until the turtle reaches the edge. Then she pulls the wrinkles out of her neck and swivels her head to stare at me.

Eyeing that face, I can understand why Turtle has carried tales throughout human history. Some tribal people said Grandmother Turtle carried the earth on her back, and carries it still. Both American Indians and Celts told of an Egg floating on warm water in the first sea, tended by the Sun and Moon as it absorbed knowledge. From Turtle's egg came lovely daughters who became spirits of

Celtic tribes, honored with stone circles like those where I walked, whispering ancient chants, in northern Scotland.

I tilt the turtle to examine her yellow breastplate, sometimes intricately patterned in woven lines. Yellow and red stripes adorn her neck, legs and tail. Indian warriors painted challenging symbols on their chests when preparing for war or celebration; this tiny scrapper wears them all the time. I put her down close to the pond, so she can slip under water before a coyote trots past. Lower, her enemies are larger turtles. When her snout breaks the surface, flying predators—hawks, eagles, and herons—have to be quick to snatch her.

Once, I rode with a friend on a two-lane blacktop across the western part of South Dakota. Leonard was my cousin's husband, a long-haired musician and puppeteer. Ahead, we saw a pickup parked beside the trail, in the breaks of the Bad River. Two burly men bent over a round object on the ground, shouting and waving brawny arms. At first I thought they were fixing a tire. Then we realized they were arguing about the best method for loading a big snapping turtle without losing a finger. One man held an axe-handle in front of the turtle's beak, jerking back each time it snapped. The other tried to wrap his arms around the shell so he could pick up the monster, destined to become soup.

I yelled, "Leonard, they're going to kill it! Stop them!"

He glanced at the sweaty men, who glared back; he scanned his own thin frame; then he raised an eyebrow, and hit the gas pedal. Eventually, we laughed about it.

I opened one eye. The rising sun shot a shaft of light past my nose to collide with the prism hung from the light fixture. The light shattered over the room; I opened the other eye to count the colors. Pink and blue; gold and orange. Green.

I couldn't stand it any longer, and hugged myself. Twelve! I was a woman! Flinging the covers back, I dived into the closet. My jeans from yesterday and the day before and the day before that were tangled on the floor. I kicked them aside instead of putting them in the laundry basket, and pulled a clean pair from the shelf. My favorite shirt was on top of the stack of folded ones—a soft orange t-shirt Mark's mother washed once, in hot water. Poor Mark. He always came over to show me his new shirts.

"Isn't this great, Linda? Bought it with my trapping money."

"Yeah, Mark. That blue goes good with your brown eyes. It won't look as good on me; when's your mom going to wash next?"

He'd roar, reaching for me, but I could bolt into the willows before he untangled his feet; he said the work boots slowed him down, but I was wearing work boots too. He'd crash and wallow behind me while I dropped into the weeds and held my breath. After awhile, he'd call, "Aw, come on, Linda. I won't strangle you. Let's talk for a minute. I got to get back before the old man misses me."

If Mark caught me first, he'd throw me in the tank or a mud hole. But once he hollered quit, he was done. Then I'd crawl out, sometimes right under his feet. We'd sit on a grass hummock, and listen to the birds while Mark told me what his drunken old man and his tomboy sister had done lately. Mark's stories were better than the adventures I made up, almost as much fun, I figured, as having real brothers or sisters.

I shook myself; things to do before breakfast. I pulled the t-shirt over my head and buttoned the Levis. My favorite socks, orange and brown ones I'd bought at the grocery store with my egg money, were rolled up in the drawer. The riding boots my father had given me two birthdays ago still fit. Good thing my feet weren't growing like the rest of me.

Was twelve too old to go out the window? If I tried to tiptoe through the house in my heavy boots, Mother would ask where I was going and want me to eat first. I pushed the screen out and dropped to the ground.

Eyes closed, I breathed deep in the sun a moment, then ran to the garden. I dropped to my knees in the cool soil and peered down at a row. Yes! The lettuce was up! My mouth watered and I crawled to the next row—onions too! My father wouldn't eat them; he said a woman shouldn't eat onions until she was married, but I ate a few on my walks. In the next row, feathery carrot tops uncoiled beside a row of radishes. My marigolds were three inches tall; I willed them to raise their faces fast.

From the tall grass at the edge of the garden I ran, crouching, through the alfalfa; I ducked through the fence into the ditch, and trotted to the willows. Back against a cottonwood trunk, I faced the sun and shut my eyes. Dew on the long marsh grass sparkled in the darkness behind my eyelids. Surely the minister wouldn't approve, but my morning ritual felt like prayer to me.

Then I peered at the moss at the base of the tree; in the willow-patch, I could look for fairies even if I was grown up. Sure enough, a tiny frog bounced out of the moss two inches from my nose. Every time I looked for fairies in the willows, I saw the little frogs. Once I found a miniature pool in the limestone on the ridge, perfect for a fairy swimming pool; the next time I rode by, a frog sat in the center. When I sat down, the frog bugged his eyes and flicked his tongue. Then he hopped to my knee, and didn't move when the horse blew her hot breath over him.

I leaned back against the rough cottonwood bark and took a deep breath. I pictured myself grown up, slim and lovely as a willow. Wishing could do it; I had proof. For years, my mother called my eyes "hazel" when I wanted them to be green. In stories, secretaries and nurses had hazel eyes, but the slinky, luscious blondes with silken limbs all had green eyes. One day my father spanked me. Afterward, I locked myself in the bathroom to cry, and when I washed my face, my eyes were gray, like my mood.

After that, I slipped into the willows every day to stare at their fresh green leaves, and picture my eyes being green. I probed the moss until I could slip a finger under it and find the hole under the roots. From a heap of my treasures, I picked a mirror and held it up. Yes! Today they were definitely greener.

A sharp whistle pierced the willows. Breakfast. Oatmeal, even on my birthday. Father demanded bacon and eggs every other morning, but Mother said eggs weren't good for people, because of cholesterol; she always explained it to us while the eggs burned.

I glided to the edge of the willows like a sexy blonde, and looked out. Cows were outlined against the green and gold grass on the south ridge, headed for water. Rebel stood by the tank, whinnying when she saw me. I petted her nose while she snuffled at my hands and pockets.

"Nothing today, baby; I forgot." I remembered to close the screen door gently as I stepped inside.

"Wash your hands; you've been handling that filthy horse."

"Yes, Mother." I splashed my face too, and used my father's brush to get some of the knots out; I'd forgotten to braid it again.

"Good morning, daughter," he said, smiling. "How does it feel to you, twelve?"

I sat down with dignity. "Oh, about the same I guess."

He grinned. "You can take it easy today; we don't have anything we can't put off. There will be a fellow coming later with the new tractor. I guess that's your present from me. And do your chores, of course."

I nodded, drinking milk. Mother called from the kitchen, "Did you invite some kids to have birthday cake after supper?"

"Yes, Mark and his sister. And Denny, and I suppose he'll have to bring his little brother. Icky!"

"Careful! Your face will freeze that way. Maybe John can put a card table out on the porch for me. I don't want those kids running through the house tearing up things."

I grinned at Father; he'd sat me down last night in the barn to suggest we let Mother have her way without fighting. More likely, the kids would have sat on the couch trying not to drop crumbs on the carpet, their backs as straight as when they were banished to the corner at school.

"What about Marlene and Darlene?" Mother said.

"Do I have to? They'll wear dresses just alike and tell me how much they cost."

"Their folks have been my neighbors for a long time," Father said. "Call them right now."

During breakfast, Father told us the cows' sides shone with fat when he drove through them that morning; the three-month-old calves lay still, curled in the green grass, their red and white hides shining like new pennies. "We'll have to brand pretty soon, and then get them over east. Think Mark can come down and give us a hand some day? I know he needs the money and he's good help."

"I'll ask him; he'll be glad of a chance to ride the pinto."

Mark's father had come home one night a little more sober than usual with a pinto horse tied to the bumper of the truck. At first, Mark was afraid to ride it, for fear someone would drive in and say it was stolen. "But just because he's a drunk doesn't mean he's a thief," he argued to himself.

After breakfast, I brushed my teeth and noticed that the crooked ones were straighter. I was looking in the mirror, struggling to braid my hair, when Mother called, "Don't forget to brush your teeth!"

"I did that ten minutes ago, Mother."

"I forgot; you're twelve now."

Twisting in front of the mirror, I finally made a single braid. In one of my father's books, the slim, green-eyed heroine wore a single braid that bounced from "one delicious buttock to the other" when she walked. I felt my rear; a little flat, but it would fill out. Anyway, I didn't ever want to swing it around the way Julie Seale did. I grinned; no boy-crazy redheads at my birthday party.

While Mother was outside feeding the cats, I extracted six cookies from the jar and opened the refrigerator. Her private store of candy bars was half full; I took two, and slipped everything into the big pockets of Mark's old Army surplus jacket.

"Mom, after I do my chores, I'm going to walk over toward the tracks to pick flowers for my party."

"Why, that's quite a walk, honey. Would you like to take some cookies along?"

"Uh. Yeah, that's a good idea." I sat on the porch step while Mother chattered from inside. "I'll just put them in a plastic bag, and how about a bottle of pop? You need some meat on those skinny bones. You have a nice walk, and I'll get busy and bake those cakes before the kitchen gets any hotter. I think we're going to need two."

First I fed the chickens and gathered the eggs. After I pitched hay to Donna, the mare with the new colt, I walked down the road to the alfalfa field and slipped into the willows.

I tried to move softly and still not step on bluebells, but deep footprints wrinkled the bottom of the draw, still spongy from spring rains. Plum petals tangled in my hair. This year I couldn't wait to make jelly; grandmother would teach me how.

The long draw corkscrewed for a mile through the flat fields, deep enough to hide me as I walked on the bottom. On both sides, dark green alfalfa rolled away; I'd soon mow it down with the new tractor. Cool air blew over me, but the sun scorched my head. Forgot my hat again.

The bushes swished; a doe leaped into my path and paused, staring with dark eyes. The twiggy legs jerked, and the doe bounded up the side of the gully and into the alfalfa, then paused with her white tail erect. A fawn tiptoed out of the willows an arm's length away from me, and lurched up the slope. The doe sniffed once, then turned and went slowly off, looking down at her little one and back at me every few steps.

I stopped by a broad cottonwood stump; after lightning split the tree, my father cut it for firewood. A gold crack stabbed across the broad surface, ending at a dark red stain in the middle. I whispered, "Still got it?"

The stump made no sound, but that was part of the test. Only a dead tree knew who I really loved. A tree stump was more trustworthy than a best friend.

Besides, since I hardly ever saw other kids except at school, I didn't have a best friend. Unless it was Mark. But I couldn't tell a boy, and anyway, I only liked him in the summer. In the winter, when we all rode the school bus, he sat with the other boys and told dirty jokes. I'd always liked boys better than girls, but lately everyone had started acting funny. Mark's eyes got hard and darker brown; he swaggered and sometimes got in fights. When he cut his finger nearly off branding, I tied a handkerchief around it, and held his hand while my dad drove him to the doctor. His dad was drunk. But when he got a black eye or a cut on his lip in school he turned his back on me.

Sitting on the stump to keep my secret in, I ate three cookies and a candy bar, then knelt at the bottom of the draw and scooped water from a seep under a rock. Even in dry summers, I found enough water here to lap like a cat; my tongue tickled the callouses on my palm. The doe and I shared the gully and the water; sometimes I stretched my neck and tried to walk as lightly as she did.

Hunkering back on my heels, I sensed water trickling through my muscles, as it seeped through every nerve in the willow and deer. I swayed in the wind, nearly asleep, until the sun felt hot on my eyelids. Then I trotted to the curve in the draw and raised my eyes level with the edge. A half-mile away, the railroad tracks glinted. No one was in sight, but I practiced sneaking anyway, crawling out on the gully's lip to wiggle into the shadows. Once I stopped to rest and reached in my pocket to touch the hammer and chisel I'd swiped from father's tool box.

Watching the muscles slide up and down my brown arms as I swung the hammer, I thought of Aunt Lenore's bulging biceps, and wondered if my arms would look like hers someday. When she picked up a baby calf, the tan skin on her arms looked like burnished cedar. Mother said Lenore was coarse; whenever she swore in front of me, Mother would put her index finger to her lips and say, "Not in front of a child!"

But when Lenore crammed her ample haunches into a saddle, she was stunning. She'd lift the reins in her fist, wrap her legs around the horse's belly and spur. Back straight, she'd gallop after a cow, leaning with the horse.

Finished, I nudged the stone into darkness at the high end of the overpass where spring floods wouldn't wash it away. Chiseling my secret name in the stone was magic. I sat down to drink the pop, thinking of my future, solemn and a little frightened to know for sure I'd grow up long and slinky, with green eyes. I'd break horses no one else could ride, and use them to check the cows on my ranch. Evenings, I'd bring tall cold drinks to a shaded porch, handing one to a man with a black mustache. Side by side, wearing faded jeans and cool white shirts rolled up over muscular arms, we'd talk to the tune of clinking ice about novels and Paris. Once in awhile I'd get in the man's white Jeep and go away with him, and come back speaking French. On matched Arabian stallions, we'd canter over the prairie, our children racing around us. My dream would happen like the flowing lines of the song because I'd carved my secret name in stone. Mariah. The Wind. The one who is everywhere free, mistress of breeze and hurricane.

My orange shirt was dark with sweat, sticking to my chest. The sun said it was nearly noon; Mother would be sure the coyotes had eaten me. I stuck the pop bottle in my pocket with the tools, and slung the jacket over my shoulder.

Just before I stepped out of the shade, I looked back. The rock was invisible. I walked away, my braid bouncing against my shoulder blades, smiling at the green alfalfa. My mare Donna had just foaled a filly, and Father said I could name her; she'd be Mariah, a secret in plain sight.

When I was almost to the stump, I stopped to listen. Footsteps coming down my draw. Then silence until a redwing blackbird complained *cherk! cherk! cherk!* I looked toward the nest, hung on three willow branches. The male swayed above it, tipping his head to look into the willows; I saw a hint of black in the green. "Mark?"

He stood up, laughing. "Took you long enough. Got any of those cookies left?"

"Yes, and I swiped a candy bar," I said, handing it to him. "I've had quite a few cookies and one candy bar already."

We sat together on the stump. "What are you doing here so early? I thought you'd just come over for the cake."

"My dad suggested that a girl twelve might be able to learn how to fish; the old lush must have a few brain cells left. I thought we could go up in the Hills and find a creek. We can be back in time for your party."

I looked up at him and batted my eyelashes for practice. "But how are we going to get there? My dad won't want to quit haying to take us."

"Oh, did I forget to mention my dad loaned me the pickup?"

"Really?"

"Your dad already said it's OK, and your mom is packing sandwiches. How come you're blinking so much?"

"Never mind. Get your lazy body up off that stump!"

He sauntered; I skipped and sang, "I love to go to the Hills. Where shall we go? Remember that place with all the moss?"

"I brought your present," he said, looking at the sky.

I stopped. "Where is it?"

"Oh, it's somewhere around. You'll have to find it."

"Find it? Did you lose it?"

"No, no—it belongs outside. I put it somewhere around, and you'll have to find it. You might not even know it's your present if you don't think about it when you find it."

"Is it a rock? Is it alive?"

"Well, I'm not going to *tell* you. You have to figure it out. It was alive when I brought it."

"Where shall I look? There's so much space!"

Hands in his pockets, he grinned. "It's kind of closer to the corral than the house, I think."

"Will I like it? Does it bite? Is it pretty?"

"Well, *I* don't know if you'll like it. I didn't have any money to buy you a present. When I found it I thought you might like it. Yes, it might bite."

"I don't want to be bitten by a present! What color is it?"

"Oh, kind of greenish and brownish and yellowish."

"I give up." Mark said nothing. "Well, aren't you going to tell me?" I was staring right at him with my brilliantly green eyes. He shook his head and looked away.

"No. You'll have to find it yourself." We stepped out of the willows; his dad's old pickup was parked in front of the house.

"If you get the lunch, we can go. Your dad said you could use his fishing pole."

"Would you get it, Mark? Mother will give you more cookies than she would me. I have to run to the corral a minute."

I lifted the latch on the gate and ran down to the tank. An idea so ridiculous I was afraid to say it had crawled into my mind. I crouched by the tank so my shadow wouldn't show on the surface of the water, and watched the board float my father put there so birds wouldn't drown when they came to drink.

After a minute, thick moss on the other side of the tank rippled, and a head like a hatchet poked up. A clawed foot reached out of the moss, and a turtle heaved herself up on the board and peered at me with yellow eyes. Brilliant orange rimmed her mouth. I grinned at her and stood up. She tilted her head to look at me, then stepped off the board, and sank under the moss.

When we were in the pickup and headed for the highway, I asked, "Is my present wearing orange lipstick?"

Mark made a face. "You found him that fast?"

"I don't know why. I'd never have thought of it, except from you. That's really neat, a turtle in the tank. That's the nicest present I could get. Maybe she'll have babies."

"Oh, some of those rich kids will bring you something really good; he's all I happened to have around. Why do you call it a her? You can't tell."

"She looked wise; I just know it's a she."

During the heat of summer in 1990, I walked one of our pastures often, watching the water level in the dam and collecting seeds from unusual prairie plants. One year when I was still in grade school, my father sold water to the construction crew that built the highway. Even after they pumped water into trucks all summer, the level never fell as far as during recent dry years. When it had shrunk thirty feet from its normal shoreline, I looked one afternoon for exposed treasures, and found a few old shotgun shells, evidence of duck hunters who had slipped past our watch. A huge turtle bumbled around in the shallows, gobbling frogs. Watching her, I tried to remember how many years had passed since I'd found leathery turtle eggs shattered on the south side of the dam bank. When the turtle saw me, she paused and raised her head; black eyes glittered. I'd never seen the one Mark put in the tank again after my birthday. A hailstorm a couple of years later flooded the alfalfa field so I had to ride out on my horse to rescue the barn cats, yowling in the cottonwoods east of the house. Later that summer, I searched for my name rock under the railroad trestle; it had washed away, or been buried in mud.

The winter of 1990–91 was dry and ferociously cold; the thermometer registered thirty below for nearly a month, with almost no snow on the ground. Spring brought little rain. When scattered wildflowers began to bloom in April, I walked the pasture hunting for curlew nests with a friend, a wildlife biologist and bird-watcher. He didn't believe they nested this far north, but I'd seen them fluttering through the grass ahead of my horse's hooves, crying.

On the opposite side of the water, I saw a dark shape. The sour smell of rotting meat reached me before I recognized the turtle, half-buried in mud. I slid my shovel under the carcass and carried it high enough on the rocky hillside so cattle wouldn't walk on it. And if we ever got another heavy rain, the bones wouldn't wash back into the dam. Each time I checked the cattle that summer, I furtively scanned the decaying remains. One sunny fall day, I picked up the empty shell and skeleton, and hauled them home. I washed the bones in bleach, and took them to the rock pile my husband George built on our hillside. Since his death, the cairn has become a shrine. I've slipped into crevices between the stones articles of George's too precious to lose.

One by one, I dropped the small bones into cracks, listening as they clinked among the other secrets inside. I lit a little fire of sage on a blackened ledge, and waved the smoke toward the six directions. Then I placed the breastplate and coat of mail on top of the cairn, against the sky.

David Rains Wallace

Tapir's Gourds and Smelly Toads

Life in a Little-known Rain Forest

from *The Nature of Nature*

I hesitated when Pedro José Mejía and his family invited me to mount a small, reluctant-looking white gelding at their house in the town of Quebrada Grande. I'd never ridden a horse, so the idea of riding one eleven miles up the slopes of a volcano in the Costa Rican rain forest seemed fantastic. Señor Mejía had recently sold his dairy farm on the volcano to the Costa Rican National Park Service as part of Guanacaste National Park, a new park in the northwest part of Guanacaste Province. The Park Service had then hired him to build and manage a biological station on the site of his former farm. He built it, as he built his farm, with trees from the pastures he cleared, sawing them into boards with a chain saw.

I wanted to visit the biological station, and the Mejías evidently considered horseback the appropriate way to get there. They were unimpressed with my hesitation and avowals of inability, and Pedro's son Walter got on his horse and started to ride away, with my backpack slung over his saddle horn. I imitated the thousands of Westerns I've seen, and got on the little white horse. It seemed as uneasy about the situation as I did, but after some stumbling at my tentative urging, it followed Walter up the dirt road.

The American biologist Daniel Janzen had arranged my visit to the Volcán Cacao Biological Station as part of a tour of the park, which stretches from the Pacific to Costa Rica's central cordillera and contains a transect of ecosystems: mangroves on the coast; dry deciduous forest on the volcanic plateau; rain forest and cloud forest on the peaks. Including deforested areas as well as some of the last significant forest remnants on Central America's heavily populated Pacific coast, the park is an innovative attempt not only to protect enough forest to maintain healthy wildlife populations but to restore damaged land and develop management techniques that will reduce conflict between local people and conservation goals. Hiring the Mejías to run the biological station was an example of enlisting neighboring ranchers in the project.

Janzen had been studying the dry deciduous forest (a much more endangered kind of forest than rain forest) below the volcano since the 1960s and had been living in the area for six months out of every year since the 1970s, but it wasn't until 1986 that he visited Volcán Cacao itself. The volcano was almost unknown, although it stands in sight of the Pan American Highway. Clouds continually cover its summit, so that parts have never been photographed by geological-survey planes, leaving topographical maps with sizable blank spots. Although rain seldom falls from November to May on the Pacific lowlands, the Caribbean trade winds carry almost daily rain to Volcán Cacao. Janzen had discovered that many of the insects he was studying in the lowland dry forest migrated to the volcano's rain forest for parts of their lives. He knew little about the volcano's ecosystem, however, because it had never been studied.

Janzen did know that Volcán Cacao was unusual. It is covered with evergreen rain forest and cloud forest (a forest typical of cool highlands) at elevations of between two thousand and forty-five hundred feet, whereas most Central American cloud forest grows at higher elevation—in Costa Rica, above five thousand feet. Towns, pastures, and coffee plantations have replaced most of the Central American forest growing at elevations between fifteen hundred and three thousand feet. Such forests were extensively cleared even before Columbus, because of their fertile volcanic soils. At Volcán Cacao, Janzen had come upon a kind of forest that wasn't simply disappearing, as most tropical forests are, but that had virtually disappeared. The grizzled biologist seemed slightly bemused by this discovery, as though he had found a living specimen of the elephantlike gomphotheres that inhabited Central America ten thousand years ago. (One of the theories that Janzen has developed about Central American forest is that many of its trees depended on large mammals like gomphotheres to spread their seeds.)

As I urged the little horse uphill, I at first saw no sign that the Volcán Cacao forest still existed. Windblown grassy hills stretched to a horizon fitfully obscured by racing clouds. A few tattered trees stood here and there, but it was hard to believe that rain forest had once covered the hills. Although they were startlingly green after the brown pastures of the dry-season lowland, only a certain brilliance to the rising sun's light and a small flock of emerald-colored parrots indicated that this wasn't, say, eastern Kansas. The air was downright chilly. Volcán Cacao is less of a barrier to the trade winds than are the higher peaks to the north and south, and it has been called one of the coldest parts of Central America.

Riding through these foothills wasn't too hard, because the ground was firm and fairly level. The horse jogged along steadily, with some encouragement from my heels. The wind was the main obstacle: at times, it blew my feet out of the stirrups.

Then the slope steepened, and we came to a gully. Walter said that there had been a sulfur mine there. The gully contained some forest, but my mind was on my horse, who couldn't seem to get a foothold on the gully's brim. It stopped, as though incredulous at being asked to follow the steep, slick track that led down one side of the gully and up the other. I was inclined to agree with it. I dismounted, and we picked our way carefully into the gully after Walter and his bigger, braver horse had thundered across. When we reached the other side, I thought I'd keep walking, but horseback really is much faster, and Walter soon dwindled to a speck below the now dimly visible forested volcanic slopes. I remounted, got back off again to chase my hat, then mounted again. Eventually I caught up with Walter, who was waiting for me by a barbed-wire fence at the mountain's foot.

We crossed a fast, cold stream, and the rain forest began with peculiar abruptness. Almost no intermediate zone of shrubs or saplings stood between the pasture's low bunchgrass and the primary forest's huge trees. The pasture had not been grazed recently, and in a similar North American setting it would have been full of seedling trees. Daniel Janzen later told me that the volcano's rain forest is extremely slow about moving back onto land that has been cleared. He thought that most of the forest's trees needed forest animals, like pacas or tapirs, to spread their seeds, and that since these animals avoid pastures the seeds would stay in the forest. Nobody was sure about this theory, however, because nobody knew much about the volcano forest's trees and animals. Costa Rica has had more success in restoring the dry deciduous forest that grows in the Guanacaste lowlands west of Volcán Cacao, because many trees have seeds that can be carried into pastures by wind or by cows or horses who eat the fruits and deposit the seeds in their dung.

The Cacao forest looked different from other rain forests I'd seen, but it was hard to say how. There were fewer orchids or tufts of epiphytic bromeliads on branches, perhaps because of the windiness or the dry season. The underbrush was taller and denser than is usual under full canopy forest, and the shrubs bore a bewildering diversity of flowers and fruits. Some had flowers like tomato plants and glossy pepperlike fruits, evidently wild forebears of common vegetables. A large shrub with big leaves and blue berries was common—but so were countless other plants.

I dismounted again as we started up the forest path, which

seemed too muddy and rocky for my poor stumbling horse. The animal became surprisingly more nimble without me on its back, and vanished uphill. I had to walk only another fifteen minutes until I came to the biological station, a sloping pasture with a bunkhouse at the top. Suddenly I could see westward as far as the Pacific—forested canyons, grassy foothills, brown coastal plain, all part of the national park.

"What a place!" I exclaimed to Walter, who was unsaddling my horse.

"*Pura vida,*" he replied nonchalantly (a Costa Rican expression that translates roughly as "real nice"). He was used to it.

A trail led into the forest above the station, and I walked up it after leaving my pack in a rustic bunkhouse made of tropical hardwood. The forest here was different from the streamside forest below. The trees were smaller and seemed to be of different species, and the undergrowth was sparser. This was only an impression: it's hard to see clearly in a place where most things are unfamiliar, and where one sees more unfamiliarity the more one looks.

The Mejías were ranching people, like most of the people of Guanacaste Province, and weren't intimate with the forest. Lupe, Walter's mother, was afraid of the *terciopelos* (also called fer-de-lance, a very poisonous and aggressive but seldom-seen tropical snake) that lived in the forest, and she wouldn't let Walter's younger brother, Elmer, go into it because of them. Once Walter chased Lupe, Elmer, and a hired girl halfway across the pasture by waving a small nonpoisonous snake at them, the only snake I saw there.

So I was on my own when it came to identifying things. Instead of writing the names of plants in my notebook, I had to draw them, in the hope that I would someday learn what they were. I did see many kinds of plants I'd seen in other neotropical rain forests—*Clusia* trees with succulent, club-shaped leaves; *Cephaelis* bushes with flower bracts uncannily resembling the wax "hotlips" sold by novelty companies; tree ferns; begonias, hibiscuses, philodendrons, heliconians, and climbing aroids. They were probably not members of the species I'd seen before, however; the "hotlips" plants, for example, had purple flower bracts instead of the scarlet ones I remembered. Tropical genera tend to have dozens or even hundreds of species.

Smaller plants were confusing enough: trees were impossible, because their leaves and flowers were a hundred feet in the air. Central American mountain forests usually contain a lot of oaks and laurels, but I didn't recognize any oaks at Cacao. I found some decayed nuts on the ground that might have been acorns, but looking up with binoculars revealed nothing noticeably oaklike about the treetops. Many fruits on the ground probably came from laurels, because they resembled little avocados, which is a Central American member of the laurel family. I knew the trees weren't wild avocados, though, because the fruit of the wild avocado is spherical, unlike the pear-shaped commercial variety, which these Cacao fruits resembled. The only trees whose identities I could be sure of were the figs, whose small green fruits, usually marked with small teeth, littered the ground under their silvery-barked parents. (Figs are the commonest rain forest trees.)

A few days later, Daniel Janzen arrived, with a party of aquatic biologists and potential donors, and I tagged along as he showed them around. He led us into the pasture (in which Señor Mejía had left some trees growing) and showed us a small tree I'd noticed earlier but hadn't recognized. I'd noticed it because it was odd: the bell-shaped white flowers grew from the knobby, whitish trunk instead of from the branches. The trunk had also produced a glossy chestnut-colored pod-shaped fruit, about six inches long.

Janzen said that the tree was *Parmentiera valerii*, a member of the catalpa family. There had been only three herbarium specimens of the species in the world when he came to Volcán Cacao in 1986, but the species has proved to be fairly common in the volcano's forest—convincing evidence that Cacao is a refugium for an almost vanished ecosystem. The tree is also called *jicaro de danta*, or "tapir's gourd," Janzen said, because tapirs are thought to eat the fruit. He speculated that *Parmentiera* might have become rare elsewhere because of a scarcity of large animals to eat the fruit and spread the seeds.

I hadn't seen any *Parmentiera* along the forest trail. As I walked it during the next week, however, I kept finding *Parmentiera* right beside it, as though they'd stealthily planted themselves there when I wasn't looking. They weren't inconspicuous trees: unlike the pasture specimen, with its six-inch fruit (which, however, doubled in size overnight), the forest trees bore two-foot-long objects that resembled a giant cross between a cucumber and a potato. I found one tree when I stumbled over its fallen fruits. I found another when a hummingbird I was watching started to feed on its flowers.

Cacao's animals were easier to recognize than its plants. There were plenty of them—Janzen had seen fresh jaguar scats on the trail—but they faded into the background. Walter told me that he'd never seen a jaguar there and didn't believe that they lived on the volcano; he had seen only a smaller cat, which he described to me in Spanish beyond my grasp. I didn't see any kind of cat, and the animals I did see I saw largely in glimpses. Agoutis—deerlike rodents—slipped across the trail. Small red squirrels eyed me from the canopy. Often I saw only parts—legs or tails of coatis, opossums, spiny rats.

The only conspicuous mammals were three species of monkeys, who seemed surprisingly comfortable in weather that made me very glad I'd brought a down sleeping bag. When I met troops of white-faced capuchins along the trail, the males walked out on overhanging limbs to glare at me, grunting and stamping threateningly. Howler and spider monkeys frequenting a gorge north of the station were less aggressive, but also made their presence felt. They usually saw me before I saw them. Then a male howler with a reddish cast to the long black hair on his back would make deep coughing sounds and pivot back and forth on his forefeet in a way that reminded me of an old black bear. The rest of his troop would just gaze at me, in the profoundly tranquil way that howler monkeys have. Although their howls rival a lion's roar, they're the most peaceful of monkeys.

The spider monkeys, which were a rusty café-au-lait color, with black faces and hands, made squeaking sounds, which I first mistook for tree limbs rubbing together. Adult spider monkeys evidently didn't mind my presence once I came into the open where they could watch me. They would bark a little, then sit quietly on a branch. Once, a half-grown one got excited, squealing and slamming branches around, hanging upside down, then diving headlong into a leafy patch. This apparently annoyed the adults: one of them got up stiffly and departed, while the remaining two grabbed the youngster and tried to quiet it. But it broke away and went into its *enfant-terrible* act again, so they also left. The youngster looked around a moment, then hurried after them.

The forest rang with birdsong, some of it startlingly loud, but I seldom caught more than a glimpse of the singers. Once, I strained my eyes to see a bird that I thought was calling in the treetops, not realizing that it was perched on a branch a few feet away. It was a long-tailed manakin, a chickadee-size blue-and-red bird that looks conspicuous in field guides but is hard to see among the forest's intricate vegetation, even though it spends most of its time calling and performing intricate dance rituals to attract a mate.

The gaudy exotic birds that figure on the jackets of Latin American novels—toucans, trogons, motmots—were common on Cacao, but their colors didn't make them much more visible than the brown or black tree creepers, wood quail, and guans. A trogon with a tomato-orange breast might be a few feet away, but I wouldn't see it unless it moved. There were too many other tomato-colored objects in my field of vision—bromeliad or heliconian flowers. The same was true of collared araçaris and emerald toucanets, although the latter at least made a lot of noise. But I kept forgetting that their harsh croaks and squeals came from birds and not frogs.

Frogs were surprisingly scarce for such a damp place. This might have been because it was the coldest time of year—as Walter and Lupe told me. (They kept remarking on the cold, although they seemed to mind it less than I did. Lying in the bunkhouse at night, I sometimes thought that the entire biological station would become airborne, as the wind strained at the tin roofs.) I thought I heard some frogs calling at dusk—some of these turned out to be cricket calls—and I found some tiny brown frogs in leaf litter. But it was very different from the din I've heard in other rain forests.

Walking the trail early one morning, I first noticed a foul odor, and then encountered a small purple-gray toad. It resembled no other toad I'd seen. Its skin wasn't warty but ridged, like worn leather. Black dots around its eyes gave it the appearance of wearing false eyelashes. When I touched it with a stick (tropical toads can have poisonous skins), the fetid smell increased markedly. It didn't struggle, even when I turned it over with the stick—just sprawled there, belly up. I certainly had no desire to capture it, and when I let go it unhurriedly righted itself and ambled off.

The nasty smell departed too, and so I inferred that the toad had produced it somehow, perhaps as a defense. I'd never heard of a toad doing that, but then little is known about the hundreds of amphibian or reptile species in Central America, many of which have been named only in the past few decades. The toad was probably a known species, but I couldn't be sure even of that, since no field guides for nonspecialists were available.

The rudimentary state of Central American herpetology was the cause of my visit to Volcán Cacao, as it happened. David Wake, a herpetologist who headed the Museum of Vertebrate Zoology at Berkeley, had told me about it; he'd been at Cacao the year before, looking for salamanders, his specialty. Daniel Janzen had found what he thought might be a new salamander species, which wasn't unlikely, because Wake and his associates had found dozens of new species in the past twenty years.

Central and South America are the only parts of the tropics known to have salamanders—amphibians that live mainly in temperate forests. A single North American family—the lungless salamanders, or plethodontids—migrated south, evolving into more than one hundred and forty tropical species in the process. These species live throughout forests from Mexico to Brazil. All use their tongues to snag insects and other prey, as frogs do. Some have become so thin and elongated that they can live in the soil like worms;

some have prehensile tails and live in the treetops. (David Wake showed me some of the latter in the museum, placing them along a string like a row of elfin acrobats.) As many as thirty individual salamanders have been found among the leaves of a single epiphytic bromeliad of cloud-forest canopy.

Wake and his students had spent weeks at Cacao, examining moss and epiphytes and digging in the forest floor. They found only one species besides Janzen's, however, and both species appeared to be known, common ones. This seemed an unusual lack of diversity for a country in which twenty-one salamander species have been found within a forty mile transect of lowland, foothills, and mountains.

Janzen evidently still had hopes for new salamander species, because he told me to "hang on" to any I encountered on Cacao. Then he returned to the lowland with the aquatic biologists, who also seemed puzzled by Cacao, although it was insect abundance rather than salamander scarcity that puzzled them. They couldn't understand why there were so many caddis-fly larvae in the streams, because these larvae eat algae and the streams were too shady for algae to grow well. But the larvae's abundance was undeniable. The local species lived in a case that it constructed out of circular pieces of leaf; the shrubs overhanging the streams looked like Swiss cheese.

David Wake had found new salamander species in the California desert, a more unlikely place than even the chilliest of Central American volcanos, so I didn't expect to find any new salamander species if he couldn't. I had already turned over dozens of logs trying and had found only a small brown crab.

Cacao was capricious with its secrets, however. The day after Janzen's visit, I climbed farther up the volcano than before, following a recently cut trail through the dwarf cloud forest. Because the trees beside the steep trail branched only a few feet above the ground, it began to seem as if I were climbing in the forest canopy. Bromeliads grew at eye level or on the ground, which was often hidden by sprays of flowers and low bamboo thickets so rain-soaked that I sometimes felt as if I were doing more swimming than climbing.

First, there were stubby light-green bromeliads, with white flowers. Then I passed through a zone of slimmer, dark-green ones, with a reddish tinge; then through another zone of the stubby light-green variety, striped with pink. I looked inside all these and found grubs, bugs, worms, cockroaches, a large colorful weevil, and an iridescent green jumping spider, but no salamanders. The volcano was constructed of a series of steep ridges, and they began to seem endless. I'd reach the top of one only to see the next looming through the mist. I saw little else in the distance, although open patches that drifted by gave me glimpses of the forest canopy below. It was brilliant with flowers I'd never seen from the trail.

Fallen trunks increasingly entangled me, and I found myself more and more *in* the trees, climbing several feet above the ground and sometimes falling through slippery branches. I sat down to rest in a temporarily sunny ridgetop glade full of pink-striped bromeliads. I'd examined dozens by this time, but I summoned the energy to glance into one perched beside me on a branch. A chocolate-brown silver-speckled salamander was curled up in one of the leaves and remained motionless until I touched it. Then it exploded in such energetic wriggles that I barely managed to get it into a plastic bag. I stuffed moss and leaves after it to keep it moist, and climbed back down to the station.

I hung the bag in the dormitory for the remaining days I spent at the station. I could hear the salamander moving around in it. I didn't dare open the bag, for fear it would get away. I knew Janzen would be unimpressed with hearsay evidence.

When it came time to return to Janzen's headquarters in the lowlands, I feared the salamander wouldn't survive the horseback ride down the mountain. The Mejías provided a bigger, bolder horse than the little white one I came up on, perhaps hoping to hone my equestrian skills. When I'd kicked my heels into the white one, it went into an equable walk, but when I tried this with the new horse it broke into a bone-jarring trot that threatened to crush bag and salamander between my thigh and the saddle.

In Janzen's cinder-block cottage at park headquarters, I described the medium-size chocolate-brown, speckled creature, and Janzen said that it had to be a new species for the volcano, because it wasn't like the two he and Wake had found. His salamander had been big, with a pale band around the tail; Wake's had been small, with a prehensile tail. Then we opened the bag.

"I don't see anything," Janzen said.

Anxiously, I pulled out the wad of leaves and moss, and the salamander emerged onto the table. It appeared as glossy and bright-eyed as when I'd found it, although the lowlands' ninety-degree heat must have been a new experience for it.

"Yes," said Janzen, "that's different." He whisked the salamander away into his inner sanctum, where a computer sat in a nylon tent under a ceiling festooned with plant and insect specimens in plastic bags. He eventually sent the salamander to David Wake in Berkeley, and that was the last I heard of it for a while.

It was intriguing to think that I might have discovered a vertebrate species new to science simply by climbing partway up a small mountain. It also seemed unlikely. The next time I talked to David Wake, I asked him what it was. He said that it probably was a species called *Bolitoglossa subpalmata,* which is among the commoner Costa Rican salamanders between three thousand and eleven thousand feet, and is known to live in bromeliads at lower elevations. He wasn't sure, however. My salamander was unusually small for that species, and no other specimens of it had been found at Cacao. Since there are over thirty species in the genus *Bolitoglossa,* identifying one from a single specimen is dubious. Wake added that the small salamander he had found at Cacao, which he'd thought belonged to a common species, had turned out to be a new one.

Hearing how scarce salamanders continued to be at Cacao made me a little regretful about having collected one. Although I knew that my salamander was extremely unlikely to be the last of its kind, extinction is such a pervasive threat in the tropics (particularly the extinction of amphibians, which are rapidly dwindling worldwide for unknown reasons) that I felt an almost superstitious apprehension.

When David Wake began studying tropical salamanders in southern Mexico and Guatemala in the late 1960s, in some places he and his colleagues found salamanders in half the bromeliads they examined. They identified fifteen species in a transect running from the continental divide to the Pacific slope. But in 1980, after political violence had put an end to his biological work in Guatemala, Wake wrote:

> The forest had been removed and pasture occupied nearly the entire area between 1500 meters and 2300 meters (4500–6900 feet). Below 1500 meters traditional coffee plantations, which feature large shade trees and extensive plantings of bananas, had given way to a near monoculture of coffee grown in hedgerows without any suitable cover for arboreal salamanders.

Since my days at Volcán Cacao, I've found another obscure salamander in Central America. It was a big brick-red-and-cream-colored salamander in a rotten log at the base of Pico Bonito, in Honduras's north coast. This is one of the most beautiful landscapes in the world, with cloud-forested, waterfall-hung peaks looming startlingly above the golden-green gallery forest and the crimson boulders of the Bonito River, so the salamander's resplendence seemed appropriate. David Wake thought it might be *Bolitoglossa dofleini*, a species that he'd seen in Honduras, but he couldn't be sure—partly because on this occasion I had let the salamander go. Pico Bonito is one of Honduras's national parks, so perhaps there will be time to learn more about its resplendent salamander, as there will be time to learn about Volcán Cacao's small brown one.

Jan Grover

Cutover

First publication

It's the sort of logged out, burned over district that makes westward migration seem like a good idea. A land so used, so brutalized, that to stay with it, to endure it, must often have seemed like a penance. Miles of black oak and jack pine, much of it dead and down. Sand roads lined with scrub. Beaten-down trailers and perpetually unfinished houses, their composition walls dulling to grey as the seasons pass. Hills and grades scraped nude, gullies branded into the thin sand soils by ATVs. A place visited mostly when the bogs freeze over and hunters from cities to the south—the Twins, Milwaukee, Chicago—spread across the scratchy hills in search of bear and white-tails. The white and red pine here is anything but natural, the result of Civilian Conservation Corps reforestation in the thirties, when much of the Cutover was replanted to pine as the only practicable solution to the region's depopulation and failure as farmland.

The Wisconsin Cutover is a profoundly altered land, a profoundly damaged culture. Logged over two to three times between 1860–1920, the northern tier of Wisconsin's counties became all but de-populated by humans and forests alike. Sold in the 1910s and '20s to naive would-be farmers by the railroad and timber companies that had felled the forests, the Cutover's soils were too thin, its growing season too short for farming. By 1921, taxes on a million acres in the

Cutover were delinquent and over 40 percent of the tax deeds remained unsold. By 1927, over 2,500,000 acres were in tax delin-
quency and 80 percent of tax deeds were unsold. In 1927, the
University of Wisconsin Experiment Station reported that the total
acreage under cultivation in the "resettled" Cutover was only 6 percent.

Up here in the extreme northwestern corner of Wisconsin, on
the pine barrens of Douglas County, there's seemingly a bar for every
resident—bars hidden back on sand roads, bars tucked back in the
trees. My neighbor says the impressive ratio of bars to people gives
fresh meaning to the term "Build it, and they will come."

They're out there for a reason.

The Cutover isn't pristine wilderness. It's the topography of more
than a century of relentless abuse and adaptation to that abuse. The
long glacial hills sliding away from the road are densely covered in
knee-high popple. Beyond lie moraines bereft even of seedlings, a
denuded pine barrens of sandy orange soil, piled slash, and the crisscross indicia of earthmovers' treads. Stumps like broken yellow beaver teeth. Only under snow cover is it conventionally beautiful. I
could call it damaged, but that would be to emphasize only its scars;
what surprises and moves me is the nimbleness and unexpectedness
of its recovery.

The sand road to the last cabin the agent shows me winds past pulp
tree plantations of jack pine. Turning onto County Road 50, we dip
past thickets of oak and popple toward a low, boggy appendix of
Crystal Lake. This is no managed landscape. Instead, it bears all the
signs of a neglect neither benign nor malign, merely indifferent.
Downed pine and oak everywhere. The few small birch choked by
anonymous, weedy shrubs. With the exception of several near-dead
red pines, not a tree is over 15 feet tall, so the landscape looks
dwarfed, ignoble. A dead porcupine lies across the road, its viscera
turned out on the tar surface like items at a yard sale. The hole in its
abdomen is as smoothly incised as an eye tuck.

We flash past him, my doubts increasing. Up ahead someone has planted idiot strips of young red and white pine. Their soughing beauty makes the jack pine and black oak behind them look even more scrofulous and less North Woods-idyllic.

The northern black oak (*Quercus ellipsoidalis*) of the Great Lakes states isn't meant to stand alone; it's a forest player, inconspicuous and comfortable *en masse*. It doesn't spread like the bur oak of the prairies, luxuriating in wild space. Instead, it reaches, in an apologetic, arthritic way, just high enough to wave its tips at the sun and provide room beneath for browse. Lichens crowd its trunk and branches; its brittle twigs snap easily in wind, returning accommodatingly to the ground. Tree fanciers have nothing good to say about it. Donald Culross Peattie, author of the magisterial *A Natural History of Western and Eastern Trees,* is typical in his dismissal: he calls the black oak "peculiarly unkempt and formless in its winter nakedness," a graceless tree "you will never see it in cultivation . . . for it has no charms to recommend it."

The jack pine, the black oak's companion in northern Wisconsin, grows with equal humility: here "a mere runt as to height and grace, a weed in the opinion of the lumberman, fit for nothing but pulpwood," sniffs Peattie. Farther north, it's a straight, stately tree, but here on Superior's south shore, jack pine looks self-effacing. It lacks the breathtaking height of reds and whites; as it ages, its branches rise popplelike toward the sky, diminishing its profile. At sixty, a jack pine is ancient, ready to fall; at sixty, a red or white pine is just attaining adulthood. Unlike the reds and whites, with their soft fans of needles in threes and fives, jacks produce blunt, short-bristled clusters and cones that recoil on themselves in tight gnarls. The French-Canadian *voyageurs* regarded the jack as unnatural, as bad luck—a conifer whose cones were mysteriously sealed shut. But jacks are the first conifers to reestablish themselves after a fire. Intense heat melts the resinous glue of their crescent-shaped cones, which open then like blowsy flowers, scattering their seed to the hot winds. The result, write Clifford and Isabel Ahlgren, "is extremely heavy jack pine reproduction, 'thick as hair on a dog's back.' " Jacks are the toughest and most adaptable of northern cone bearers, boreal trees that can thrive on the thinnest sand soils left behind by glaciers. Rangers celebrate jacks' tenacity and homeliness in doggerel— "There, there, little jack pine, don't you sigh. You'll be a white pine by and by"—but the Cutover's first loggers despised them. Their wood is soft and light, unsuitable for timber, unworthy of the loggers' art, useful only for pulping.

Above all else, jacks are survivors.

Seeing the cabin for the first time, I know none of this. I am innocent of the temptation to metaphorize every tree, shrub, lichen. I know only that the landscape seems vaguely distressing and ugly, the forest mournful and neglected—not at all what I have imagined and hoped for. Against the hard white April snow, the forest lacks any beauty I can understand. I see trees with scoriatic bark, rheumatoid branches, the torn flags of last season's leaves. I sense that such trees are the result of damage done here, but I am not sympathetic to their homeliness. Like most city-dwellers dreaming of a forest retreat, I am seeking an unblemished North Woods of tall, stately trees. I want no part of these scarred veterans or of the opened earth, the trailer camps back in the trees, the sandbanks riven by ATVs. I am eager to move on without wasting any more time.

The cabin lies at the end of a sand road by a bay still opaque with ice. Far out on its horizon, something black and liquid dips and loops, pouring itself into the ice, reappearing in a skivvying line. With binoculars, the dark coil resolves into an otter. The agent brightens at my new show of interest and quickly piles on other points in the property's favor: bald eagles, bobcat, bear.

I hear her as if from a great distance. Already something else completely unexpected is working in me: a slight, not yet traceable intimation that this ruined land can be my teacher if only I will agree to become its pupil. What surrounds me I can see now only through the eye of convention, but I sense that through the eye of love and knowledge, I may one day find this place beautiful. I am eager to be schooled, to nurse what twitches of hope, of feeling, I can.

There are dangers in reading landscapes and other cultural artifacts as texts. The meaning of any text greatly exceeds the words used to constitute it: this is what intertextuality is about—the excess of cultural baggage we bring to reading something seemingly circumscribed and specific. The references we bring tend to be from other textual systems—films, music, literature—which for all their differences are still a particular kind of human artifact: symbolic representations of real acts.

Treating landscape as text is a dangerous project because land is not merely a representation. It is also a physical palimpsest of complex human, animal, and geologic acts, most of which are not primarily symbolic but written in flesh and soil and rock. While most landscapes are unquestionably cultural, it doesn't follow that theories devised for analyzing cultural representations are particularly applicable to reading them. The Cutover is a deep cultural landscape: even if I look back no further than the arrival of the first documented Europeans, the *voyageurs,* that still leaves almost four centuries of European, Ojibway, and Dakota actions on the land to account for and interpret. These woodlands have been fretted by the pathways of peoples west and south, then north and east, then south and west again. If the European settlers' arrival and displacement of earlier inhabitants seems to us now somehow more decisive, more tragic, than the Ojibway's displacement of the Dakota, it is partly because it is more recent and better documented *as text.* Anguish is kept alive in writing as well as in landscape by both displacer and displaced, heightened by the cultural differences between victor and vanquished.

Suppose I choose to look deeply at the area surrounding the cabin: what do I call such a search? Is it a textual reading? Because it

involves the ways cultures shape land, I might instead call it landscape study or a species of cultural studies, with all that the latter
term implies about eclectic methods and intentions. Does it matter
at all what I call this project? Well, yes: depending on how I conceive
it, certain data, certain methods, suggest themselves. My observations might be turned toward the jack pine's life cycle in one case and
the history of European-American logging in another.

I ask myself why I find a landscape this damaged so beautiful, or at
any rate so touching. Answering this question brings me to the lip of
a personal abyss—the eight years I spent under the brand, the whip
of AIDS.

   I no longer believe there will be time, and time enough, for everything I want to do. That I can control many events. That my culture's
standards of beauty and virtue are attainable or even desirable. I
know how easy it is to stand outside my own body and watch it strain
toward feeling, any feeling, at whatever cost. I've learned to find
beauty in places where I never would have searched for or found it
before—in an edematous face, a lesioned and smelly body, a mind
rubbed numb by pain. Pain. A burned-over district. Mortal lessons:
the beauty of a ravished landscape. Now middle-aged, I find mortality doubly my possession, keeper and kept.

   The diminishment of this landscape mortifies and therefore dis-
ciplines me. Its scars will outlast me, bearing witness for decades beyond my death of the damage done here. Fat-tired ATVs and their
helmeted riders lay the land bare, pock and deface it until it runs red
and open, as disease has defaced the bodies of my friends. I am learning to love what has been defaced, learning to cherish it for reasons
other than easy beauty. I walk after the ATVs, collecting beer cans
and plastic leech tubs from the banks of the bass hole, tutoring myself in the difficult art of loving what is superficially ugly. Beauty
flashes out unexpectedly. I try not to anticipate its location, try only
to trust its imminence.

   There are exceptions: curving in a hook southwest of the cabin is a bog that ends in a point forested with a stand of ancient red and white pine, immense and still, grave with age and uninterruption. These pines shelter an eagle couple who wheel over the bog every afternoon. The bog is thick with the improbable feeders who thrive on a peat-acid tea: tamarack, sundews, leatherleaf, pitcher plants, bog rosemary, Labrador tea. The pines beyond the bog on the point survived the felling of millions of their fellows because they were too difficult to log out. Crystal Lake is spring-fed; no rivers to merrily lead away fallen giants. Thus they stand on the point still, one of the few remaining stands of ancient whites in Douglas County.

There's no more lesson in this than in why some people with HIV survive ten, twelve years while others die after three. These things happen. I have learned to be deeply suspicious of metaphor, resistant to the pretty conceits I once used to explain pain and disaster. When I gaze south toward the black rampart of the surviving pines, I try to resist reading a moral into it—try to abjure the lessons that spin so readily to mind, like files summoned from a whirling disk. The pines have no more intrinsic meaning than the eagles or me. If I choose to read particular lessons in any of us, I must remember that they are *my* meanings, just as the comforts I drag from friends' deaths— heavy, cold, resistant as wet laundry—are not for or by them but for and by myself.

It's common to associate damaged landscape with open dumps, with suburbs shorn of the forests that preceded them, with prairies plowed under for four-bedroom, three-bath strip malls. There's little evidence of such damage here. Other than hillsides altered by the all too aptly named all-terrain vehicles, pines continue to double over in the northwest winds and blueberries to fruit underfoot. Deer flash like glimpsed dreams across the bog, and in late fall, old beater pickups prowl the sand roads, jammed with galvanized kennels and bawling coon hounds, sound as ancient as the cry of cranes. The woods are reputedly full of bear, the sky is thick with waterfowl, the lakes, so clear and deep, filled with muskie and pike. Oak leaves, ox-blood in fall, flutter against the navy sky, the bay water is black with cold—natural, natural, all so natural. So *what's the problem?* Why my heart-stopping conviction of measureless damage?

If explaining this is hard, it's because landscape presents itself as an epistemological puzzle. Can we understand a landscape by recurring to what it once was? The sentimental response to this would be yes: merely invoke the "preinvasion" or pre-European forest as a measure of what's been lost, and the job's apparently done. But it's not: *which* pre-European forest do we mourn the loss of? Forests in this sand-skinned country succeed each other with a slowness beyond human scale. Only pollen core samples taken from peat bogs provide a scale of change over forests' time sufficient for tracking how this land has responded to human and other alterations. If the Cutover's most visible recent damage was caused by European-American logging, it's also true that lightning-caused fires have altered these northern forests as dramatically, as conclusively, as loggers have. Or wind: in 1977, a 200-mile-an-hour straightline wind flattened miles of forest just south of my cabin as low and ugly as any logging operation ever did. The hills down there are covered now with six-foot popple indistinguishable from what succeeds a clearcut. In the spin of centuries, forest succession barely registers the damage done by European settlers and loggers. So which forest am I mourning? Whose deaths?

Today on my dawn walk, I see for the first time a small meadow obscured all summer by the deciduous undergrowth along the road. Now I crash through the leafless shrubs to look at it more closely. It's perfectly round, knee deep in frost-stiffened grass. A former beaver pond, silted up, wind- and animal-seeded, moving through the lists of succession on its way to becoming a forest clearing, then a patch of forest. But what kind of forest? Jack pine and black oak? The trees around its edge are birch, suggesting that soil here is deeper, more moist, than in the surrounding pine barrens. So a hardwood thicket, perhaps: a small puzzle for people a hundred years from now, who

will wonder at this unexplained ring of deep-soil hardwoods surrounded by dryland jack and oak.

Like that small meadow, the bay outside my door is slowly trans-
muting, silting up to become a bog. Already it is lapidary with peat
eruptions marooning unwary canoeists when the water draws down
in midsummer. If the next century is unusually dry and warm, the
breakdown of water plants in the bay will accelerate and the bog
along the western shore will expand; eventually the bog will dry to
meadow. At that point, trees will begin to move in from the edges
and form a swamp forest.

Should I call this process damage, should I call it succession?
What model—too inappropriate, too human—do I use when I embrace this landscape as altered, imperfect? According to what and to
whose sense of time?

I am watching the resident vulture soar on wings like ironing boards,
rocking faintly on a thermal. I think about Perry's leg.

Shortly before he died, I got my first look at Perry's dying leg. I'd
been uncomfortably aware of it for several weeks—a faintly sweet,
overripe smell in the house, an undertone of rot.

He was reluctant to let me change the bandage. "Are you sure you
want to do this? It can wait until morning. Are you sure? Are you *very*
sure?"

I wanted to do it: It comforted me to think of him going to bed
dry and clean when there was so little else I could do for him. I knelt
in front of him like a subject before a king and slowly peeled his pant
leg away from the soaked bandage. Yards of puke-green gauze, which
I unwound and threw into a reeking pile.

How much of the world can I find in something so altered—in a leg
no longer smooth, intact, encased in a tan skin but instead burst
open, eruptive, returning to orderless matter?

I am very tempted to touch it, to find out what something so

formless-looking can possibly feel like. Are there still nerve endings
in this mass of dead and sloughing cells? Does it feel, this leg?

Is there a sense in which this leg can be viewed as a creation instead of only an annihilation? Its world is an entropic one, moist,
swirling with energy turned on itself, no longer producing orderly
structures. Dermis, epidermis, capillary, vein, artery, ganglion. Instead, hyperbolic replication that guts out needed systems, floods
cells, drowning them. The surface looks like deep night sky, dark,
light-absorbing, starred with drops of serum winking back my reflection, the room, me kneeling there.

Light gathers up chaos, shapes it. Perry's leg shapes death: here is
where it most visibly enters my friend, through this swollen leg. He
hauls his death around with him; it comes this way. The leg, or what
used to be the leg, midwifes urgent talk. *Talk death,* it urges. *It's present; you can smell it, you can see it.* It creates a faint sweet stench, deep
as formalin, as ineradicable, as deeply remembered.

I debride Perry's leg with hydrogen peroxide, much as I would
pour soda over a ham or meatloaf. The bubbles wink back at me,
catch light; they might be stars wheeling in an unfamiliar galaxy.

Perry talks disparagingly about his leg.

I ask him, "How does it feel, seeing your leg like that?"

"Sometimes I simply can't bear it." As if he can't believe it's his.

"What do you do then?" I ask.

And the curious thing is that as soon as he answers, I forget what
he has said. I have tucked away his reply, an unopened valentine, a
lost letter. I have tried to remember, have fallen to sleep hoping I'll
catch his answer when it bobs unguarded from sleep's deep hole,
bursts through the skin of resisting consciousness. But I can't. His
reply lies in some shaded place, guarded against memory.

Perhaps he doesn't answer me at all. Soon afterward he says he has
developed a high tolerance for pain. And perhaps that is his answer:
he has learned to dissociate himself from the slow dying of his body.
But that can't be right. Perry hasn't apportioned himself into the
comfortingly disengaged blocs of Body and Soul. He knows that the

KS festering in his left leg has also laid siege to his lungs, his liver, his esophagus, his soul. None of him is unaffected by what now mac-erates his leg's flesh. He is turning into something else, rich and strange—a dead organism, human peat. Dear bog.

I rewind his leg's burial sheet.

Richard K. Nelson

The Embrace of Names

from *Connotations*

I was born in Madison, Wisconsin—a place named for a politician who had never been there. The city is nested among four lakes—Wingra, Waubesa, Mendota, and Monona—names whispering the language of ghosts. Who among the living hears them?

When I was twenty-two years old, these whispers finally came alive for me, in the voices of hunters speaking names that rooted them deeply into the land. An aspiring cultural anthropologist, I had come to the arctic coast of Alaska to live with Inupiaq Eskimos. On a midsummer day, six of us were hunting walrus in a traditional sealskin-covered boat. We had traveled so far offshore that the flat expanse of land became a thin stain along the eastern horizon, then sank completely out of sight.

Sitting beside me was a man named Kuvlu, who had designated himself my benefactor and teacher (partly, I suppose, to keep me from dying on the tundra or sea ice and partly to savor the endless entertainment of my blunders). Kuvlu gestured toward the hard seam where water met sky. "Before the White Man came, Eskimos knew the world was round," he said. "The elders warned that if you went too far offshore it was hard coming home, because you'd have to paddle uphill." Later on, after we shot and butchered two walrus, a solid wall of fog swept in around us. For hours we groped blindly through congested ice floes, relying on one man's genius for dead reckoning to keep us headed toward land.

Then, suddenly, a clay bluff loomed ahead, like the prow of an on-coming ship. Kuvlu inspected the land for a moment, turned to the others and challenged: "Who knows what place this is?" To me it looked like everywhere else along this coast—the same high bank, same gray beach, same capping fringe of tundra grass, and a narrow ravine that seemed indistinguishable from a hundred others I'd seen on earlier hunting trips. To my amazement, Kuvlu's older brother had it immediately: *"Aqlagvik,"* he said with assurance, "Place to Hunt Grizzly Bears." I was incredulous. How could anyone know the country so well? But Kuvlu only smiled and nodded, as we turned to follow the shoreline home.

Over the next hour, Kuvlu recited the names of camps and aban-doned settlements along the coast: *Nullagvik, Pauktugvik, Milliktagvik, Avgumman, Aqisaq, Imnaurat.* For a few, he offered translations: *Qil-amittagvik:* "Place to Hunt Ducks with Ivory Bolas." *Mitqutailat:* "Arc-tic Terns." *Nannugvik:* "Place to Hunt Polar Bears." *Inuktuyuk:* "Man-Eater," a spring hunting camp used by those willing to overlook its ominous name. The fog cleared as we traveled north, and finally we saw the village—a scatter of weathered houses in a place called *Ul-guniq,* "Where a Standing Thing Fell and Left Its Traces."

Reflecting on those times twenty-five years later, my mind whirls with Inupiaq names and the memories they bring: how each place looks, events that happened there, and stories I heard about it. *Qay-aiqsigvik:* "Place Where a Kayak Was Accidentally Lost." *Pingusugruk:* "Big Pingok" (a hill thrust up by heaving permafrost). *Kangiich:* "Where Tributaries Join at the River's Headwaters." *Aluaqpak:* "Big Coal Outcrop." *Anaqtuuq:* "Many Droppings." *Qiqiqtasugruk:* "Big Is-land." *Umingmak:* "Musk Ox." Some names I remember without knowing what they mean: *Singauraq, Minnguqturuq, Aquliaqattat, Aqia-gugnat, Kaulaaq, Ivisauraq, Amaktikrak . . .* and dozens more. Each one evokes for me a place set apart from all others and braided into the events that have made my life.

On my first caribou hunting trip, a man named Annaqaq gestured away from the frozen river where we stood: "Take your dog team to the top of that hill," he said. "We call it *Nasiqrugvik,* 'High Place Where You Look Out at the Land.'" I was confused by the name and by his instructions. Unaccustomed to the subtleties of a nearly flat tundra plain, the hill was completely invisible to me. What would it mean, I wondered, if the people who carried its name disappeared like the ghosts of my Wisconsin birthplace? In a deep and vital way, *Nasiqrugvik* would vanish into a monotonous, undifferentiated terrain. And the earth would be diminished as a consequence.

During the years I spent with Inupiaq people, I was interested in place names because I loved the language and because they were vital as a map when I traveled alone by dog team or kayak. I never considered writing down the names, making them part of my work as an ethnographer; not until years later, when I began recording them as a way to establish people's tenure on their traditional homelands. I did this first with the Inupiaq and then with Koyukon Indians, who live in the forested interior of Alaska just below the Arctic Circle. Koyukon place names chart the landscape, and they color it with beauty and meaning, much in the way of Inupiaq names. I spent long evenings with Koyukon people in their village cabins, maps scattered across the floor, penciling down names, listening to stories that gave each place history and significance.

I also traveled widely in Koyukon country—hunting moose from camps along the rivers, searching for bear dens in the fall, following traplines through vast forested wildlands, fishing in the lakes and sloughs. In a small way, I experienced how their lives were connected with places we discussed in our map sessions. And I was left with an array of names that are still lodged in my mind—not empty words but *names,* filled with memories, filled with the land's beauty, filled with stories from ancient times. What little I know of these things is at least a shadow of how the Koyukon people and their natural world are conjoined through names.

In the Koyukon tradition, many names tell you something about the places to which they belong—how the terrain looks, what animals or plants are found there, what has happened there in the near or distant past. These are names born from the land itself, as much a part of it as the spruce forests, the bedrock outcrops, and the twisting rivers. They are also rich in sound and sometimes aglow with spiritual power that renders the landscape sacred.

Let them speak for themselves: *Sis Dlila'*: "Black Bear Mountain." *Bidziyh Kohunaatltaanh Dinh:* "Where a Caribou Is Lying on Its Belly." *K' itsaan' Yee Hukuh:* "Big Grass Lake." *Ts' eydla:* "Black Spruce Hill." *Tin Lootleetna:* "Hanging Ice Place," a creek so named because dwindling flow in early winter leaves a hollow space under the ice, so an unsuspecting traveler could easily plunge through. *Dolbaatno':* "River of Young Geese," where people hunt fledglings in midsummer, when the birds are big and fat but cannot fly. *Diniyh T' oh:* "Bearberry Place." *Oonyeeh Tilaah Dinh:* "Where the Blackfish Run in Season." *Gguh Tlitl't' o Tiya:* "Hill Named after the Nape of a Snowshoe Hare's Neck." *Tlookk' a Ts' ilyaan Dinh:* "Lake of the Fat Whitefish." *Dilbaagga Ts' oolneek Hu:* "Where Somebody Grabbed a Ptarmigan." *Toneets Ts' ibaa La' onh Dinh:* "Spruce-Covered Island in the Middle of the Lake." *Ts' atiyh Dinaa Dakk' onh Din:* "Where a Forest Fire Burned the Hill to the River." *Dotson' Kkokk' a Gheeyo Din:* "Where the Great Raven Traversed the Length of a Lake."

Each of these places is aswarm with stories. There is an invisible life in the landscape, one known only through the mind and memories of the Koyukon people. At a place called *Tsotlyeet* there is a one-room cabin, half hidden among birches and aspens, a cabin that would vanish entirely if left unused for a few decades. A stranger would think little of this place today, and nothing at all if the cabin were gone.

But *Tsotlyeet* is the place where one of my Koyukon teachers grew up—where he spent all the years of his childhood and early adult life. The surrounding woods and thickets, muskegs and lakes, creeks and rivers were the neighborhood for young William, and for his mother and father, his sisters and brothers. This is where he acquired his intimate knowledge of moose, bear, grouse, whitefish, wolverine, caribou, and the rest of the living community to which his family belonged. It is where William perfected his skills as a hunter and trapper. In later adulthood, he often stayed there with his wife; and in the forty-odd years since they settled in a nearby village, *Tsotlyeet* has remained the family hunting and trapping headquarters. This place is the nexus of William's life. It would be impossible to understand one apart from the other.

Yet sometime, perhaps not long from now, *Tsotlyeet* could cease to be a place. Without the Koyukon people and their collective memory, it would vanish from the significant world. And the same is true for literally thousands of other places, named and intimately known by Koyukon villagers.

One night I was poring over maps with William and his old friend Joe. During a break from our work, Joe looked at me, his eyes filled with sadness, and he spoke: "I'm really glad we're putting these names on the maps, because our kids don't know a lot of them." He thought quietly for a moment. "The names might get lost. And if I died, then that country would die with me."

By this time I knew the Koyukon homeland was saturated with names—the hills and mountains, the lakes and sloughs, the river bends and islands, the ridges and valleys; places where animals congregate; places where people fish or gather berries; places known for wind or calm or deep winter snow; places with trapping cabins, hunting camps, or burial sites; places of historical importance; places known from *Kk' adonts' idnee,* stories of the Distant Time, when animals and people shared one society and spoke a common language; places alive with sacredness, where the land listens and the earth underfoot can feel.

As Joe and William turned their attention back to the maps, my own thoughts slipped away, to imagine the entire North-American continent in a time before living memory—this enormous sprawl of land, sheathed and cloaked and brilliantly arrayed with names. Names covering the terrain like an unbroken forest. Names that wove people profoundly into the landscape, and that infused landscape profoundly into the people who were its inhabitants. Names that gave a special kind of life to the terrain, as Joe and William knew so much better than I.

I imagined how these names had dwindled with the deaths of elders, beginning five hundred years ago; a steady impoverishment of names, as the Europeans spread west, knowing too little of the land and its people to realize what was being lost. The continent was plundered of its names, left desolate, emptied of mind and memory and meaning.

But all is not lost. Many Native American names survive, others are now being recorded, and some are finding their rightful places on maps. North America is also embellished with thousands of European place names, although many are opaque to the land itself, as if the earth were shaped into mountains and rivers as a way to commemorate the famous and the dead. There is no better example than Mt. McKinley, our continent's highest peak, named for a little-known politician who would later—coincidentally—become president. McKinley never laid eyes on the mountain, which Koyukon people know as *Deenaalee,* "The High One." Our maps are littered with such names. One of my favorites is Goulding Harbor, on the southeast Alaska coast, named by Captain Nathaniel Portlock to honor, flatter, or court favor with the publisher of his book.

I can think of few more worthy endeavors, few gestures that could better show our respect toward the environment that sustains us, than to remove this blight of numb, invading names. Where elders remain to teach us, we could resurrect original names and put them back where they belong. If all memory has vanished, we could find names through the land's own guidance and inspiration, as countless generations of inhabitants have done before us.

We could also follow the examples given by trappers, prospectors, lumberjacks, fishermen, homesteaders, and others who bequeathed to us names reflecting the land and its nexus with humanity. The wild country of Alaska is filled with wonderful examples. Some are purely descriptive: Dogtooth Bend, Flapjack Island, Splitrock Point, Skull Cliff, Naked Island, Ottertail Ridge, Coffee Can Lake, Three Tree Island, Ragged Cape, Bearnose Hill, Twoheaded Island, Bay of Pillars.

Some carry useful information: Hell Roaring Creek, Moose Pasture Lake, Dog Salmon Creek, Over-the-Hill Portage, Rotten Fish Slough, Peril Strait, Walrus Island, Logjam Creek, Whalebone Cape, Caribou Snare Creek, 197½ Mile Creek, Crab Trap Cove, Fishless Creek, Sealion Rocks, Plenty Bear Creek.

Some are warnings for travelers: No Thoroughfare Bay, where extreme tides create terrific currents and reversing falls; Williwaw Point, named for its sudden and violent winds; Boiling Pinnacles, where tidal currents thrash over a shallow reef.

Some commemorate personal experiences or historical events: Slaughter Island, Easy Money Creek, Cow-and-Calf Moose Lake, Strangle Woman Creek, Threetime Mountain, Lost Temper Creek, Deadman Reach, No Grub Creek, Sore Finger Cove, Tired Pup Mountain, Broken Snowshoe Creek. And Saddler's Mistake, where an erstwhile navigator guided his ship into a swale joining two mountains, thinking it was the pass between neighboring islands.

The meanings of some, of course, are anybody's guess: Big Skookum Creek, Dull Ax Lake, Seven Egg Creek, Blue Mouse Cove, Helpmejack Lake, Zipper Creek, Mooseheart Mountain, Red Devil Creek, Bear Blanket Slough. And we can speculate about the whimsies that brought forth Seduction Tongue, Doctor Beaver Creek.

Look at the map for any state and you can find dozens of names like these, expressing every possible connection between humanity and earth. They are a powerful source of hope. Given time and a return to intimacy, we newcomers to this continent may yet learn to inhabit its myriad places, may yet become worthy of the gifts it offers us, may yet find the humility and grace of those who lived here for millennia before us, may yet learn to honor the land that nourishes us, gives flight to our imaginations, and pleasures our highest senses.

The names we choose, I believe, will be a fair measure of our success.

Note: I am grateful to the people of Wainwright, Huslia, and Hughes, Alaska, for sharing their lives and traditions with me over the years;

and to Eliza Jones and James Nageak for help with Koyukon and Inupiaq translations. I am solely responsible for inaccuracies and awk-
wardness of the place name translations. An anthropologist writes
with the air of an expert but is seldom more than a raw apprentice,
so I can only hope the elders will be patient with the inevitable errors
and shortcomings in my work. Personal names used in this text are
pseudonyms. Finally, because of typescript limitations, I have simplified the spelling of Inupiaq and Koyukon words; by doing so, I intend no disrespect for the beauty and complexity of these languages.

Adrienne Ross

Return of the Falcons

First publication

In late winter 1994 what had been an open secret in the bird-watching community became public knowledge: Two peregrines were courting in downtown Seattle. The falcons, nicknamed Stewart and Virginia after two downtown streets, had been seen diving in courtship or perched on the ledges of bank buildings and condos, giving each other courtly horizontal bows. Stewart was even observed bringing Virginia gifts of starlings, tangible proof of his fitness as a hunter and worth as a mate.

In their choice of habitat, Stewart and Virginia were hardly unique. Long associated with craggy cliffs and open skies, these rare and remarkable birds—penultimate aerial hunters capable of flying seventy miles an hour and performing killing dives, or stoops, of up to two hundred miles an hour—have become increasingly common in urban areas. What made Stewart and Virginia unusual is that these were not captive birds raised and then released in a city. These were wild birds who returned spontaneously to colonize a city that happened to be within their species' ancient range. Because peregrines show a strong tendency to mate and rear their young in the same areas where they were raised, for years Seattle's peregrines had left the city in the late winter, returning to their mates and their traditional breeding areas to the north or in Canada. Stewart and Virginia were the first peregrines to stay past the winter and use the downtown area as their breeding grounds in the spring. Visions of their descendants establishing territories and breeding sites in cities up and down Puget Sound began to dance before the eyes of birdwatchers, biologists, and urban planners.

The story of Stewart and Virginia demonstrates just how blurred the once firm line between city and wild, natural and artificial, has become. As the wild and untouched places slip further into shadow and myth, more and more animals, birds, and flora are turning to the city as their new refuge. To turn Thoreau's oft-quoted sentiment inside-out: Perhaps in cities lies the preservation of the wild.

Few city dwellers, however, realize that they are surrounded by a rich and secret wildlife. Ask which animals now share their habitat, and most people will name the stray dogs and lost cats they occasionally leave food for on their back porches. They know about rats, perhaps raccoons their dog has sniffed out during the evening walk, and, of course, pigeons. But they probably are unaware that high above them, on the ledges of skyscrapers and bridges, endangered falcons now make their home.

Peregrines (the name means "wanderer") are found on every continent except Antarctica. During the fifties and sixties, as a result of DDT build-up in the food chain, the falcon's North American range was reduced to tattered fragments. Extinct in the northeastern United States by the late sixties, peregrines in the west numbered perhaps 10 percent of their original population. The severe restriction of DDT in the early seventies, coupled with captive breeding and release programs begun in the late sixties, prevented what could have been the peregrine's rapid slide into total extinction.

Wintering peregrines were first seen again in Seattle in 1986. By 1993, there were eight wintering birds raising storms of terrified pigeons at grain terminals or chasing starlings between Seattle's waterfront office buildings. Following the falcon's return have been bird-watchers and biologists, their spotting scopes set up under bridges or in parking lots, their binoculars and cameras poised in the early dawn, ready to catch a glimpse of a white-chested bird with a thick stripe down the side of its face, its sharply pointed gray wings cutting through the cold morning air.

Even those of us who have spent months learning the birds' territories and favorite hunting and roosting sites have no guarantee that a day's outing will result in a sighting. Today, however, I am lucky. A sudden leap, and the female, Virginia, flies into a cloudy sky, her dark crossbow silhouette reflected in the shimmering blue windows of an office tower. She returns with Stewart, a smaller bird, who takes her place on the nest box, allowing her a chance to feed. I watch as she rips feathers from some city bird, a pigeon perhaps, or an unlucky starling. Bits of bloody fluff and pieces of wing drift down the air currents, past the windows of secretaries, architects, and vice presidents for marketing.

I lower my binoculars, catching sight of a portly, middle-aged woman, her silver and black hair pulled back in an old fashioned bun. She glares at me as she walks past. With my rucksack and red Eddie Bauer jacket tossed against the tire of a blue Mazda, I wonder if I look more like a homeless woman than I do a bird-watcher. The woman shuffles past me, huffing out, "What are you staring at, crows? Is that those falcons I've been hearing about, is that what's up there?"

On the door leading to the rooftop ledge of the Washington Mutual Tower, the bank management has attached a sign: HOME OF THE PEREGRINE FALCONS. PLEASE BE QUIET WHILE PASSING THROUGH. Once the peregrines showed a marked preference for this building, a coalition of community groups called the Seattle Peregrine Project installed nest boxes on the top ledge of the building's east and north sides. Stewart and Virginia chose the east side ledge for their nest, making the north side their food cache and preferred roosting site.

I have positioned myself in front of a flower shop in the Pike Place Market, my binoculars focused on the north side of the Tower. The proprietor of the flower shop, a handsome man with curly brown hair, stands beside me as he dumps a bucket of petal-stained water down a storm sewer. "You won't see the birds up there any longer," he says in a smug, almost conspiratorial tone. "The TV crews spooked them off. They sent up a helicopter to get shots of the nest box and those birds just took off and haven't been seen since."

I thank him for his information, even though he speaks of rumors and urban legends. News releases and TV shows have been following the progress of Stewart and Virginia's courtship through the early spring, and the birds are now local celebrities. Earlier, when I set up my observation post on a hilltop parking lot, the lot attendant, an elderly African American gentleman, gave me updates on how often the birds would change incubation shifts. Until recently, I doubt if he—or many other people in the city—knew exactly what a falcon was, much less a peregrine.

For Seattleites, who like to think of their city as unique, having it be home to nesting peregrines feeds the local vanity. Yet Seattle is one of many cities that provide food, winter range, and breeding areas for peregrines and other raptors. Peregrines now winter and breed in cities such as San Francisco, Denver, and New York City.

What we see as a skyscraper of chrome and steel, its windows reflecting clouds in a turquoise sky, a peregrine can see as a cliff, full of crevices for nests and ledges for the clumsy first flights of young. Walking along a city street, we look down watching for traffic and avoiding the eyes of strangers. High above us a peregrine is perched on a tower watching pigeons flying far below. The falcon will wait until the time is right, when a pigeon has left an area of cover and is flying careless and unsuspecting. Then, at high speed, the falcon will slip behind its prey, just outside of the pigeon's range of vision, striking first with its talons and then fatally biting the bird's neck.

Without our realizing it, our artifice, in an animal's eyes, recreates the natural world. Far from being isolated from nature, our cities are playing an active role in evolution, favoring certain species over others and helping determine what degree of biodiversity can exist into the twenty-first century. While peregrines like Stewart and Virginia have been able to find an urban home, not all species will be so lucky.

Cities tend to be warmer and drier than the surrounding countryside. This makes them appealing places for species such as mockingbirds, which have been extending their range from southern states into the north, but poor choices for creatures that require wetland or water habitats. The near constant landscape disturbances from construction, traffic, and pesticide use tend to favor exotic, introduced plants over the native species that have evolved to fit relatively stable and long-term environments. Habitats can also vary greatly within a city, with plants and animals that are thriving in one area nonexistent just a few blocks away. Nocturnal mammals such as raccoons or opossums do well in cities, as do jays, crows, gulls, magpies, and house sparrows.

Here in Seattle, eagles nest in city parks and harbor seals haul themselves onto local beaches for an afternoon sun against a background of sewage treatment plants. One winter day, a year or two before Stewart and Virginia's arrival in Seattle, I spent hours monitoring a female peregrine at her perch under a bridge. The hunting was juicy pigeons, tame and easy for the kill. That winter, the peregrine fed both herself and an immature red-tailed hawk who routinely stole her first kill of the day. By spring, she left for her northern breeding grounds fat and robust, looking better, some said, than a bird that had hunted in wild lands.

But the urban brave new world is not without its dangers, even for peregrines. The mortality rate for a city-raised falcon chick, called an eyas, is very high. On average, one chick in three will survive if it takes its first flight, called fledging, from a bridge. The odds improve if the fledging occurs off a building; two out of every three eyases tend to survive under those conditions. Young peregrines have been known to land inadvertently in city streets alongside cars or buses, flutter clumsily down ventilator shafts, become entangled in wires, or drown in nearby bays.

From the time the courting peregrines were first spied darting behind the Federal Building or exchanging bows on the ledges of Washington Mutual Tower, Seattle's bird-watchers and biologists recited the survival odds, to keep hope in line with reality. Virginia's blue cere, an area just behind the beak, revealed her to be an immature bird. For a bird so young to engage in courtship was surprising. The odds were that she wouldn't be able to lay eggs her first year. And even if she could, the eggs would probably be infertile.

Soon enough, the Seattle Peregrine Hotline, originally set up to report sightings of the rare birds, became a community message center on the status of Stewart and Virginia. Interest in the birds became so high that the owners of Washington Mutual Tower, at the urging of organizations such as the Falcon Research Group and the Seattle Peregrine Project, allowed a hole to be drilled through one of their walls so a video camera could film activity in the nest box. By the time a remote monitor was set up in the building's lobby, Virginia had already beaten the first set of odds by laying three reddish-brown eggs.

During lunch hours, after five, and through much of the day, up to two dozen or more people could be found watching the peregrines. Bank officials kindly put up a small sign by the monitor informing novices which bird was on the nest. Hard-core birders, falconers, and raptor enthusiasts, staring at the flickering gray screen would quickly exchange the latest news on feeding patterns or on Virginia's tendency to leave Stewart on the nest and take in a bout of flying. Because their bodies are conspicuously larger than the males', female peregrines normally stay continuously on the nest, providing warmth to the eggs or newly hatched eyases, and deterring potential predators such as gulls. But Virginia, perhaps because of her youth, would frequently leave the brooding responsibilities to Stewart. Whoever was the nest sitter of the moment, whether Virginia or Stewart, the shifting of blue-grey wings, spread like a protective mantle over the nest box, would elicit a gasp from the crowd, anticipating a glimpse of the three red-brown eggs.

"Like many of our customers," joked a rotund, horn-rimmed banker one day to a crowd staring at the monitor, "when they came to Washington Mutual, they took their nest egg with them."

Another afternoon, during my daily falcon watch, a silver-haired woman turned to me and said, "Look what they did for us. They brought us together. Imagine strangers in a bank lobby having something we could talk to each other about."

Yet before we became strangers in a bank lobby, divided by age or race, sex or religion, class or desires, we were members of the same species. Somehow the fact that we all struggle to love our families and find meaning in our lives was not enough reason to come together and simply talk. Now the sight of the peregrines establishing a home, simply and determinedly against such odds, was putting the weary and cynical hearts of city dwellers to flight. Amid the squealing of brakes and poisonous fumes of cars, alongside love affairs in red Audi's or mothers walking down 6th Avenue arguing with their grunge daughters, something was opening the doors of our city. Another creature, as vital and alive as us, was entering, bringing with it an odd but palpable feeling of hopefulness, and even of community.

"Where's Stewart?" I once heard someone ask, a voice in a crowd of two dozen people staring at the monitor.

"She told him to go get a latté," said one of the bank employees, a regular at watching the birds.

"Isn't that just like a man? Ask him to go to the corner store for coffee, and he comes back hours later. Who knows where he's been."

Virginia beat the odds again by having one, then two eyases emerge from their eggs. Bank employees put up a cardboard poster of a peregrine and two eyases with a word balloon above them reading *One more egg to hatch and our family will be complete!* A Hatching Party was thrown, complete with cake, which was being served just as the third eyas broke through its shell. The three downy chicks hardly resembled birds, much less falcons, except for their dark eyes and sharp, if miniature, beaks.

Virginia had proved to be a lucky bird so many times that no one could have expected her to die a week after her first eyas had hatched. Virginia was flying near Freeway Park early one afternoon. An office worker sitting outside a nearby building reported hearing a loud thud, followed by the sight of a large dark bird dropping limp out of the sky. "Perhaps," a coworker suggested, "it's just a pigeon?"

No one knows exactly what happened, but it's possible Virginia was on a hunting flight. Although it is unusual for a mother peregrine to leave the nest so soon, Virginia, a first-year bird, had a great deal to learn about survival. What the office worker heard might have been the crash of a diving peregrine into a reflecting glass window. Where blue sky should have been was instead that sudden, fragile border between life and death.

Just as the hatchings and feedings were televised, so too was the removal of the eyases for temporary placement with a foster pair of captive peregrines. Week-old eyases require a parent bird with them 24 hours a day, providing warmth and protection from predators. Stewart could not hunt and brood the young at the same time. This early in their development, the eyases were dependent on two parents.

News of Virginia's death spread quickly through the city, even making the front page of the *Seattle Times*. In addition to reporters and TV news crews from the major networks, some two dozen people waited for hours in front of the bank's TV monitor as zookeepers from the Woodland Park Zoo and the head of the Falcon Research Group prepared to remove the chicks from the nest.

"Who's going to tell Stewart?" a man asked, only half-rhetorically.

"They die in the wild all the time," I heard another man say. I wanted to add, *And they die in cities all the time, too*.

"But we don't know about that," a woman replied. "We don't give them names."

The flickering images on the monitor showed Stewart standing in the nest box, his wings spread wide but still too small to properly cover the tight, fuzzy cluster of rapidly growing eyases. Perhaps there was something inspiring, something not seen often enough, in a parent's remaining to care for his young regardless of circumstances. Watching him, a diminutive woman with a dangling, battered pair of Bushnell binoculars moaned, "Poor Stewart! He's going to be absolutely devastated when they take the little eyases. He's trying so hard to be a good father."

In the monitor we saw Stewart hopping to the edge of the box. With a swift motion his wings were open and he flew off, leaving three pale chicks huddled together. He returned with a decapitated prey carcass from the food cache on the building's north side. We watched as he tore the flesh and soft organs into dark red strips, dropping them into the eyases' gaping and eager mouths.

"Take good care of our babies!" a woman called out as she stared at the monitor screen. We watched as biologists brought a window washing stage up against the ledge. Stewart flew off, circling closer and closer to the trestle, a gray crossbow cutting through the evening clouds. Then one of the men reached over to gently pluck the three eyases from the nest box.

When Stewart returned it was to an empty ledge. For a moment he sat twisting his head, looking up and about. Then he sat quietly beside the empty nest, not entering it, not moving.

"That punched all my father buttons," muttered a man standing next to me.

Do animals feel grief? Or do we need to feel it for them? In my education and training as a lay naturalist, I had been taught that these kinds of comments were wrong. By projecting our experiences onto an animal's reality, we miss a species' unique essence, the fine and glorious brush strokes it gives to evolution's vast and ever changing canvas.

Yet as romantic as people's responses were, they held a genuine compassion. Perhaps we were simply being human, and doing what

Stewart, a being of speed and instinct, could not do. We watched the monitor as Stewart's head began to bob rapidly and he flew off, presumably in search of new prey.

Stewart and Virginia's eyases were placed with a captive pair of peregrines who bonded to their young charges immediately, providing food and parental care. To keep Stewart in Seattle, another eyas was loaned by a peregrine breeder. Two weeks older than Stewart's young, this eyas did not require constant parental attention. Stewart also bonded quickly with his foster eyas, hunting for it and providing care and companionship.

For a time after the eyases were removed, the bank switched off its lobby's remote monitors. Explained a spokesperson in the *Seattle Times,* "Because of the tragedy, it's part of the healing process." Yet calls continued to come in to the Seattle Peregrine Hotline, from people eager for information on how all the eyases were doing with their respective foster parents.

A few weeks after their mother's death the eyases were returned to their original nest, high atop the Washington Mutual Tower. Stewart's foster eyas was returned to its breeder, and people began to gather again in the bank lobby to watch the reunited falcon family. Some people who were present when Stewart rejoined his young say that he seemed to hesitate for just a second. His charges suddenly multiplying from one to three did not stop him long, however, and Stewart immediately began to feed the ever hungry eyases.

With Virginia no longer present to hunt with him, the burden of finding food for himself and three young falcons fell solely on Stewart. A feeding tube was attached near the nest box so that bits of quail or pigeon could be surreptitiously dropped onto the ledge, preventing the eyases from identifying humans as a source of food.

Of the three eyases, one died of natural causes before it was old enough to take its first flight. Another eyas, a male, did fledge but experienced several flight-related injuries; he was eventually euthanized by a local wildlife clinic after he broke one of his wings. The third eyas, a female, successfully fledged and was seen flying around the Seattle office towers with her father and on her own.

It is too soon to tell if Seattle can become a peregrine breeding ground, but the city—and others like it—can take steps to provide badly needed habitat for wildlife. Our world is becoming too small for us to continue focusing our efforts exclusively on protecting distant wilderness areas. Nature lives in those open and wild places we must continue to protect and cherish, just as it lives in the hive that bees set up in a church yard or in the dance of spring butterflies in the flower planters of a local shopping mall. The same drama and beauty we search for in far-off lands can be found in the urban wild—if we learn to look up, watch carefully, and take less for granted. But we will have to make our cities far more livable—for humans and for wildlife—if this beauty is to survive into the next century.

If Stewart's eyas survives her first year, she will probably return to Seattle to find a mate. Her father already has. By the early fall, Stewart had returned to the Washington Mutual nest box with a falcon known as Belle.

David Petersen

Knee-deep in Its Absence

First publication

Awhile back, I was asked by Tom Lyon, editor of *Western American Literature,* to contribute an essay to a special issue he was putting together. The theme of that issue, and what Tom wanted me to ponder and write about, was "nature and place." Specifically, Tom posed the question of why I have chosen to make my career (such as it is) writing about nature.

The answer is easy: I have no choice; it's in my genes.

To wit: The best scientific guess is that crude, "proto" language first appeared among the progenitors of our species more than two million years ago. Full language, it is thought, evolved forty to one hundred thousand years ago, in parallel with the triumphant emergence of *Homo sapiens sapiens.* (In fact, the ability to communicate intricate thoughts may have been what gave early *H.s. sap* the competitive edge over his contemporary, *H.s. neanderthalensis,* Neanderthal man.) At that time and until the most recent moment of human history, our hunter-gatherer ancestors had no cultivated crops, no domesticated livestock, no industry beyond small-scale production of crude implements. And since we also had no writing, all accumulated knowledge—social and religious values, tribal and family histories, myth, law, legend, ritual, everything—had to be precisely memorized and orally transmitted from generation to generation.

And what better vehicle for condensing, organizing, making memorable and transferable the spoken word than . . . story.

Which is to say: for the overwhelming bulk of human tenure on this lovely earth, our world, spiritual as well as physical, was *inseparable* from wild nature; it *was,* we *were,* wild nature. And naturally, the characters who breathed life into ancestral story would have taken (and in surviving primitive cultures, still take) the form of animals, animal-humans, animal-gods, and even (as in Navajo creation myth) animated landscapes.

Only ten to twelve thousand years ago did we learn, here and there around the planet, to domesticate wild flora and fauna, trading spear, atlatl, and digging stick for plow and shepherd's crook, thus beginning our separation from wild nature, our divorce from Eden. In due time came industry, that irresistible magnet for urban growth. Thus, only in the last second of human history did "progress" insidiously separate the majority of men and women from daily association first with wild, then pastoral, nature.

Simultaneous with and due to this estrangement, the ancestral literature of nature and place that had been kept alive for countless millennia began to fall out of favor, out of use, being replaced first in oral tradition, then—beginning some 3,500 years ago with the invention of the first true alphabets—in written literature by stories focused ever more on the increasingly un-natural human-constructed world. In the second half of the fifteenth century, *Herr* Gutenberg's printing press appeared, facilitating and speeding that transition.

But what goes up must return to earth, and now, in this living generation, as we witness the last remnants of wild nature being clear-cut, bulldozed, and blacktopped toward extinction, as the spiritual quality of our lives atrophies even as our material "standard of living" continues to bloat, nature writing is regaining its deeply historical popularity and significance. Literate, thinking readers are increasingly expressing what may well be a genetic craving (*à la* Edward O. Wilson's *Biophilia* hypothesis) for nature-based story, ancestral story, story that reconnects us to our roots and rejoins us, at least in spirit, with the natural world that was and is our one true home . . . story which, like religion, gives direction and meaning to our increasingly complex lives and offers hope for the future by embracing values from the past.

Consequently and by and large, the character of the place in which a nature writer lives and works (or longs to return to) colors his or her work. For Wendell Berry it is rural Kentucky, for Terry Tempest Williams the Great Basin and Colorado Plateau, for Richard Nelson coastal Alaska, for Edward Abbey the desert Southwest, for A. B. Guthrie, Jr., the Big Sky country of Montana, for Harry Middleton wherever wild trout yet swim pristine waters.

My own physical and spiritual place is the southern Rocky Mountains. I thrive on the crisp clean air and cold clear water, the heartbreaking beauty of the creased and crenulated landscape and its abundant wildlife, the quiet and the solitude and the personal freedom it all adds up to. These are the things I have come to cherish most in life. It follows that these are also the things I am happily compelled to write about. In my case at least, the nature of the place has become the nature of the man, of the writer.

During the first few years my wife Caroline and I lived here, we had a most pleasant habit of walking or snowshoeing a couple of miles down the mountain to spend Sunday mornings lazing around an antique wood stove drinking coffee and chatting with an octogenarian rancher friend named Helen.

Helen has spent her entire long life on the verdant riverside spread where she was born in 1905. She is living local history and a captivating storyteller. Among my favorites is her tale of the Naked Fat Man.

In the summer of 1913, when Helen had just turned eight, her father went hunting up the tight little creek valley where my hillside cabin now squats. There, "in blow-down timber so thick you couldn't ride a horse through," Helen's father killed an exceptionally large bear that could have been the dead-last grizzly in these parts.

With helping hands and horses, the hunter wrestled the bruin home and hoisted it by the hind legs into a sturdy tree, then skinned it in preparation for butchering. (Few country folk in those lean and pragmatic days wasted fresh meat of any kind, and "woods pork" was widely considered a delicacy.)

It was then, with the bare bear hanging there and her father standing beside it, bloody knife in hand, that young Helen wandered onto the scene. Horrified at what she saw, she burst into tears and fled. Eighty years later, Helen laughed when she recalled how the flayed bear "looked like a naked fat man hanging there. I thought Dad had killed somebody and was fixing to cut him up and feed him to us. I haven't been able to stomach bear meat since."

Story spawns story.

Some years ago, while exploring a secluded bench aspen grove a few miles up the mountain from my cabin, I stumbled upon a hidden spring. Abundant spoor announced that deer, elk, bears, turkeys, and other wildlife visited the place regularly to drink from the little pool, to browse the lush vegetation watered by its brief overflow and, I like to think, just to be there. Shadowy and quiet and almost spooky at twilight, the place exudes a preternatural ambience. Since that day I have visited this sylvan shrine often; it has become my local refuge from Babylon. And among the most significant elements of the spirit of this place are its bear trees: across the decades, the soft white bark of several of the larger aspens ringing the spring have collected hundreds of blackened bear-claw tracks.

This in itself is hardly unique. I've seen scores of bear-scarred aspens near dozens of secluded spring pools throughout the Rockies. Most often, it's black bear cubs that do the climbing and whose needle-sharp claws scratch and gouge the impressionable bark, leaving distinctive curved parallel signatures. As the aspens grow, these modest tracks harden, blacken, stretch and puff, eventually coming to look as if they were made by the most monstrous of bruins.

But two special aspens near "my" spring wear a different sort of signature entirely: heavy, widely spaced vertical claw marks more

than a foot long and at just the right height, allowing for eight decades of subsequent growth, to suggest that an exceptionally large
bear once stood upright, stretched as high as possible and raked its
claws heavily downward. Exactly as grizzlies are wont to do.

Like my friend Helen, those storybook aspens have survived
nearly a century rooted firmly in this lovely little corner of the silver
San Juans. I find it a deeply poignant experience to sit quietly in that
enchanted refugium and study those crude autographs and imagine
them being scribbled by Helen's Naked Fat Man himself. As perhaps
they were.

On one of the last occasions Caroline and I visited Helen, I found
myself admitting to her that I was terribly envious of the simple, self-
sufficient, quietly satisfying life she'd known growing up and living
on a working ranch in the good old days of a still-wild West. "I'd give
anything," I confessed, "to have lived your life."

"Hell," said Helen, "you can *have* my life. I wish I'd been born fifty
years sooner."

Surprised, I asked why.

"So I wouldn't be around today to see what the sonsofbitches are
doing to these mountains."

The thing you've got to watch out for with progress, my old friend
Bud Guthrie was quick to point out, is that once you've got it, there's
no going back. Helen is ninety now and no longer guides elk hunters
and fly fishers into the wilderness or plants a big garden or keeps
chickens or tractor-hauls hay out to feed snow-stranded cattle or
drives a horse-drawn sleigh thirteen miles to town in January blizzards. No more grizzlies in the neighborhood either. Instead, we
have ever more new roads slicing like daggers into the heart of recently former wildness, ever more urban refugees arriving to build
ever more houses along those new roads. My magical bear trees are
in mortal danger of being "harvested" for the polluting pulp mill
that makes the waferboard used to build those new houses. Wal-
Mart is coming.

Progress.

"The thought of what was here once and is gone forever will not leave me as long as I live. It is as though I walk knee-deep in its absence." Wendell Berry said that, and I live it with him daily.

Standard advice to aspiring writers is "Write about what you know." For aspiring nature writers, I'd refine that to "Write about what you know and love."

Why do I write about nature?

I have no choice. It's in my genes. And in my heart.

Judith Larner Lowry

Gardening at the Seam

from *Orion*

Once I spent some time at a hot springs in Mendocino County, whose accommodations included a "cool pool" for swimming, built by damming the creek on three sides with poured concrete. The fourth side of the pool was formed by the rocky base of the hill, along which flowed the creek. On the hillside, native clarkias cast a pink net through the grasses.

When, after swimming my laps, I came to pull myself up and out of the pool, I found that one hand was on concrete and one hand on native rock. Regarding the seam between the two materials, it occurred to me that this was the place where I have come to garden. At the seam between the wild and the cultivated, where they merge and mingle, the shape of one giving shape to the other.

Moving ten years ago to this small coastal town, I was entranced by the constant glimpses of ocean all over town and by the miles of protected land that surround us. My first walks into that land revealed the beauty of the coastal scrub plant community. Low mounding shrubs and subshrubs of all kinds of greens, grays, and gray-greens made a rich foliar tapestry, punctuated in spring and summer with the oranges, reds, blues, and golds of coastal wildflowers and flowering shrubs. I couldn't look enough. Yet, when I visited the gardens of my town, these local plants were conspicuous for their absence, as was any conversation about them. I came to see that I lived in a uniquely protected location that reflected little of the vast surrounding riches. Without quite knowing what I was doing, I began to try to work myself into this place through gardening with these plants.

My town is bordered on the north by Jack Creek, which feeds a rancher's stock pond, then wends its diminished way to the ocean. One bank of this creek has been planted with a windbreak of eucalyptus trees. Under these trees, which continually drop large, acidic leaves, little is able to grow except French broom and brambles, all shallow-rooted plants. The bank on that side is crumbling and eroding rapidly. The eucalyptus trees, forest giants, become increasingly top heavy as their trunks shoot skyward. On the other side of the creek, the north-facing bank is covered with coastal scrub plants, a low-growing plant community which includes monkey-flower, sagebrush, coyote bush, lizard tail, mule's ear, and cow parsnip. The bank on this side is intact, verdant, complete even down to the smaller plants, such as the tiny, narrow-leaved native plantain (a larval food plant for the endangered bay checkerspot butterfly), and the spring-blooming bulb named "cat's ears" for its fuzzy white petals.

Where Jack Creek empties into the ocean, the bank becomes a steep bluff. On the eucalyptus side of the creek mouth, the tree currently nearest to the end of the bluff clings precariously for years or months, as the case may be, providing dramatic photo opportunities, then falls, taking with it a huge hunk of cliff. The beach is littered with these bleached eucalyptus trunks, resembling an elephant's graveyard. The other side of the bluff erodes at its own West Coast pace.

I saw other situations where homeowners, seeking to save their bluff edge properties, had planted species reputed to help in erosion control. Iceplant, one such plant, installed in many places throughout California, quickly covers the ground, but it is not deeprooted and doesn't tie the soil layers together as do the native bluff species. Indeed, its succulent leaves are so heavy, their weight can pull down sections of cliff. The salt stored in its leaves changes the chemical properties of the soil when the plants die. Walking and looking, I came to hypothesize that the group of native bluff and coastal scrub plants that hold these cliffs have just the right characteristics for the job. Their leaves filter rain to the soil in the right way, their roots dig into the cliffs in the right way, and the habitat structure they provide enables the greatest number of fauna to thrive. I began to explore the ways, both obvious and subtle, that we could benefit from the incorporation of the wild into our gardens.

So I began my own garden, juggling its creation with trips into the nearby wildlands, for seed collecting, and for idea collecting. I never drew a plan but depended on visions, gained through explorations of the surrounding wildlands. I haven't been tied to these visions but have kept open to surprises; indeed, I have come to see surprises as the highest kind of gardening experience. Gardening with our local flora has allowed me to study and live with the plants in such a way that I have discovered qualities of which I was previously unaware.

Take coyote bush, for example. On my piece of land, the only species from the coastal scrub plant community was coyote bush, which is often removed when a garden is made. We left islands of coyote bush, good places for mysterious rustlings from wildlife in the early morning. As I talked to people about coyote bush, information began to emerge. It turned out there were more coyote bush appreciators than I had thought. What had begun as a lonely conversation expanded to include many talkers, and eventually a loose association formed, dedicated to protecting and restoring habitat in our town. At first jokingly and then as a matter of course, we called ourselves "Friends of the Coyote Bush."

We learned that coyote bush is an indispensable source of nectar in the autumn, when little else provides it. Hundreds of insects take advantage of its nectar, including *Paradejeania rutillioides,* an insect critical for the control of insect pests on agricultural crops. The soil under coyote bush is rich, good for growing vegetables or for sheltering native herbaceous plants like checkerbloom or brodiaea. Its distinctive honeyed fragrance in the fall and winter locates me in this place. Some birds live their whole lives in coyote bush, finding there all they need for perching, nesting, breeding, eating, and resting. Coyote bush is enough for them. We pondered the mysteries of its many forms, from the graceful mounds, like clouds on a hillside, to the low-growing, ground-hugging form, to those individuals that unaccountably shoot up to tree size. As we learned more, my friend Lea said, "It's hard to remember that once I thought coyote bush was just . . . coyote bush."

What came to me slowly was a vision of my home nestled into the intricate earth, surrounded by those trees, shrubs, grasses, and wildflowers that at one time graced it, and surrounded also by those birds, insects, rodents, and mammals that have slept in, eaten off, hidden in, bred in, and otherwise hung out in these plants for the last ten thousand years. The white-crowned sparrow, famous for its different dialects, has a clear, sweet whistle heard only in the area reaching from my town to a lake three miles away. The California poppy occurs in a lemon-yellow rather than a crayon-orange variety along our coast. Home was becoming more particularly defined, more specific, more tied to the details of smell, color, and form, as we searched out the clues and looked at the pieces.

While the land around my house, and in my town in general, can no longer be called pristine, the kind of gardening I have become interested in appears at the place where my plant choices and the general direction of the wild landscape meet, where I can work to locate myself and my garden in the ongoing evolution of life forms as they have become evident in this post-Pleistocene era, on this marine terrace, at the edge of this sea. I am increasingly eased by my association with these plants. Collecting, cleaning, and sowing their seeds, planting and transplanting them as young plants, collecting seeds from them in turn, all create a long intimacy somewhat reminiscent of, though not nearly as rich as, the complicated, layered involvement of the native Californians who used and continue to use them. When Mabel McKay, recently deceased Pomo basketweaver and doctor, heard somebody say that he had used native medicinal herbs but that they hadn't worked for him, she responded, "You don't know the songs. You have to know the right songs." With no one to teach us, we don't know the songs either. The native practice of dreaming songs about the nonhuman world seems as valuable and elusive as a piece of pure bunchgrass prairie or the truth about this land.

Our retreat hut in the garden is called the "Coyote Bush House," and its door handles are made from the hard, twisted limbs of its namesake. We use this hut for restorative naps, on a cot so situated that what you see out the open door before you fall asleep in April is the intense blue of lupines, against the creams, yellows, and golds of tidy tips, goldfields, and the lemon-yellow form of the California poppy. What you see in the winter months is coyote bush regenerating after the long time of no rain, its new leaves the freshest of greens. The structure sits low to the ground, providing a good place for guard quail to perch while watching their flock feed—their calls spring through the garden. Here, our first plant songs might be dreamed.

Eighteen years ago, when I first began working in a California native plant nursery, I wasn't sure why I was drawn to work with native plants. In the middle of a major drought, they seemed important in water conservation, though now I no longer focus on the drought-tolerant aspects of native plants. The reasons to garden with locally occurring native plants have more to do with joining in, with setting in motion interrupted processes that are unique to this place. It has to do with recreating a garden that connects the gardener with that larger garden beyond the fence.

In that larger garden, many plant/animal relationships are finely tuned and easily disrupted. Certain butterflies, for example, are called "host-specific," meaning that they will lay their eggs only on one or a few different plant species. When the larvae hatch, they require the kind of food that the leaves of their host plant provide and the kind of shelter that the leaf litter at the base of the plant provides. Without that particular plant, they will not survive. One example is the pipevine swallowtail, whose larvae are found only on the leaves of one of California's most beautiful native vines, *Aristolochia californica,* Dutchman's pipe. Without this plant, you won't be seeing the huge iridescent greenish black wings of *Battus philenor.* It all starts with the plants.

Gardening this way has changed me in ways I couldn't have predicted. My previous employer, Gerda, a venerable German woman whom I regard as a mentor, also has a demonstration garden of native plants, but around the house is a cutting garden, a formal rock garden, and some of the beloved plants that reflect her European ancestry. Accordingly, when I set up our demonstration garden, I followed her model, starting at the edge of the property with natives and working my way up to the house, where I half-consciously assumed I also would grow exotic plants that caught my fancy.

By the time I got to the house, which took years, I was different. What I wanted to be greeted by in the mornings was the rusty-green roughish leaves of the California hazel, its horizontal twigs slanting against the office wall. I wanted not to have to go anywhere to experience the sleek gray limbs of the California buckeye, or the deep-green leaves of the handsome coffeeberry. I wanted our fog-gray house to melt into the grays of the coastal sages. These are the friends whose seasons and graces go beyond novelty, the friends with whom I have become quite comfortable.

I want to be able to walk outside into the coastal scrub and see it jumping with those resident birds that favor it for nesting and feeding, such as the wrentit, the bushtit, and the white-crowned sparrow. Quiet makes me nervous now, reminding me of what Robert Michael Pyle calls "the extinction of experience—the loss of everyday species within our own radius of reach." He says, "When we lose the common wildlife in our immediate surroundings, we run the risk of becoming inured to nature's absences, blind to delight, and, eventually, alienated from the land."

When I hike into the surrounding wildlands, I have a purpose, a reason to be there. As well as collecting seeds, I'm seeking inspiration and information. We think we know what these plants can do, but surprises are the name of the game. Led by my friend John, who has made it the business of his retirement to know and protect this watershed, we once went deep into a coastal canyon, past marshy grasses, to a grove of Pacific wax myrtles so large that their ancient limbs created a sheltered glade, where we reclined and picnicked on its foot-deep, cinnamon-colored leaf litter. Having only seen these plants in their shrub form, we could only guess at how old these individuals were. I brought back a bit of the duff to scatter at the base of my own small wax myrtles, in case some mycorhizal connection in the soil has enabled the spectacular growth of these plants. These treasured bits of information let us know what was once and what might be again.

In the way that our coastal creeks spread out over the land in a broad floodplain before they empty into the lagoon, so the plants in this garden and in these wild gardens have begun to spread and seep out into our lives. At the end of a performance at our community center, we threw handfuls of coyote bush seed into the audience. The shining fluffy white seeds floated and drifted and landed in people's hair, adding to the layers of memories about coyote bush. Some people grabbed at them and put them in their pockets, as though the seeds were something valuable they had never seen before. The electrician working on my house opened some buried electrical boxes to find deer mouse nests made of the brushy pappus. People stop me on the street if they have something to say about coyote bush.

One part of the garden where the seam between the domestic and the wild is particularly evident is the food garden for humans. In this area, I have planted both domestic and wild bush fruits, which include the domestic raspberry and blueberry alongside the wild huckleberry and thimbleberry. In the greens department, we have miner's lettuce, every backpacker's favorite green, side by side with domestic lettuces. The California woodland strawberry sends runners alongside Fragaria "Sequoia," asparagus beds flourish next to a plant of cow parsnip, said to have shoots that taste like asparagus. Native alliums and Bermuda onions share a bed.

In order that the smells and colors particular to this place be joined by the tastes particular to this place, twice a year I immerse myself in food preparation tasks involving our local plants. At our open houses, we offer the public roasted bay nuts, pinole made from blue wildrye, sugar cookies studded with chia seeds, miner's lettuce on cheese and crackers, manzanita berry tea, and chia seed lemonade. We may not eat like this most of the time, but the ritual acknowledgment and honoring of this aspect of our local plants has come to feel compelling enough that I find myself preparing these foods and adding to the menu every year.

Once I went to visit a friend on First Mesa on the Hopi reservation. Inquiring as to her whereabouts, I was told that she was "whitewashing the kiva." She emerged from that task with a certain virtuous glow. This glow is what I feel while roasting the seed of red maids, while shelling bay nut seeds, while roasting bunchgrass seed to make pinole. It is a mundane activity that sets the stage for important events. It is a time for honoring continuous ways, in this case, ways having to do with the plants. Like whitewashing the kiva, this food preparation is the background activity for a sacred experience, in this case, the incorporation of the molecules of local foods into our bodies.

Where you see coyote bush, you often see its partner in the coastal scrub plant community, that plant of ineffable shining silvery-gray green, California sagebrush. The smell and the color are the essence of California shrublands, both interior and coastal. A good medicine smell, a heart-easing smell. A smell with some of the sharpness common to these chaparral plants, a smell that tells us where we are, that seems to cut through grief or ennui.

I walk through the garden with Ann, who has worked here with me for seven years. She hands me a wand of pungent, palest silvered-green sagebrush and says, "Smell this." Wandering on, we stop at a large soaproot plant and look through the stems and leaves to the shadow they cast on the leaf litter at the base of the plant. We experience a certain lack of ambition. We note a strange lack of plans. Now that we have reinjected the native virus, it is, to a greater and greater degree, out of our hands. Not that there isn't plenty to do; weeds are forever, especially in a Mediterranean climate, but the balance has been tipped in the native direction. Now that the California hazel is established and thriving, we can let the rose from France next to it arch its long canes in the hazel's direction.

As the years go by and the plants develop their character, I begin to accept them at their worst. The California sagebrush, during its long summer and fall dormancy, turns a ghostly pale color, and looks, with its empty seed stalks, like it just got out of bed. But ours is not a relationship based only on looks. The wrentit uses scrapings from its bark to make its nest, bound together with cobwebs. My partner's son Sasha cut twigs to make smudge sticks and sold them at our Christmas fair as local incense. If, as you walk through the scrub, your coat brushes the sagebrush, you become redolent with a fine fragrance, at once spicy and sweet.

Twice a year, a Pomo Indian named Milton "Bun" Lucas puts a chair between the two elderberry bushes in the garden. From there, he directs us, as we scurry about cutting shoots from the elderberry for him to turn into carved clapper sticks and flutes (musical instruments used by many Californian tribes). Our cutting goals include fostering those stems that next year will be the right width for a clapper stick or flute. Gardening can be an anxious pastime, as the demands of weeding, watering, fertilizing, and pruning accrue. I have never experienced such peaceful gardening moments as when we plan for next year's "music bush" harvest. "Cut here," says Bun, "and cut here."

Basketry materials are not as available to native Californian basketmakers as they were in the past. Basketgrass, used by a number of Californian tribes, is hard to find and often not of suitable quality. At the same time, this grass has become extremely popular in landscaping. A large, fine-textured handsome grass easily grown horticulturally, it is being planted by thousands throughout California and seems to be adaptable to many conditions; there is no reason for indigenous basketmakers to go without. This fall, I was able to offer sheaves of its beautiful pale seed stalks to a Yowlumni basketmaker.

I have talked with other indigenous Californians about plants they used to see but no longer can find, plants of cultural importance to their tribe. There is a plant gathered for its root, an elusive mention of a grass with seeds as large as wheat, a variety of wild tobacco no one has seen for a while. All these could be found and brought into the native garden. Recent anthropological theories about Indian land management indicate that, to the indigenous people of California, there was no "wilderness," but that human activities have always transformed the landscape. The distinction between the garden and the wild blurs further. The seam shifts, cracks in some places, holds more closely in others.

I have become a patron of used book stores, looking for the odd find that may illuminate some hitherto unknown aspect of this kind of landscape and these plants, of previous human interactions with them and reactions to them. The coastal plants, except perhaps the redwoods, have no John Muir. They are largely unsung. Easily removed for development or ranching, of little evident economic value, they are the underdog of plant communities. I think of myself as becoming of them. I am "of the coastal scrub."

For this kind of garden, plant lists are not taken from charts in glossy garden books. Ideas for plantings come from local floras, from hikes with naturalists into nearby undisturbed areas, from visits to botanic gardens, from the recollections of old-timers, and from the oral histories stored in our museums and libraries. They come from the diaries of early Spanish explorers, from the journals of wives of doctors living in gold-mining communities, or from the casual asides of English tourists.

This garden isn't the wild, but it looks to, and is in conversation with, the wild. It backs on, and is backed up by, natural systems. The goal is that the quail in the vacant lot next to us will find in our arranged mosaic of coastal prairie, coastal scrub, and wildflower fields the forbs they need for greens, the seeds they need for protein when nesting, and the habitat structure for shelter and protection in our shrubs. The ubiquitous subclover, a plant widely sown for forage, will not be found in our garden, as it is in nearby lots, since it is now known that this plant contains chemicals that inhibit reproduction in quail. Nor will the naturalizing pyracantha, for though its berries may seem to make birds amusingly inebriated, they actually set them at risk for predation and interfere with the activities necessary for their survival. Instead, we plant toyon, the shrub for which Hollywood was named, with its bright hollylike berries at Christmas time.

With plantings of toyon, we have joined the great feeding schedule, whereby food is available at the right time for the right creature. In early summer, the buckeye blooms, sometimes for three months. Its great pendant blossoms attract the insects that nourish the protein-hungry nesting birds. Even birds that are usually vegetarian often require animal food while nesting. In midsummer, the annual and perennial seed crops come in, bee plant, poppy, miner's lettuce, clarkia. By early fall, the native honeysuckle drapes succulent red berries on trees and shrubs. Mid-fall brings the acorn and hazel harvests, and late fall sees the ripening of the madrone and toyon berries, while the coyote bush pumps out the nectar. The arrival of the rufous hummingbird is tied to the blooming of the flowering currant in January and February.

Some might say it is not truly representative of the fine art of gardening to use local natives, to use natural models. But choices have been made, plants have been arranged, an aesthetic has been developed. It embraces all I know, all I hope to know, and all I wish I knew about this set of ancient processes and associations. Some have said it is the way of a lazy gardener, but I find that horticultural challenges are many.

For example, I want to establish a stand of Indian paintbrush here, which probably grew here once but has so far not survived in my garden. Appearing in a radiant palette of apricot, scarlet, and yellow, it hosts a particular kind of aphid-eating mite. This mite lives in the flower, where it eats nectar, until a hummingbird comes along to share the nectar. At this moment, the mite runs up the hummingbird's beak and into its nostril, where it sits tight while the hummingbird flies down to Baja. As the hummingbird approaches a nectar-producing plant, the mite gets ready, rears up, and races from the nostril, down the beak, and into the flower. Since it must run so quickly, it is estimated that this creature is as fast as the fastest animal on earth, the cheetah. By establishing this flower in the garden, with its as yet elusive cultural requirements, I may be facilitating this mind-boggling nasal journey.

Some might call it xenophobic to remove or exclude nonnative plants. The fact is, on all but one side of us, where coastal scrub still exists, our garden stands out startlingly from the surrounding vacant lots, filled as they are with escaped exotic plants like eucalyptus, pampas grass, passionflower vine, German ivy, and French broom. Here the native plants have become the exotics. I can justify my gardening choices with data on habitat for songbirds, butterflies, insects, voles, and lizards, with quotes from scientific journals and studies. And knowledge of the qualities of these plants seems to fill some of that cavity of longing for knowledgeable connection with our tribe, both human and other, that some of us carry around like an empty burden basket. But the truth is, some of the creatures we long to see around us may not come here at all, so isolated are we in this diminished habitat.

And too, those who say that this way of working with plants isn't really gardening might be right. Maybe my piece of land is neither the wildlands nor a garden, and maybe the activities involved aren't really gardening at all but more like inserting yourself into the long dream of this solemn, fog-bound, silvered land. Though protecting, enhancing, and bringing close the coastal scrub and other native plant communities has become my business, though life is punctuated by phone calls and seed orders and scheduling, at the back somewhere always is the color of the litter made by wax myrtle leaves, and the smell of coyote bush in the rain.

Gary Nabhan

Finding the Hidden Garden

from *Desert Legends: Restorying the Sonoran Borderlands*

Murrieta, California, April 8, 1993: I stared at the hole in the ground in front of me, a hole in the manicured grass. Above it hovered the huge box holding one of my heroes inside it, Howard Scott Gentry. He hated green grass, preferring to sow wild, unruly native plants wherever he lived. It was not only his preference but his trade as well. He was a plant explorer who had spent more than half a century roaming the desert border states, collecting agaves and other wild plants with promise, many of which he brought into cultivation for the first time.

As of April Fool's Day, he was done roaming; this would be the last time he was headed for new ground. His daughters, his wife, his Mexican sidekick Juanito, and many old friends were there to see him off. Some of us served as pallbearers. Others just stood back and cried.

They were ready to lower him into the grave, but I was not ready to let him go. I wished I had one last chance to "talk agave" with him. It would have been too hard to tell him all that he meant to me. Instead, I simply wanted to tell him that I had recently found people still growing, eating, and celebrating the Hohokam century plant, *Agave murpheyi,* a rarity that had posed an unsolved riddle for him for almost thirty years.

When he and I "talked agave," it seemed that the rest of the world stood still. I could listen to that old man tell me of his plant-exploring adventures for hours. It was odd that we were completely on the same wavelength on that one subject, because whenever we talked about anything else—farming, business, politics, love, marriage, the work of friends, or even the origins of beans—we seldom saw eye to eye. He was forty-nine years my senior, and we had come from different cultures. And yet, we had ended up loving some of the very same things: the smoky taste of home-brewed mescal, the sound of *campesinos* tending maguey, and the diversity of shapes, sizes, and circumstances in which agaves grew.

Once I had invited him down from his home so that he could "talk agave" to a bunch of my friends in a desert garden at night. We sat and drank the fermented, distilled juices of the very plant that was the subject of his rambling lecture. He spoke within the shadow of a giant maguey, and near the end of his talk he glanced over his shoulder at it and declared that, "being a man, I think and speak as a man, but today I also speak for agave. You see me held in the arms of this giant maguey. I am a son of Mayahuel, the goddess of maguey. What I have told you today is what she told me to tell you."

And so old Howard baptized me into some ancient rite, not by water but by firewater—a shot of bootleg *mescal bacanora* distilled from wild desert agaves. Howard became a father figure for me, one whom I sometimes saw as legendary, other times as limited by his own flaws. In turn, I became one of the many grandsons of that Native American goddess, Mayahuel.

I was adopted into Mayahuel's family not long after I left my boyhood home for good, and not too long before my own father died. I had been cooped up on the midwestern farm where I had been working, so I moved to the Sonoran Desert with the hope of devoting my life to tracing the natural history of its plants in the wild. I can now confess I had no idea how I would ever make a living doing such a thing, but I tried. The first regional field guide I purchased after my arrival was a peculiar little book written by Dr. Gentry in

1972: *The Agave Family in Sonora.* I hoped that it would lend me some of the confidence that I sorely needed at the time.

Using it on a long hike down the southern slopes of the Bradshaw Mountains late in the winter of 1975, I easily identified the first two agaves I encountered at higher elevations. I then came on a third that somewhat fit one of Gentry's descriptions but didn't jibe with the distribution map for the same species.

Instead of having flowers on its stalk, it had a bunch of miniature plantlets called bulbils. Judging from what Gentry had written, bulbils seemed to occur regularly only on one species within the Sonoran region, *Agave murpheyi.* However, that species was apparently not known from the lower elevations of the Bradshaws at the time. And so I pressed a specimen, dried it, and sent it off to Gentry a few weeks later. I had learned in the meantime that he had "retired" to Arizona, leaving the U.S. Department of Agriculture as its chief plant explorer to take on the somewhat honorary position as senior research scientist at the Desert Botanical Garden.

Within a week of sending off the specimen, I received a letter from Gentry on some self-designed stationery embellished with a sketch of a flowering maguey: "Welcome to the Agave Family!" he proclaimed.

His letter went on to inform me that if a certain kind of agave is damaged by freezes as it begins to flower, it will abort its blossoms and reproduce vegetatively, spawning through bulbils like the ones I saw. "I don't think it would be much fun if we could replicate ourselves that way," he added dryly. In short, the identity of my plant was not definite: it could be *Agave murpheyi,* or a related species that didn't normally produce bulbils. Gentry encouraged me to make more collections at the same site. In that way, we could verify whether or not bulbils were characteristic of the entire population. He also invited me to pay him a visit sometime. I did.

Within a year of that first dispatch from the old man, I embarked on my own agave-collecting trips in Sonora and tasted bootleg mescal for the first time. My father had died while I was out of reach, in

Mexico. After the funeral I took my dried plants to Gentry, to see if the master would help me interpret their value. We soon found something to talk about on a fairly regular basis. Within another year, I took a few weeks off to work with him. We began by drinking tequila in an agave patch on a Fourth of July evening and stayed together until the end of the summer, when I left for more plant collecting. We split our time between two places, the Desert Botanical Garden in Phoenix and his family's homestead in Murrieta, nestled within the Sierra foothills an hour south of Los Angeles.

That summer, ethnobotany and the horticulture of native plants became more than technical sciences for me; they harbored a reservoir of stories about rural peoples and their ties with the natural world. Nearly everywhere in the American deserts, agave fibers formed the rope that secured those ties. Gentry considered this link a "mutualism between two disparate organisms"—a true symbiosis—for without agaves as his companions in the desert, "man would be a lone egocentric without a single other organism in the whole world to counsel him."

The old man would draw upon the counsel of mescal or scotch each afternoon before wandering off to his bedroom for a siesta, or falling asleep, glass still in hand, in his easy chair on the patio. He always kept a good field hat on while he was outside and often kept a little wild stubble on his chin to go along with it. Lubricated by his afternoon drink, he might recall the views of scholars (Webb, Sauer, or Xolocotzi) on some arcane horticultural practice of Mexican Indians. Then he might give me an Indian perspective on the same practice, by referring to a conversation he had with a Guarijío, Mayo, or Tarahumara elder forty years before. If I was lucky, he might recall one of his own adventures while out exploring the *sierras* with Juanito Arguelles, who had often traveled with Gentry as his *mozo,* or errand boy. Arguelles has ended up being the second most prolific collector of agaves in the history of northern Mexico, but the collections with his name on them hardly rival the twenty-five thousand or so that bear Gentry's name. A fourteen-year-old when Gentry first met him in San Bernardo, Sonora, in 1933, Juanito learned to take care of Gentry's mules and plant presses. He later moved to Murrieta and found jobs tending cutting horses; he decided to retire years before his former boss had to force himself to stop working.

Once Gentry began his stories from the trail, they would unwind naturally. He often returned to a point he had wanted to demonstrate to me earlier in the day. When recording folk taxonomies for plants, he insisted, be careful of *campesinos* making up provisional names for plants in areas unfamiliar to them. Then he would laugh heartily and confess that in 1951, he had provisionally named one species *Agave jaiboli* after what he thought was an Indian name. In the Sierra de la Ventana, he had encountered a *gente de razon* (non-Indian) who told him that a fine distilled drink could be made from this unusually sweet plant. The man had called the distilled drink *jaiboli,* to distinguish it from the mescal that the Guarijio Indians made from *temeshi,* another local agave.

Fourteen years later, Gentry ran into the man again and learned that he had worked as a wetback years before on the U.S. side of the border. While in the United States, the man had taken a liking to the highballs that the Gringos made with their liquor. *"Aquí, hacemos jaibolis con mescal,"* he told Gentry, who belatedly realized that *jaiboli* was no Indian word after all. The name stuck nonetheless, and Gentry used it for the official scientific name when describing the plant as a new species in 1972.

While we were over in California, Gentry took me for my first drive through the heart of Los Angeles. We were on our way to the Huntington Botanical Gardens, one of the most heavily visited horticultural displays on the West Coast. There in the middle of its outdoor exhibit, the old man pulled out a rope and made it into a lasso. He deftly tossed the loop over a twenty-foot-high agave stalk in flower and fruit. Once he caught its candelabralike bouquet, we wrestled it down to the ground, much to the horror of the tourists passing by.

"I've been waiting for this plant to flower damn near since the year you were born," he said, taking his hat off and wiping the sweat from his brow on his shirtsleeve. Gentry had planted dozens of seedlings of unknown species at Huntington in 1951 and 1952, but it took some of them another quarter century to flower for the first time. It was only then that he could fully describe them.

"Take my machete," he ordered, "and cut three or four of those leaves off. Skin 'em out and section them so that they fit into the plant press. I'll finish up pickling the flowers while you're doing that." The entire effort took nearly two hours and filled an entire plant press. Every day the following week, I swabbed each leaf section with alcohol to keep it from molding and dried the blotters out in the sun. After waiting twenty-five years to finish his work on this collection, Gentry was not about to let a specimen go to waste.

Hundreds of such specimens informed his 670-page masterwork, *Agaves of Continental North America,* which was finally published in 1982 nearly fifty years after Gentry had begun his first agave collections. By that time, the old man seemed tired and frustrated by what he had done. "It only makes evident how little I know," he said sadly. "But I just can't do any more. These damn plants have nearly killed me. It's up to you young lads and lassies now."

Even before he reached this stage of exhaustion, he had encouraged me to ask O'odham friends questions he himself had not resolved. He was especially curious about their knowledge of *Agave murpheyi,* because its distribution puzzled him. He'd seen it just north of Phoenix, then not again until one hundred miles south in an O'odham Indian village, and then not for another hundred fifty miles southwest in Sonora, near another O'odham village. His masterwork contained just three cryptic lines about its origin and distribution: " . . . *murpheyi* has never been observed in extensive or dense populations: Some of the clones appear to have been associated with old Indian living sites. The propagules are easily transported and transplanted."

The plant happened to grow in the garden of Laura Kerman, the namesake and godmother of my daughter. Laura was an O'odham potter, teacher, and storyteller who was older than Gentry but just as horticulturally curious. When I asked her about the origins of her plants, she nodded toward the Baboquivari Mountains.

"When I was a little girl, we would stay with my grandmother back in those mountains during the dry season. We took these plants from there. There used to be hundreds of them up in the canyons, and that is what my people would harvest to eat. They would dig them up, chop off the long leaves, roast them in a pit overnight."

Her eyes would get wide as she began to visualize scenes from her childhood. "Next day, they opened the pit to take them out. If the coals were still warm, they took the leaves they had cut earlier and dried them over the coals. Then they would make rope or other weavings out of the fibers taken from the leaves. We never made mescal to drink, like the Mexicans do, although some of the old men would buy it from the Mexicans and then get drunk. We just ate it and used it to make rope."

Then she looked up at me, blinking. "You take me up to the mountains for a picnic, and I'll show you those plants."

One summer, I did take Laura up to the canyon home of her grandmother. We had a picnic with a small band of Pima, Papago, and Navajo friends, then she sent us up the slopes looking for plants. But as we scrambled around the abandoned village, we could find only the more common species of desert agave, no *murpheyi*.

I was sure that she had not confused the two. She simply called the common desert agave *a'ud* but knew the one in her yard as *a'ud nonhakam,* "the agave that has eggs or progeny." In fifteen years of hiking the Baboquivaris, I had found only a single *murpheyi*-like plant that had "progeny" or bulbils on its stalk where flowers might otherwise be. As with the first agave I ever collected, I could not be sure of its identity by this one trait alone. Its leaves were too dried to allow for identification. My only guess is that Laura's ancestors had cultivated this special agave around their homes in the last century, but it had not survived the droughts, freezes, cows, or harvesters. Its fiber and food qualities were so superior to those of *Agave deserti* that younger O'odham harvesters may have finished off (or transplanted to their own homes) the plants their forefathers had tended.

I later decided to return to the only area in Sonora where Gentry had seen *murpheyi* growing. It was an area that I knew had old, mostly abandoned O'odham villages and ancient hillside terraces nearby. Gentry had found *murpheyi* cultivated in a yard across from a truck stop, but its owner claimed that it came from the nearby hills where it grew wild. And yet, when Gentry got up to go and explore the hills, the Sonoran dissuaded him, saying that the plants there had already been cut for eating and for making bootleg mescal.

It seemed easy enough to travel forty miles south of the border and explore the hills surrounding San Luisito to find what might be a truly wild population of the plant. But, like Gentry, I would not see any plants in the hills. As my friends and I drove into San Luisito one summer day, a roadblock loomed up just fifty yards past the garden where the plants grew. Since we weren't going any farther south, I pulled into the truck stop rather than driving right up to the Federales and their barriers. Unfortunately they thought I was dodging them.

The next thing I knew, five Uzi machine guns were pointed at me, and two other armed guards had me up against the hood, frisking the daylights out of me. Two hours later, after my Jeep Cherokee had been scoured for every smidgeon of plant debris, and each leaf analyzed for traces of drugs, the narcotics squad released me and my friends.

"This is drug country. Why did you come down here anyway?" the *jefe* asked me. I pulled out Gentry's *Agave Family in Sonora* and showed him a picture taken in the garden across the road some twenty years before. He was not impressed. He doubted that I had any legitimate reason to be there and discouraged us from wandering around in the hills nearby. "There are drug traffickers who think they can go around us. They are not the kind of people who will like you getting in their way."

The following winter, after I had heard that drug running through that part of Sonora had waned, I did find four or five more ranchos with little patches of *a'ud nonhakam* in their yards. Always, the O'odham and mestizo cowboys would tell me the same thing they told Gentry. Years ago, they had brought these plants in from ones in the hills, but now they were no longer sure if there were any left in the wild.

About that time, however, word came in from a friend in New River, Arizona, that caught me off guard. I had begun to work at the Desert Botanical Garden, joining Gentry's department. Another one of Gentry's understudies, Wendy Hodgson, had been collaborating with an amateur botanist, Rick DeLamater, tracking the distributions of agaves in central Arizona. One day Rick heard me complain to Wendy about my trouble finding truly *wild* populations of *Agave murpheyi* anywhere on the O'odham Reservation or in Sonora.

"Crap, I know where a bunch of wild *murphs* are right by my home. You know Encima de la Mesa near New River?" Rick said casually.

"There are prehistoric terraces all over there!" I blurted.

Rick didn't follow me. "What do terraces have to do with it?"

"There's this archaeologist named George Gumerman who had a big project up there in the seventies, and I went up there with him one time. He had a whole team of students mapping hundreds of terraces and rock alignments built prehistorically, thinking that they might have been used for agriculture. Funny thing was, in all their excavations and analyses of pollen and soil, they never figured out what people could have been growing up there. You haven't seen any prehistoric agricultural features where the agaves are?"

Rick looked at Wendy and scratched his beard. "All I know is where the plants are. And where a few hilltop ruins are above them. I wouldn't know a prehistoric agriculture feature if it reared up and bit me on the . . ."

By the end of the week, Wendy, Rick, and I went up to New River

with some biologists visiting from Mexico and the Navajo Reservation. As we walked out across the *bajada* toward the plants, I began
to see rock pile after rock pile, rock alignments, check dams, terraces, and stone tools. Rick led us to one particularly large clone of
agaves. There in the middle of it was a prehistoric agave knife, the
same kind that had been found near agave roasting pits throughout
the Southwest for decades. And there, beneath the *a'ud nonhakam,*
was the lip of a cobblestone border that had been put there to slow
the flow of water down the slope at least five or six centuries before.

The hidden garden. There, amid the paloverde and mesquite, the
bur sage and the barrel cacti, a prehistoric Hohokam crop had persisted at least half a millennium after being last tended. The same
plant—the identical genetic stock that had been transplanted here
in prehistoric times—had reproduced vegetatively on its own, clinging to the same terrace where it had been originally placed. Rick had
discovered the hidden garden, a horticultural experiment so well
adapted to the desert that it ultimately needed no human interven-
tion to keep it going.

By that time, we knew that tens of thousands of acres of similar
rock-pile fields, cobblestone alignments, and terraces had been
found between Tucson and Phoenix by Paul and Suzanne Fish. At
first, they too were baffled because Suzanne's pollen analysis revealed
no obvious candidate for the crop that the Hohokam had grown
there.

Then one day, Paul's survey team stopped to eat lunch on the *bajada* slope. Nudging his bootheel into the slope overlooking a wash,
one of them noticed that they were sitting on ash and charcoal, not
soil. The team had stumbled upon a huge roasting pit, and within a
few weeks their coworker Charlie Miksicek had sorted out fragments of agave leaves mixed into the ash. The leaves were too beat-
up to identify, but when Charlie heard of Rick finding *Agave murpheyi*
up at New River, it didn't surprise him. Most of the agaves would
have been cut and roasted before they flowered anyway. If *murpheyi*
aborted its flowers so early, it's no wonder that Suzanne could find

little pollen where Charlie had found an abundance of charred leaves.

Suzanne, Paul, and Charlie gradually fleshed out the details of a prehistoric horticultural tradition in North America. It was a tradition that had escaped the notice of dozens of archaeologists who had worked in the same region over the last century. They had presumed that agaves were aboriginally cultivated nowhere north of Mesoamerica. Paul and Suzanne Fish have now shown otherwise, that agaves have been intentionally cultivated in Arizona since A.D. 600. The one hundred fifty square miles of rock piles on the middle *bajada* above Marana captured and conserved water for each vegetative transplant, augmenting food production in an area too high and dry for conventional irrigation agriculture.

The agaves grown from Marana to New River were not simply transplanted wild species but specially selected variants. They had all the characteristics of other domesticated plants such as the maize and thornless prickly pear brought in from Mesoamerica. The Hohokam leaders living down near the better-watered ceremonial centers had likely grubstaked workers to cultivate agaves, offering them maize and beans grown on rich floodplain soils in exchange for mescal and fiber. Thus, the scenario that Gentry had earlier imagined for prehistoric agave cultivation in Mesoamerica rang true for arid America as well:

> They cleared wild land and put agave into it. They opened up new niches for the random variants of the gene-rich agave. . . . They selected the genetic deviants of high production by planting vegetative offsets. Generally, this is what man did for agave in this Mesoamerican symbiosis.
>
> In return agave has nurtured man. During the several thousand years that man and agave have lived together, agave has been a renewable resource for food, drink, and artifact. . . . As man settled into communities . . . agave fostered the settled habit, attention to cultivation, and the steadfast purpose through years and life spans, all virtues required by civilization. . . . Agave civilized man.

It is even more amazing that the agaves did not become civilized. The *a'ud nonhakam* had never lost its capacity to survive, to thrive in desert climes without the aid of irrigation or gardeners.

Over the following years, Rick DeLamater and Wendy Hodgson found remnants of more than fifty previously neglected stands of *Agave murpheyi* in the forests, parks, and ranchlands of central Arizona. Rick's eye for this plant became legendary. Every once in a while, he would come into our office, sure that he had found a truly wild population. On further inspection, Rick, Wendy, or I would find artifacts, rock alignments, and other cultural remains to indicate prehistoric cultivation. I found another five sites in Sonora on my own, but all of them were associated with historic homesteads and prehistoric settlements. They could persist amid wild vegetation but were never found in "pristine wilderness"—their presence always spoke of earlier cultural presences, of man-made desert gardens from long ago.

Even their genetic history showed human imprints. We sent leaf samples to geneticist James Hickey, who discovered that all the plants had the same chemical markers regardless of whether they came from Sonora, Papaguería, or New River—they had none of the heterogeneity from site to site found in wild agaves. Perhaps they were all of one clone, transported and then transplanted over hundreds of square miles in the heart of the Sonoran Desert. And yet, they all took that desert to heart, adapting to its droughts and freezes, resisting its pests and plagues in a way that few of today's pampered crops could if cut loose from human attention. The hidden garden could get along with or without the intervening hand of Hohokam horticulturalists.

In the end, that is what Dr. Gentry let us do. He never intervened with our agave studies, all of them ultimately grounded in his own. He never expressed any worry over whether younger investigators would come along to revise parts of the story that he had spent most of his life compiling. He encouraged Mexicans as well as North Americans to get out into the field and prove him right, wrong, or somewhere in between. After he retired, he would still listen to our new reports as they came in, but he would never try to give these new details his own spin. He would shift uneasily between his respirator and his afternoon drink, then mutter in his throaty voice, "Pshaw, laddie, you've come up with something there that I would have never expected!"

The last couple years of his life, I saw the old man less than I had seen him over the previous fifteen years. He could no longer get out into the field with any frequency, and I guessed that confinement killed his spirit. I could not stand to see him captive in a domestic scene—a field man relegated to the subtle insults of idle retirement, nursing homes, or hospitals. Instead, I took the memory of him into the field with me, trying to seek out the kind of *campesinos* with whom he had loved to talk since he first crossed into Mexico sixty years before.

Francisco Gámez Valenzuela was one such man, the kind of Sonoran that Gentry would have fallen in with—two kindred spirits. I rounded a corner in Querobabi, Sonora, one summer day, and there was this yard, spilling over with all kinds of desert plants, including a long hedgerow of *Agave murpheyi*. I stopped my van in the middle of the road and looked around to see if anyone was hidden within all that verdure, working in the yard. And there was Francisco, who was more than willing to talk about the plants he called his *lechuguilla*.

"*Hace diez años que se trasplantó aquí. Se crece en las lomas de piedra cerca de Ranchos San Jacinto, El Saucito, La Sesma . . . ,*" he told me, rattling off the names of abandoned historic outposts from which he had salvaged these plants a decade ago. I asked him if they were truly wild, or whether they appeared to have been associated with the former plantings of his *antepasados*.

"*Pues, se crece silvestre, pero hay corrales de piedras, trincheras, y rastras de minería en aquellos cerros.*" With cobblestone corrals, terraces, and remnants of rustic mining operations, the sites could have been from the colonial period, if not earlier.

Francisco told me how he occasionally roasted a single plant into

the smoky, carmelized foodstuff called *mescal tatemada*. He also loved
to join forces with an elderly neighbor now and then to pit-roast
twenty to forty "pineapples," then distill them into *mescal lechuguilla*.
I took a look at his hedgerow. It was obvious that he took good care
of the plants—they were a deep blue-green and stood waist high.

I asked him if they needed much pampering. The answer he gave
me made me realize that *Agave murpheyi* would still do fine long after
Howard, Francisco, and I were all long gone. I thought about it long
after translating it in my head: "Oddly enough, it produces much
better during the drought than it does during wet years," he said,
tipping his cowboy hat back on his head.

"What?" I'd never heard of such a thing for a domesticated plant.

"*Pues, sí, durante la sequía, se da más ley.*" During the hardest of
times, a Sonoran folk-saying goes, a good plant still "gives the law."
The Law of the Desert. Not only had *Agave murpheyi* persisted as part
of local diet and drink, it also remained strongly rooted in the folk
expressions of the village.

When I returned to visit Francisco the following December, I was
just in time to catch the Hohokam agave resurrected in a new spiritual role. As I entered Querobabi, I began to notice shrines erected
for the Virgin of Guadalupe, who was honored during a series of
processions culminating on her feast day of December twelfth. The
families in Querobabi had each constructed what looked like miniature desert gardens in front of their homes, replicas of the hill of
Tepeyac, where the Virgin communicated with the Mexican Indian
Juan Diego in December of 1521. There on the little hills erected
around the village, *Agave murpheyi* rosettes stood alongside pictures
and statues of the Virgin.

According to legend, Juan Diego had converted to Catholicism
from his native religion but still felt that this was not the path for all
his people. As he climbed a hill one day, the Virgin appeared in order
to assure him that she would remain within his indigenous community. He went down into the Valley of Mexico and spoke of his
vision to Bishop Zumarraga, who refused to believe that the Mother
of Christ would offer anything of import to a lowly Indian.

Juan Diego prayed to the Virgin to receive some sign that he could take to Zumarraga, to convince the bishop of the veracity of his claim. That is when the Virgin appeared again, urging Juan Diego to climb to the very top of the Loma de Tepeyac to pick flowers for the bishop. Juan Diego hesitated, knowing that few flowers grew on the arid, rain-shadow slopes of the valley in winter. Nevertheless, he decided to follow her instructions.

By all accounts, he found roses of Castille "growing in a place where Nature produces only cactus and maguey." He wrapped these domestic roses of European civilization in his cloak, and when he offered them to the bishop, he found the miraculous image of the Virgin imprinted on the inside of his serape. This began the veneration of the Virgin of Guadalupe as the matron of Mexican Indians, a tradition that became strongly rooted as far north as Sonora by 1740.

In the Sonoran folk tradition, cacti and agaves from the local desert are transplanted into shrines for the Virgin to commemorate the arid landscape where she first made contact with their people. Organ pipe, fishhook, and pincushion cacti are nestled side by side with the *lechuguilla* offshoots taken from Francisco's hedgerow, and visited by the processions for the week prior to the Virgin's feast. Then, crepe paper flowers of the Castillian Rose are added to the shrines, while the matron of all indigenous people sees her miracle observed once again.

From the embrace of the goddess of Mayahuel to that of La Virgen de Guadalupe, this native plant had somehow survived the collapse of the Hohokam ceremonial life to be resurrected and integrated into the folk Catholicism of Sonora.

From deep in my memory, I heard Gentry's prophetic words:

> As civilization and religion increased, the nurturing agave became a symbol, until with its stimulating juice man made a god of it. . . . Mayahuel, the principal goddess of agave, slaked the parched throat, relieved the duty pressures, altered the spirit, provided at least temporary surcease from hard life, and, being god-like, protected the home. Altogether, this was another contribution of agave to man during the centuries of the symbiosis.

It seemed the agaves joined with the Virgin in desert gardens to produce many of the same effects. Mayahuel now stood in the background, but her work, too, was being carried on.

In April 1993, Mayahuel witnessed one of her sons rejoin the earth—one who felt more comfortable on the cactus-and-maguey-stippled slopes of Mexico than in the suburbs of the United States. He was being buried in one of those suburbs, and neither Mayahuel nor the Virgin were being mentioned in the funeral service. I stood in the back row, listening to the cadence of the ceremony, scanning the surroundings. The memorial service was not all that different from those offered for other well-respected elderly men in Protestant enclaves within southern California. As the minister closed his hymnal, and the audience began to stir, I felt crestfallen, as though something were desperately missing.

Marie Gentry, his widow, must have sensed that same feeling, because she stopped us all dead in our tracks right as the service ended.

"Thank you, all of you, for being here with us for this service. But because it has all been offered in English, someone who is here was not able to share in the eulogies. It is someone who spent nearly as much time as I spent with Howard in those early days, and because Spanish is his native tongue, I would like to ask Juan Arguelles to say something in Spanish before we all go. Juanito, *por favor* . . ."

There were a few Spanish speakers among us, but this request caught most of the crowd off guard—they shifted uneasily in their Sunday clothes as Juan moved forward through the crowd. He came to the hole in the earth and spoke to it, as if beginning a slow but steady mouth-to-mouth resuscitation.

"*Pues, este viejito—es uno de mis grandes amigos. Con este señor, he caminado a todos partes de la sierra, buscando para plantas . . .*"

And with that first step, Dr. Gentry's sidekick began to conjure up the trails they had traveled together, on horse, on foot, in Model T; he told of the amazing plants they had discovered, the mescal they had sampled; he called up the campfires they had hovered around and the stories they had heard there—stories that had never been written down, but had been passed from mouth to mouth, campfire to campfire, for centuries, and still no doubt lived on wherever Mayos, Guarijios, Tarahumaras, and others came together around a mescal pit in the dry *sierras*.

And that was when I remembered that ethnobotany is not just a science. It's a reservoir of stories that link humankind with the verdant earth, a reservoir of legends we need to dip into now and again. The stories are not restricted to indigenous peoples. They honor the spirited plants they relied on for food, for drink, for miracle. Because we all owe the land and its plants our lives, such stories speak for all of us. They must reach from the past into the present, to hook farmers and ranchers and even suburban gardeners, linking them to what nourishes and inspires us. The best remind us of that capacity for symbiosis, a capacity one old crusty ethnobotanist found in the legend of Mayahuel. If we leave behind that capacity to be part of mutualisms larger than ourselves, then the rest homes, suburbs, and plant engineering labs will turn darker and lonelier, more sterile than ever before.

Adele Ne Jame

Poems

First publication

Compensation

On the Puna coast two dark men ease themselves over the high ledge
a hundred feet down to the wet volcanic boulders—
huge and mostly submerged by the rising sea, a harvest of opihi
their intention. As one deep wide wave moves, as if in slow motion,
to meet this high wall of lava rock, it falls in on itself throwing
a punishing break of white water over the one who works the black
slippery boulder to her left. She thinks he will die, crushed
against the severe lava wall below her, the air suddenly
sucked from his heavy lungs. But somehow he manages—
clings to the rock flat on his belly, hugging it
spread eagle in the sun, a gorgeous spectacle
against the white foam spilling over him,
arms and legs like taut steel cables,
each hand and foot finding a crevice, he holds on
as if born to this punishment. Like the power of barnacles
he is loving it, really. He tosses his wet hair back
working fast between waves, slicing opihi off the rock
with hard jabs of his metal blade; he fills the mesh bag
tied to his waist then effortlessly rises

and dives into the next swell—falling for long minutes below
the shining water, surfacing far away to climb the next boulder—,
and after that, the next. He moves over
their hard angles with pure grace and
pleasure as if no harm could come of this
so that she begins to see it as a kind of dance choreographed,
a loving dance requiring careless perfection. For him
death only a possible afterthought. All else
work and pleasure and pure perspective.
And she is simply watching
from the ledge above amazed, stunned into the present,
envious of the risk, the erotic pleasure of danger
here where every heavy loss seems suddenly lifted from her,
here where it is so clearly
the feral heart and air to breathe or nothing at all—,
to be completely taken over, against reason,
while there is still time— and in return an exceeding
happiness she will remember for years, when
there is no one calling her name in the dark.

from *Equinox*

Natural Science

This afternoon when the sun's glare wears away
the edges of the trees to pure glimmer,
the local man who sharpens knives has come
to my neighbor's cottage. And in this white heat

the sound of his grinding wheel a constant,
shrill intrusion in a world that is all
light and lotus. Walking down the pathway
through the blowing gates, the mock orange

overhead is so heavy with blooms and
sweetness, the white clusters have broken
apart, petals falling from a vaulted sky
in such profusion I imagine snow over

a wide green river, and the body, for instance,
altering that way: formed grace to disorder,
a steady dispersal. Through the filtered light
I find him hunched over his machine

in the wooden lean-to where he hardly notices
I have set my ruined knives alongside the others
that he will work, with punishing attention,
from rust to gleaming cobalt. A splendid

wearing away. The blade pressed
to the whirling disk shoots a stream of fiery
particles into the air, evidence of the way
steel loves heat, of the violence that perfects.

Soon he nods for me to take them.
I want to speak, make more of his accomplishment,
but stop, regarding his silence,
and go from this back to the steady afternoon,
back to nothing at all.

First publication

Letter from Wisconsin

Because it's winter and Lake Monona
is frozen white—five solid months now,
I want to mention water birds, diving mallards,
even the trumpeter swan, something extravagant
to relieve an expansive, blank sky,
this fog that has lasted for days.
My friend says he walked on the frozen lake
last night, that walking in the cold and fog is
like being in heaven, like being dead
and coming to life, everything less
visible, more tentative, except for the clear
sound of rare birds. He speaks of
patience, the pleasure of subtle
variations of grey, says that in this we have time
to prepare for the flight of Canada geese,
the promise of wisteria as if
desire could be bargained with. And there,
on the window ledge, my hibiscus—
the surprise of its winter blooms,
their driven beauty, pure red petals untwisting
in the cold light. How they hurry towards
their unqualified expending, their persistent
unfastening, a swift and reckless dying.

Dan Duane

Sharks

First publication

Naturally, one takes an interest in sharks, studies photographs of their gaping, bloody mouths—prostrate on the decks of fishing boats or on municipal piers, great whites always seem a ghastly and naked smear of triangular teeth and pale, fleshy gums. And the stuffed great white at the San Francisco Aquarium—thirteen feet long and somewhat deflated in its freezer case—when stared at all afternoon, serves reasonably well as an embodiment of one's relationship to fate: you know they're out there, you even know they're more likely to be at one place than another, and yet, the odds are on your side. You either quit surfing (unthinkable), or just decide that the angel with the sword either has your number today or doesn't. A common-enough sentiment in the water: "Yeah, I figure, if a shark's going to get me, he's going to get me." But then, on the other hand, how many aspects of late twentieth-century American life involve the possibility of being devoured by a two-thousand-pound predator with razor teeth? A kid I knew in high school had once seen a coroner's photographs of a Monterey surfer bitten almost in half— he told me for years how most of the man's ribcage was gone and how his organs spilled across the table. The board had beached first, with a classic cookie-cutter bite missing; the body drifted in the cold currents for nearly two weeks before being found. Years later, another local man was paddling out among other surfers, having a great time on good waves at a remote reef, when he felt as if someone had dropped a VW on his back—suddenly, he was underwater facing a huge eye. And in Oregon, a shark bit the board out from under a surfer who was sitting in wait for a wave; that awful mouth surged up and chomped onto the fiberglass between his legs. The shark bolted with the board in its teeth, dragging the surfer along by the ankle leash; when the shark turned to charge, the surfer grabbed its tail—two other surfers witnessed this—and they wheeled around in circles together before it let go.

With all that in mind, I took coffee and a muffin over to the lighthouse—home of the Santa Cruz Surf Museum—for a look at the obligatory chewed-up board. A small room with the air of a temple, the museum had an historical range of boards hung all over the walls, from redwood planks to the latest big wave elephant guns. Old black-and-white photographs showed smiling boys in simpler times; an older gentleman wearing a satin Santa Cruz Longboarders Association jacket mentioned that the winter of '41 was a beaut. And then I found it: huge teeth had crunched the fiberglass like a potato chip, tangible evidence of a phantom reaper; like the footprints of a yeti or film footage of a ghost. A glass case held photographs of Erik Larsen, the victim, in bed, with heavily bandaged arms; handwritten doctors' reports described deep lacerations and massive blood loss. Pieces of wetsuit, also behind glass, looked shredded as if by a tree-mulcher. A photo caption compared territorial bites to feeding bites, said Larsen was slated as dinner; they usually spit surfers out . . . expecting rich, fatty seal meat, they get fiberglass and neoprene, a little lean muscle and bone—rarely come back for a second bite. So, tide dropping, big storm on the way and time wasting, I said my mantras—"more likely to be killed by a drunk driver, more likely to be struck by lightning"—and drove north. Feeling the dread of true wilderness, of joining the food chain—something humans have been good at avoiding, like exposure to the elements and procreative sex. Changed into my wetsuit with a little reggae on the tapedeck: "Kill de white man, kill de white man . . ."

On the path, panicked cottontails scampered into the dead hemlock as I passed. I paddled out in water slate gray and disappointingly flat, caught a little nothing of an ankle-high wave, then drifted about and took comfort in the water's murkiness—concentrated on surfaces, ignored the way my legs faded down into the milky green. Smelled the brine, watched granite-colored light wave along the still outer waters—there's a rare quality of sun and shade here on cloudy days, with the dramatic contrasts of black-and-white film. Vince not around—hadn't seen him in a few days. Rose and fell a little, lying down, eyes at water level: Ishmael again: "These are the times of dreamy quietude . . . when beholding the tranquil beauty and brilliancy of the ocean's skin, one forgets the tiger heart that pants beneath it; and would not willingly remember, that this velvet paw but conceals a remorseless fang." A small man in a black wetsuit sat far outside, arms folded, watching the shifts in shadows and holding onto a kelp strand as an anchor against the current. A seal's shiny head surfaced quietly behind him, undetected. It watched the man's back for a minute, then leapt out of the water and came down with a terrific slap: thrashing and kicking, the surfer spun around on his board, utterly hysterical, face white, screaming, "What was that!? What the *hell* was that!?"

And I didn't blame him: you can think you're thinking about the super chicken burrito you intend to have for lunch, merely brush your leg against a thick boa kelp stalk and absolutely flip with terror, death by devouring just a thought below the surface. Sharkiness: state of mind spoken as a state of place—"getting kinda sharky out here, dontcha think?"—a combination of history, water depth, and exposure to open ocean. I paddled over to a patch of kelp to hide from the deep, and, thinking of the guy who'd been dragged around, sat up to avoid decapitation. A neighbor of mine had been sitting on his board near here just recently, thinking what a drag it would be if a shark appeared—so few waves, he'd have to paddle in. And just then, he'd seen a four-foot dorsal fin ten feet away from him, a huge wake displacing as it moved. He told me his eyes couldn't quite process it at first, kept trying to see a seal or a sea lion; but then another surfer had *leaned* around the fin and nodded frantically with an expression that said, *Uh huh, that's exactly what you think it is!* They frantically paddled for the beach and my neighbor turned around once to see the fin slowly following. When they'd screamed the other surfers ashore, one die-hard remained in the water, unbelieving. I had actually mistaken a sea lion flipper for a fin once and discovered a peculiar human dynamic: guys want to scorn your misplaced fear, but never quite do, the danger apparently too legitimate for teasing. Nevertheless, Shorty once felt convinced he'd seen a great white inside a wave: he paddled for shore and left without telling any of the other ten surfers in the water, didn't want to be ridiculed.

So many disturbing traits, once you look into them—sharks are the world's only known *intrauterine cannibals:* eggs hatching within a uterus, the unborn young fight and devour each other until one well-adapted predator emerges. If the womb is a battleground, what then the sea? And, without the gas-filled bladders that float other fish, if sharks stop swimming, they sink. Thus, their tendency to lurk along the bottom—21-foot, 4,600-pound benthic land mines with hundred year life-spans. Hard skin bristling with tiny teeth sheathes their flexible, cartilage skeletons—no bone at all. Conical snouts, black eyes without visible pupils, black-tipped pectoral fins. Tearing out and constantly being replaced, their serrated fangs have as many as 28 stacked spares (a bite meter embedded in a slab of meat once measured a Dusky shark's bite at 18 tons per square inch). And all of the following have been found in shark bellies: a goat, tomcat, three birds, a raincoat, overcoats, a car license plate, grass, tin cans, a cow's head, shoes, leggings, buttons, belts, hens, roosters, a nearly whole reindeer, even a headless human in a full suit of armor. Indiscriminate recyclers of the organic—my sensitive disposition, loving family and affection for life, my decent pickup, room full of books, preoccupation with chocolate in the afternoons and tendency to take things too personally: all immaterial to my status as protein.

Leftovers from premammalian times, survivors of the dinosaur extinction, sharks evolved completely and always in the sea, never in fresh water; first appearing 350 million years ago, they've descended from 60 foot, 50 ton prehistoric monsters, truly overdetermined predators—in one photo a group of scientists stand comfortably inside a pair of fossilized jaws. Capable of between 40 and 70 knots—calculated from photographic blur—white sharks swim with their mouths open; one writer describes a diver in the Mediterranean being hit so hard he exploded; another mentions a white shark leaping clear out of the water to pull a seal off a rock. "But in most attacks," this latter writes, "witnesses see neither seal nor shark, only a sudden explosion blasting spray 15 feet high, then a slick of blood on the surface." One never sees the white before it strikes, no speeding fin: it surges up in ambush, jaw distended, and tears out fifty-pound chunks of flesh. And jelly-filled subcutaneous canals on its head and sides are lined with neuromasts—Ampullae of Lorenzini—a kind of prey radar detecting faint electrical fields. (Waiting for a wave, one's very life force pulses like a homing beacon.) And their powerful eyes—with optic nerves thick as ropes—see detail quite poorly, are adapted only to separating prey from background. Among the world's most efficient predators, their kill rate is better than ninety percent (while the hawks just inland strike all day without luck).

I popped a kelp bulb just as a seal rose and looked at me, processing my presence. Perhaps wondering why I'd be stupid enough to dress like him in this part of town.

"Don't like seeing seals," said a surfer nearby.

Now I was nervous, having always seen seals as good news.

"Just paranoid," he answered, when I asked why, "because . . . I'm Erik Larsen." He sounded almost apologetic.

I looked closely, saw the resemblance to the bandaged figure in the photographs. He rolled up his wetsuit sleeve to show deep scars the length of his forearm; I let a little wave pass—had to ask, had to know.

"Kind of foggy out there," he said, telling a tale many times told, "and my brother had just gone in. I got this weird feeling a big animal was under me. Really hoping it was a sea lion. Then I saw teeth, like coming up at me."

The surfer who'd been startled by the seal—a slender, weathered man with a bright curiosity about him, drifted over to listen.

"And then my whole leg was in the thing's mouth," Larsen said, slouching like a beaten veteran. "It cut my thigh muscle in half and severed my femoral artery." He looked outside at a three-wave set; clouds still a gray continuum. The other guy said he'd heard you bled to death if your femoral artery got cut.

"If you slit it, you do," Larsen said, "but it's like a rubber band, so if you cut it all the way like mine, it'll snap back and close a little."

Not a distinction I enjoyed picturing. The one who'd asked looked toward the beach.

Larsen explained how the shark let go, circled, and attacked again, this time at his head. "I put up my arms," he said, crossing them before his face, "and it cut all the abductor tendons and my right brachial artery—the really big one under your bicep. My arms were all flopping around in its mouth. Yeah, I totally remember thinking how much room there was in there, like plenty for me. But I got one arm out and hit it in the eye."

He took a breath. I was stunned, couldn't be patient—and then?

"It let go," he said. "And I actually got on my board. No shit. And the miracle is, I could even paddle because I still had the tendons that pulled down, even though it cut the ones that lift up. I actually caught a wave." He laughed a little. "Yeah, a little one—belly-rode it in, and a lady came out with her kid and I told them how to tie tourniquets. When the chopper got there I'd lost a third of my blood."

The end of the story left an awkward silence: what to say? Larsen stroked into a waist-high right and surfed it casually, did what the wave wanted. I floated a while alone, then caught one in—waves kind of small, not real interesting.

Rosalie Sanara Petrouske

The Root of the Universe

First publication

*And the journey is an evocation of three things in particular: a landscape
that is incomparable, a time that is gone forever, and the human spirit,
which endures.*   N. Scott Momaday, *The Way to Rainy Mountain*

My grandmother was sixty-one years old when I was born, and I was
her youngest grandchild until I was ten. Her name was Katherine
Marie, but I never called her that. She was always "Grandmother"
or "Grandma Kate." I must have been about four years old the first
time she walked me to the pond near her house. It was late April and
the trees were barely budding, tight green buds that she cupped my
hand around.

"Feel this," she said, "it's a bud, and in May it will be a hawthorn
leaf."

"Will it grow like me?" I asked.

"Yes, Marl-a-babe. It will grow into a big leaf," she said, using her
nickname for me.

Although she knew little of her ethnic heritage, which was German, and she could not give me that, my grandmother did know the
language of trees and flowers, of birds and dragonflies, and she
taught me about the only landscape she knew. I can still see her
breaking two branches from the black willow tree—one for her to

lean on as she walked and a smaller one for me. Her cumbersome shape silhouetted against the sun, she carefully reached for a choice branch and slid a straight-edged knife into the verdant bark.

My grandmother was a large woman. Her feet in sturdy, flat-soled boots moved slowly, but were strong. This was long before arthritis twisted her legs. Her hair was fine, still black, but so thin that her flesh poked through each strand. She had had typhoid in the 1920s, when my mother was a baby. Before that her hair was so long she could sit on it, and she had worn it braided in a circle fastened to the top of her head with tortoiseshell combs. I have seen pictures of her, her hair blue-black, like the crows that cawed over the pond where we gathered pussywillows and the dark heads of cattails.

The house where she lived after my grandfather died was located in Menominee County, the southernmost county in Michigan's Upper Peninsula. The Little Cedar River flowed north and south about a mile behind her house. The river was more of a trickling stream that meandered slowly, and was so shallow in some places you could cross it by using a few boulders as stepping stones. My grandmother's nearest neighbors, at the time, lived in the small adjoining villages of Carney-Nadeau approximately ten miles away.

The house itself was a rickety white cottage with green shutters that clattered on windy days. Each shutter had a half-moon shape cut in its center. Her front porch was just as rickety with loose floorboards washed to a silvery gray by the years. My grandmother drew her water from a hand-operated pump beyond the back door. There was no electricity, and light glowed from the globes of heavy kerosene lamps. Her cooking was done on a cast-iron oil stove, which was also used for heating during the long winters.

Pine and apple trees shaded her front lawn and patches of June grass grew in clumps, untamed and knotty, like the burls in an old oak. In May, apple blossoms were abundant and ruby-throated hummingbirds hovered over the full-blown petals, thrusting their thin beaks into the puffy centers of each cupped flower. Early June

brought lilacs and the lacy white veils of spirea that drifted haunt-
ingly when the wind blew on moonlit nights.

My grandmother taught me about the natural world in the height
of its beneficence. She made sure I knew how to name all the inhabitants of her landscape, and I will always consider her as my first and
best teacher. She also taught me that nature could be inexorable, like
the spring we found the dead fawn.

"Nature can't always be kind, Marl-a-babe," she told me. "There
was not enough food this year for the deer. It was too harsh a winter."

There was a wooded area to the south of my grandmother's house
that held all the secrets of the wilderness. On the hill that raised before dropping into a growth of trees, blackberry brambles grew and
by mid-August burst with bountiful fruit. The path into the woods
was covered with tall grass that exploded with grasshopper song,
and poplars bent in rows in the wind all the way down to a murky
pond, where frogs hummed on summer nights until their song became a cadence that clicked and echoed in my eardrums. I would
imagine the sound was a chorus of voices and soon words would distinguish themselves until I thought the frogs were speaking to me.

During the springs and summers I spent with my grandmother,
it is the walks I remember best. This is when she taught me the
names of the flowers that grew wild in the fields and woods. The
flower names became a litany and my love for language formed as I
wound my tongue around their fragrant syllables: Indian paintbrush,
butter-and-eggs, St. Johnswort, black-eyed Susan, snowy campion,
Queen Anne's lace. Often, I stopped to chase a butterfly, and then
the naming ceremony would begin again as my grandmother helped
me identify them. There were stately Tiger Swallowtails spreading
their wings across a poplar branch, the burnt orange of a Monarch
glimpsed wheeling against the midsummer sky, the velvety black and
yellow-banded Painted Ladies perched on downy thistles, and along
the semidark paths, tawny Coppers cavorted.

Perhaps even then my grandmother knew that someday I would find solace in writing, and that knowing the names of birds, trees, flowers, and people would open my vision to the possibilities of language, and to the substantiality of being able to give all things the dignity of their names.

In the late spring, my grandmother took me to gather pussywillows at the pond. In the thicket, the pussywillows grew, dimpled white fluff perched in a brown shiny pod. We snapped their twigs and carefully placed them in her canvas gathering bag.

My grandmother always prepared for our walks with meticulous care. She covered her clothes with a leather butcher's apron. It was her father's apron, and it had come from Germany. That was all she knew about it; the apron belonged to her father. It was a russet brown with dark stains embedded in the creased leather. I pretended those stains were the blood of lambs, or deer hearts from the Black Forest. On our journeys, my grandmother wore her black hair tied into a cloth, babushka style.

"Look, Marl-a-babe," Grandma would say. She would take my hand into her own larger, work-roughened one, and place it on the soft pussywillow stem.

"This is how you cut," she would say, showing me the way to angle the knife, to slice the twig cleanly.

"Now, you do it." Reverently, I would take the knife from her, cut carefully the way she had showed me.

"*Das gut,*" she said.

In the haze of an early June midday after one of our walks, we often sat on the weathered slats of my grandmother's front porch. She put a white linen cloth trimmed with Alencon lace over the table that she used for canning and she brought out jars of thick golden apple butter, or last year's batch of blackberry jam or pin-cherry jelly along with her baking powder biscuits, browned at the edges and still warm. I sat in the miniature red rocker, the one my grandfather had made for me—that was before his stroke, before he was buried in the cemetery at Nadeau in 1955—and filled my mouth with sweet and tart while grandmother showed me the dragonflies with their red and blue bottle bodies as they dipped in and out over the yellow, feathery grass.

"They're called darning needles," she said. I trembled if a dragonfly flew close to me because I believed they would sew my mouth shut if I talked too much.

On those afternoons the air was alive with birdsong. The killdeers sloped low overhead calling out *kill-deeah, kill-deeah,* and my grandmother mimicked their calls. She would point to a dash of red cardinal wing in the thimbleberry bush or a flash of blue jay feather farther out in the woods. Barn swallows gathered when we tossed biscuit crumbs, and pecked at the brown dirt.

"*Kvik-kvik, vit-vit,*" Grandmother said, mimicking the swallow's cry. "See, look they're taking food to their little ones. Their nest is in the eaves of the toolshed. Watch, Marl-a-babe, watch them go. I saw them building their nest yesterday."

If it was late afternoon, sometimes the mournful sound of a whippoorwill drifted eerily in the quiet of approaching nightfall. If I was very still, I often saw a flutter of wing as the whippoorwill circled the copse of trees at the edge of the hill, and its refrain *whip . . . poor . . . will* echoed again and again. The northern legends, or so my grandmother told me, spoke of the whippoorwill as a harbinger of death. If someone was sick or dying, often a whippoorwill would call into the night and circle the house to forewarn of the impending death. I shivered in delight and fear. One winter when I caught a fever, my mother said I asked her over and over if she could hear the whippoorwill outside the window.

Every living creature that existed in the domain of my grandmother's yard was cared for. At twilight we carried a burlap bag of ripe apples to the edge of the wood and spread them for the deer. She kept coffee cans filled with seeds and nuts, and when the swallows and wrens crept on branches close to the house, I was allowed to fetch a can and sprinkle the seed or coax bushy-tailed squirrels and alert sloe-eyed chipmunks to take nuts from my hands. I learned to hold my hand still, to never draw back in a sudden movement. "Never let them sense your fear," she said. "Trust your instincts." At first, my small hand quivered visibly; I imagined the crunch of sharp teeth embedded in my palm, but soon the chipmunks moved hesitantly and snatched at the acorn I offered. By the end of that summer, one brave chipmunk traversed my arm and perched for a second on my shoulder to receive its prized acorn. This was the beginning of my journey in learning to trust my instincts in both animal and human worlds.

There were many times when I had to trust strangers, and to trust in my own decisions. I moved from childhood to adulthood, from a small town to a large city, from being a daughter to becoming a mother. If I kept my hand steady, if I waited patiently, if I had faith in myself, I found I was always rewarded.

As the summer nights enclosed us on my grandmother's front porch, I drew my tanned and bramble-scratched legs beneath me and leaned against her broad knee to watch the Michigan sky create a collage of stars. Then, my grandmother named the constellations: The Great Bear, The Lesser Bear, Cassiopeia, The Hunting Dogs, The Northern Crown. Soon the moths gathered around the circle of light emanating from the kerosene lantern. The pale green Luna moth slowly moved its gigantic wings and drifted closer to the light, usually landing on the front porch door. The brown and furry Polyphemus moths bore black and yellow eyespots on their hind wings like the one-eyed giant Polyphemus of Greek mythology, and some of them were as large as the back of my hand. Around these huge and shadowy moths, the smaller and swifter Sphinx moths darted, singeing their wings on the glass of the lantern. And so night came to my grandmother's porch pressing us indelibly into a moment of time, an ageless grandmother and her granddaughter listening to the peeping of frogs and the distant *hoo, hoo-oo, hoo, hoo* of a Great horned owl.

I was a child, and children are not aware of the passage of time. Those summer nights seemed endless as I grew sleepy waiting for the moon to dash from beneath a cloud, for the fireflies to make their first appearance.

"Fireflies bring good luck and good health, Marl-a-babe," my grandmother told me. "But if you kill a firefly, it means bad luck."

Sometimes, I would catch a firefly and put it in an empty jelly jar so I could watch the glow of its tiny lantern, but I always remembered my grandmother's words, and soon released it into the night.

Many times throughout the years, I have tried to capture in words on a page the joy of being that child who wound her way through woodland paths and lay down among tall ferns—all the while breathing the scent of wintergreens, of sun-warmed grass, that loamy fragrance of moss, and listening so intently to the silence that I could almost hear the dank brown mushrooms growing at the root of the universe.

This evening, over thirty-one years later, I sit on my own front porch in Marquette, Michigan, rocking my seven-month-old daughter, Senara. There are smooth floorboards beneath my feet, and as the sun drifts toward late evening and a twinkle of lights flicker out on Lake Superior, I simply hold my daughter close. I know when I turn on the overhead porch light, only a few white cabbage moths will creep toward its glow. It has been a long time now since I have seen the ethereal Luna moth, or the regal Polyphemus, although I have sat still and waited some dark nights for one to find the welcoming light of my front porch.

My grandmother recreated for me a legend of natural beauty, a respect for our environment, and for the importance of knowing how to name everything we encounter in the world.

Although I now live in the northern Upper Peninsula of Michigan, where some areas remain untouched by man's hand, I know of no cottage marked by the pioneering essence of my grandmother, no place where my daughter, who has yet to take her first steps, can run and toss herself headlong into a field of blue forget-me-nots. I cannot give my daughter a front porch where the hills spread beyond it, flower-clad and alive with voices; my grandmother's house has passed the way all such memories pass, into the vortex of the seasons. I do not even remember the directions for the country road that used to take me there. Progress and development have changed her landscape. It is only her spirit that endures, and the strength of her teachings. She is there on that path I have never forgotten, leaning her hand upon the head of her willow stick, pointing to a knobby outgrowth of hawthorn.

My daughter stirs on my lap, and as she does, I notice a movement in the lilac bush. I know Senara is still too young to understand me, but I tell her anyway.

"See there, that brown in the tree, Marl-a-babe? It's an ovenbird." And then to Senara's delight, I mimic the ovenbird's call, "*teach-teach-teach.*"

Gregory McNamee

Desert Winds

First publication

Not long ago a desert-born duststorm rushed by my window, obscuring the view of the mountains fifteen miles to the north, and that of the alligator junipers in my next-door neighbor's yard. Reddish-brown grains of sand formed small dunes in the streets of downtown Tucson, the date-palm tree in my yard bent nearly sideways, and a fury of static energy crackled in the air, warning residents of the city to stay away from telephones, computers, and most other artifacts of our time. The sight was impressive, even a little frightening, all the more so because the season of the great duststorms—from late April until, say, late September—had not yet come, bearing the promise of a spring out of *Flight of the Phoenix* for residents of the Sonoran Desert.

Deserts are noted, of course, for their lack of water, and by definition are areas where the average annual rainfall does not exceed ten inches—about twenty-five percent of the planet's surface, by most reckonings. Deserts are also noted, at least in the popular imagination, for their presumed consequent lack of life. The origin of the English word is in the Latin *desertus,* "abandoned," as in Robinson Crusoe's island home. Most deserts, in truth, are far from desolate. They swarm with life, albeit life that snarls, hisses, howls, bites, stings, or sticks. Still, the writer and amateur ecologist David Quammen frames the question well by suggesting, "a desert is one of those entities, like virginity and sans serif typefaces, of which the definition must begin with negatives." The absence of water, of the discernible four seasons, these things determine.

But the deserts of the world are not lacking in one thing: wind, and lots of it. What makes them deserts in the first place is not so much the lack of water as the fact that ever-thirsty winds pull such scant rain as falls from the clouds back skyward before it can reach or penetrate the ground. You can see this in the eerie "virga" rain phenomenon, where ghostly trails of falling water evaporate thousands of feet above the earth in the thermal-ridden air. In windy Bagdad, California, not a drop of rain fell on the earth for 767 days, from September 3, 1912, to November 8, 1914; yet the sky was full of clouds in their season, water kept from the earth by the constant flow of dessicating wind. A similar arid river blows across west Texas, so strong, local legend has it, that if it ever stopped all the cows would fall down.

Duststorms are a common enough occurrence in southern Arizona, especially now that a development boom has scraped off vast swaths of groundcover in a mad effort to reshape the lower Sonoran Desert into another Los Angeles. They are common enough in every desert of the world. This one's sudden appearance transfixed me, though, blowing up as it did in a mild season, a time of clement, even sublime weather. This one, I thought at the time, had to be one more harbinger of the El Niño current's ongoing flip-flopping of the normal jet stream, reversing centuries-old patterns of rainfall and climate.

The mythographer and ethnologist Sir James G. Frazer rightly observed in his landmark study *The Golden Bough,* "Of all natural phenomena, there are, perhaps, none which civilized man feels himself more powerless to influence than the wind." (Let us set aside the adjective "civilized." It has little meaning anyway, especially in these thoroughly uncivilized times.) Of the 5,600,000,000,000,000 or so tons of air in the atmosphere, some large part is always whistling

down, it seems, on desert rats, for it is the uneven distribution of solar energy that drives the winds—and solar energy is, of course, dis-
tributed in an embarrassment of riches across the face of the
drylands.

The deserts of the world for the most part lie in the zone between
the trade and westerly winds. At sea the "oceanic deserts," where
rain does not often fall, are called "horse latitudes." Most deserts lie
between 15 and 30 degrees from the equator, areas where constant
high-pressure systems separate the westerlies and trade winds,
which bring so much languid lushness to places like Guatemala and
Malaysia. Those deserts that dare extend into the westerlies, like the
Sonoran, are blocked by mountains that collect moisture while in-
tensifying the winds, a sort of double whammy.

For half the year, most deserts are graced by caressing, soft winds
that are nothing less than rejuvenating. In those breezes lie the
promise of new life, reverberating through scents, in the case of my
neighborhood, like that of the orange blossom—the orange, that
marvelous heat-loving berry, having first been introduced to Europeans in the first century by Greek and Roman travelers to the Thar
Desert of India, and reintroduced by Moors into the rich gardens of
Andalusia, whence most of the Spanish explorers of New Spain
arose. On such days the air hangs in the sky like a loose silk gown,
so brilliantly clear, so deep blue, that it seems almost as if you could
make out each individual molecule.

But were some master of the Chinese necromantic art of *feng
shui*—the alignment of buildings to their environment—to design a
house for a Sonoran Desert dweller in the normally clement month
of February, the plans would have to be scrapped in two months'
time. Come late April, when the orange blossoms fade into memory,
ever-intensifying winds announce the advent of summer and, not far
behind it, the monsoon season—for, as the Akimel O'odham, the
"watercourse people" of the Sonoran Desert, say, "the rain is blind
and must be led by the wind."

If you look into the literature of deserts, as I have been doing lately, you will find wind as a constant no less than heat and aridity, and that is just as it should be. One of my favorite passages comes from the naturalist W. H. Hudson's fine 1917 memoir *Idle Days in Patagonia,* describing the dreaded *pampero* wind that tears across southern Argentina:

> The wind beats incessantly on the exposed roof with a succession of blasts of waves which vary in length and violence, causing all loose parts to vibrate into sound. And the winds are hissing, whimpering, whistling, muttering and murmuring, whining, wailing, howling, shrieking—all the inarticulate sounds uttered by man and beast in states of intense excitement, grief, terror, rage, and what not. And as they sink and swell and are prolonged or shattered into compulsive sobs and moans, and overlap and interweave, acute and shrill and piercing, and deep and low, all together forming a sort of harmony, it seems to express the whole ancient dreadful tragedy of man on earth.

A related wind, the *simoun* (from the Arabic word for poison), shrieks over the Sahara, whipping up sand and dust into fearful, sharp-grained *chevaux de frise.* Herodotus, the great Greek traveler and historian whom his younger contemporary Thucydides uncharitably called "the father of lies," doubtless got it right when he reported the story of a Libyan army that marched off two and a half millennia ago into the deep Sahara to find and subdue the lord of these storms. The expedition never returned, "disappearing, in battle array, with drums and cymbals beating, into a red cloud of swirling sand." The Assyrians, it is said, did much the same, sending squads of archers to combat the approaching clouds. And for good reason: a duststorm once buried Ur of the Chaldees, cause enough to seek vengeance.

The *simoun* has many local equivalents: the Moroccan *sirocco,* the Libyan *ghibli,* the Saudi *khamsin,* the Egyptian *zoboa,* the Australian "brickfielder," the Mongolian *karaburan,* the Sudanese *haboob,* the Mauritanian *harmattan,* and the Indian *loo,* which Rudyard Kipling describes in his story "The Man Who Would Be King" as a "red-hot wind from the westward, booming among the tinder-dry trees and pretending that the rain was on its heels." The logic of those winds seems to have prompted evolution to make a few alterations in the master plan; recently, biologists have concluded that camels, strange creatures to begin with, evolved so that, standing, they can clear the sand-laden zone of air, which goes up only to about six feet, slightly lower than the average camel's height. Other creatures, like the antelope-like saiga of Central Asia and certain kinds of desert hares, have filtering tissues surrounding their respiratory tracts that give them the same adaptive advantage.

Closer to my home, the Tohono O'odham, "people of the stony barren," tell of water serpents that dwell in the boiling summer clouds that rage across deserts the world over, bringing rain to the dry earth not in nourishing drops but in great black undulating curtains of water, leaving floods and destruction in their wake. It is no sin to kill such serpents, the O'odham explain, but even their best shamans and archers rarely succeed in doing so.

Ignaz Pfefferkorn spent many years of his life trying to purge that shamanism, that ancient way of knowing nature, in his role as a Jesuit priest. Until he was expelled from the Kingdom of New Spain in 1767 along with the rest of his order—the Bourbon King Carlos III having decided to punish the Jesuits for their political intrigues in Europe—he oversaw a succession of missions in what is now northwestern Mexico, observing in his *Sonora: A Description of the Province,* the ancestors of the summer storms, now ironically called "monsoons," that swelter overhead:

> Sonora, through these daily rains, receives a pleasant relief from the heat, and at the same time its products are increased. Hence, these rains would surely be considered as priceless blessings of nature were they not always accompanied by the most horrible thunder-storms, which not infrequently do great damage to men and animals in the villages and in the fields. One cannot listen to the continuous crashing of the thunder without shuddering. At times such thunderstorms bring with them a damaging hail, which destroys all growing things in the field and garden; or there may occur a ruinous cloud-

burst, in Sonora called *culebra de agua,* or water snake, which will
flood over country and villages, devastating them. Sometimes the
thunder-storms are accompanied by violent windstorms and whirlwinds, which lift the sand in a very thick, twisted column almost to
the clouds. Nothing these whirlwinds seize can withstand their
power. . . . Hence, during these months everyone avoids traveling in
the afternoon if possible, because of the constant danger of being
caught in such a storm. Therefore, wherever one reaches a shelter
around noon, or even a little before, the day's journey is ended.

During one such thunderstorm in Arizona in the summer of 1941, a
saltwater clam fell from out of the sky on a young boy, who was
knocked out cold by the blow. (He fared better than the playwright
Aeschylus, on whose bald head an eagle dropped a tortoise, killing
him instantly.) Scarcely a summer storm goes by when a pelican or
albatross is not blown from the Pacific or the Gulf of California and
dropped down into the heart of the inland desert, there indignantly
to await what has become local tradition: a plane ride back to the
coast.

Pfefferkorn had it right: it seems that nothing, indeed, can withstand the power of those great storms. Out of them, after all, have
come gods to cow humans into obedience: in the wind-lashed Sinai
Desert, Jehovah, recapitulating his origins as a Semitic storm god
like his later rival Baal, first appeared before Moses as chain lightning. You will find in Ezekiel mention of "a storm coming out of the
north, a vast cloud with flashes of fire and a brilliant light about it;
and within was a radiance of brass, glowing in the heart of the
flames." Such storms are unique among inorganic phenomena inas-
much as they resist the tendency of all things to slip away into inertia
and entropy: instead, they swell, burst, spawn new storms, and eventually wander off elsewhere to cause new trouble. The last one to
visit my home behaved less than divinely: it split a chinaberry tree
neatly down the middle, tore up a good section of prickly-pear
fence, and sent a well-rooted agave spinning off into the street, all
within the space of perhaps a minute's time.

Desert tempests have brought down whole governments, like that of Ur of the Chaldees, like that of the worthy Jimmy Carter, who never quite recovered from the hostage-rescue debacle of 1979, when nineteen Delta Force elite soldiers maneuvered their helicopters into a funnel of whirling dust over the barren saltpans of Iran. These "dust devils"—the term comes to us from some unknown source from the Indian subcontinent—are an astonishment of nature; if you drive from, say, Phoenix to Los Angeles across the sandy lowlands of the Sonoran and Mojavean deserts, you'll count dozens of them on most hot, cloudless days of the year, miniature cyclones dancing to their own music alongside the interstate. When I was about six years old, I walked into one as it carved its sinuous course in the gypsum deposits of White Sands, New Mexico, thinking that it would take me off to Oz. I did not retrace Dorothy and Toto's adventures, but Southwestern legend has it that whole flocks of barnyard hens have been swept heavenwards through a passing dust devil's fancy. No one has personally seen this occur, of course, but then no one has seen another phenomenon that passes for fact in many parts out this way: it's so hot most days that chickens lay hardboiled eggs.

The tallest dust devil ever recorded was spotted in Utah about thirty years ago. It stood about 2,000 feet tall, lasted for seven hours—an unusually long life span for what is in essence a tornado—and traveled across the alkali desert for more than 40 miles. That it came from the comparatively mild desert of Deseret is no surprise, really, for the Great Basin is the source of most of our continental storm systems. Even the fiercest Saharan sandstorm might be preferable to a day's contending with the basin's fierce katabatic winds, which sweep down onto the desert floor from the tall Sierra Nevada and Wasatch mountain fronts, generating howling low-pressure systems like the so-called Washoe winds. Mark Twain wrote of them, "seriously," that they are "by no means a trifling matter." Not so seriously, he described what a Washoe storm hid within its dust clouds:

Hats, chickens and parasols sailing in the remote heavens; blankets, tin signs, sagebrush, and shingles a shade lower; doormats and buffalo robes lower still; shovels and coal scuttles on the next grade; glass doors, cats and little children on the next; disrupted lumber yards, light buggies and wheelbarrows on the next; and down only thirty or forty feet above ground was a scurrying storm of emigrating roofs and vacant lots.

Far on the remotest fringes of the Great Basin lies the resort town of Palm Springs, California, where I happened to spend a summer night not long ago. Trying to reach my room from the lobby, I was buffeted from one end of a Motel 6 parking lot to another by midnight winds that screamed down through the San Gorgonio Pass— the site, appropriately enough, of a giant windmill field, one of the West's countless monuments to surrealism—and the towering San Jacinto Mountains. As I careened off dumpsters and fire hydrants, I wondered why on earth wealthy celebrities like Jerry Lewis, Steve Allen, Gerald Ford, and Bob Hope should wish to spend their waning days surrounded by such gales. Perhaps, I concluded, it sharpens the edge somehow, rather like those sandblasted Egyptian pyramids are thought to do in certain mystical circles.

Those falling winds, cousins to the *maloja* of the Swiss Alps, the *yama oroshi* of Japan, and the *reshabar* of the southern Caucasus, are most famously known to Americans as the Santa Anas. The mechanism that drives them works like this: on warm days the air rises uphill from valley floors, and then cools as it ascends, creating an upward–downward (anabatic–katabatic) wind flow. In the case of the Santa Ana winds, high pressure over Utah and Nevada causes air to spill off the Mojave Desert, rushing over the Pacific coastal range and onto the coastal lowlands. The coastal air is robbed of humidity by this thirsty invader and fills with static electricity. As it envelops desert and littoral alike, the Santa Ana creates a weird atmosphere of impending doom. During its season, as Raymond Chandler wrote in his famous short story "Red Wind," "Meek little wives feel the edge of the carving knife and study their husbands' necks. Anything can happen."

Anything can, and it usually does. Most heart attacks and strokes among desert dwellers occur when the wind is blowing at force 4 or 5 on the Beaufort scale, or 11 to 21 miles per hour, about the average for a Santa Ana day. And statistics compiled by the Los Angeles Police Department demonstrate that homicide rates, already fantastically high in southern California, double on Santa Ana days. (In the Gobi the winds often blow between 15 and 25 miles an hour for weeks at a time. I wonder why contemporary Mongolians don't massacre each other daily, but understand better why the bloodthirsty Golden Horde exploded from out of the high steppes a millennium ago.) In Pfefferkorn's time, Spanish defendants could cite the wind as an extenuating circumstance in homicide trials. The dust devil, it would seem, made them do it.

Old Ibn Khaldun, the great Moroccan historian, must have been working on a public-relations campaign when he wrote, "The Desert People are closer to being good than other settled peoples because they are closer to the First State and are more removed from all the evil habits that have infected the hearts of settlers." One glimpse of the *fin-de-siècle* Southland in the windy season would have forever scrapped that sentiment.

Matters grow worse with the advent of a desert thunderstorm, a water-laden wind blown up to tremendous proportion, one that bears the energy equivalent of a dozen atomic bombs of the kind that fell on Hiroshima and Nagasaki. "Rogue" ions from air molecules cause such a storm to discharge electricity; the resultant negative ions cause crankiness, loss of production, and, yes, psychopathic impulses. You need not, of course, live in a desert to experience these moods and their unhappy effects. As we increasingly tamper with microclimates to create dry, germ-free atmospheres in office buildings and shopping centers, the bacteriologist Alfred Krueger warns, our artificial climate-regulated lives will be ever more spent with a positive-ion deficit, a situation that he calls "clearly unnatural and probably unhealthy."

Poison winds, Santa Anas, homicide, despair. The winds of the world's deserts grind down whole mountains over geological time, scrub boulders down to pavement and dust, lay bare the bleak flats of the Bisti badlands of the Navajo Nation, the clean-scoured salt-pans of the Taklamakan. Why ever would anyone choose to live among these all-devouring currents?

Perhaps because, eternal optimists, we remember the gentle days, the scent of birthing orange buds and new bunchgrass, days when the calls of birds and coyotes linger in the soft, still air. Even after escaping what turned out to be the hottest summer in recorded Sonoran Desert climatic history for a few weeks in August of 1994, I found myself missing the *culebras de agua* and howling winds when I should have been thanking my stars for a sojourn in the temperate Ish River country. Call it perverse, but I was glad to descend again into the familiar furnace of the Great American Desert, even glad to see one of its westernmost gateways down the decidedly un-friendly—*pace* Buck Owens—streets of Bakersfield, alongside which dust devils danced.

The desert winds do not tolerate our inexperience, and they assure us of our many imperfections. They test us and find us wanting. But they keep those of us who choose to live in their thrall guessing, never quite certain of what the next subtle shift of current will bring: a scent from paradise, or a blast from the inferno.

Jennifer Ackerman

The Great Marsh

from *Notes from the Shore*

The Great Marsh is a broad plain of mud and grass that lies a mile northwest of Lewes. It's roughly rectangular, five square miles, bordered on three sides by uplands and on the fourth, by Beach Plum Island. Along the southern border Oyster Rock Neck and Hells Neck run a half mile or so into the marsh, their wooded uplands reaching an elevation of about ten feet. A few islands, or hummocks, rise out of the sea of grass and support little forests of pine and cedar, sassafras, red maple, and black gum. Otherwise, this is a landscape of no relief, flat and featureless. The major tool for navigating here is the system of tortuous streams that crease the grassy plain: Canary Creek, Fisher Creek, Black Hog Gut, and Old Mill Creek, which meanders in giant loopy S-curves from Red Mill Pond to the Broadkill River and drains nearly three-quarters of the marsh. The Delaware Bay flows dendritically through Old Mill Creek and its tributaries. The creeks predate the marsh, which was born seven thousand years ago when the rapidly rising sea drowned a valley of the Broadkill River, transforming it into a small lagoon. Silt gradually clogged the lagoon and filled it, then pioneering grasses advanced over the mud, trapping soil in the tiny baffles of their roots and anchoring it to make marsh.

Just before sunrise, low tide. I walk out into the marsh in the dark, stepping around chocolate brown pools agitated with the scratching and scuttling of fiddler crabs, past delicate marsh pinks, absent their

color in the white-wash light. Waves of warm air waft up from the
mudbanks bared by the outcreeping tide, a strong sulphur smell, not
unpleasant. The beam of my flashlight catches the giant ghostly pale
blossoms of the seashore mallow, *Kosteletzkya virginica.* I linger here
for a moment, hoping to "shine" the eyes of a wolf spider, which
have mirrorlike membranes that reflect light.

The darkness of the marsh is not the close darkness of woods,
where blackness pours up from between the trees, but a thin, liquid,
open, far-reaching darkness that descends onto the grass. Silence
stretches from horizon to horizon, broken only by the occasional call
of a whippoorwill, a sound that carries easily over the flat topography, somehow amplified by the open acres of air and the drum-flat
surface of the nearby bay.

My destination is a small tower of metal scaffolding fifteen feet
high topped by a wooden blind that sits about a mile into the marsh.
The path to the tower is wandering and uncertain and moves errat-
ically between firm ground and sloppy bottom that sucks hungrily
at my hipwaders. Even in the night damp I'm sweating profusely,
bundled against mosquitoes in long pants and a flannel shirt. Beneath
the grass is a deep black brew of river silt and clay trapped over millennia, bottomed twenty feet down by hard-packed yellow sand.
Every fifteen steps or so I sink deep in a soft oozy hole. When I reach
the tower, I peel off my damp shirt and my hipwaders, coated with
a glossy mud sheen, and sit in my socks.

The sky above the Great Marsh is so broad that it hosts more than
one celestial event. This morning a sagging August moon a day or
two past full is setting in the west, and in the east, a tomato of a sun
is edging up over the horizon. Soon it's swallowed up by a reef of purple clouds, casting the marsh in monochromatic light. The tower's
open, rickety, crow's-nest platform offers a 360-degree view of the
low country around it. I can just make out the lean profile of a great
blue heron well camouflaged by stillness. It plunges its head into a
pool and comes up with a fish, swallows it, and then raises itself
slowly with deep parenthetical beats of its huge wings. I can hear the

cackle of a green heron, but can't pick it out of the ranks of green roughage.

For months after I arrived here, I did not understand the draw of this leveled, subdued landscape, couldn't focus on any one part of it long enough to penetrate its surface. This summer I spent time in the tower with a young scientist from the Delaware Division of Fish and Wildlife. Randy Cole is a native of this place who was raised on duck hunting and wears his hipwaders like a second skin. He is studying the wildlife drawn to several artificial ponds dug into the marsh a few seasons before. The ponds are part of a state program designed to control mosquitoes and, at the same time, draw back some of the wildlife that has been chivied out by earlier mosquito control efforts. In the 1930s state officials had a complex system of crisscrossing ditches cut into the marsh, not with the loops and curves of natural creeks, but with the straight lines and right angles of the planning grid. In so doing they broke the natural order of the marsh, disturbed a rhythm old and of vast importance. The grid-ditching drained the big natural ponds whose permanent waters once attracted breeding colonies of black ducks and gadwall. The new ponds, a dozen half-acre pools contoured for natural effect, are designed to bring the birds back.

Randy's job is to record the species and number of animals that use the ponds for feeding or breeding. While we sit and watch for waterfowl, he points out salient marsh plants: *Spartina alterniflora,* or smooth cordgrass; salt-meadow hay; sea lavender; spike grass; and *Salicornia,* or saltwort. The latter is an odd little thing with leaves like long swollen toes, the only plant that can survive the extreme salinity found in the salt pans that pockmark the higher marsh, where water has been concentrated by evaporation until its salt content is several times that of the sea. At this time of year its spears are turning red from the roots up, giving it the look of a bizarre Christmas ornament made of flesh.

The marsh vegetation, which to my first bewildered surveys was utterly indistinct, has slowly sorted itself into recognizable zones, not altogether different from a mountain's, where leafy deciduous woodland gives way to pines, and then to treeless tundra, only here the distinction between zones comes down to shifts of inches. In the marsh's higher reaches—the hummocks and along the landward edges, out of reach of all but the highest spring or storm tides— grow two woody plants collectively called saltbush. There's marsh elder, *Iva frutescens,* an awkward stalky shrub with thick, fleshy leaves, and *Baccharis halimifolia,* the groundsel tree. Now in late summer, its seedheads look like hundreds of tiny white plumes. Below, but still wetted only twice a month by spring tides, grows salt-meadow hay, windrows of fine light stalks that swirl and mat in giant cowlicks. Lower still, by only two inches or so, salt-meadow hay gives way to the big, coarse, dark green stalks of *Spartina alterniflora,* which are flooded by every tide. *Spartina* is remarkable for its rich ability to so- licit sunlight and its ingenious adaptations to the salt flood that sweeps through the marsh twice daily. Close to a million cubic feet of brackish water flow in during flood tide, nearly doubling the water's salt content. Salt sucks water from living cells. But by special cunning *Spartina* can drink the water while excluding the salt: mem- branes on the plant's roots pull the fresh water from the sea. What little salt makes its way into the sap is excreted by glands in the plant's leaves. At low tide you can see the exiled salt crystals flashing in the sun.

On the walk out to the tower, Randy would squat down to show me the miniature tropical forest amid the thick stems of *Spartina,* a hot, humid, nearly windless environment. On and around the stems grows a microscopic, polycultural jungle of hundreds of species of diatoms, algae, and dinoflagellates, which trap phosphorous, ni- trates, and other elements vital to marsh life. Beneath it all, the marsh mud is black, blacker than the soil of the Mississippi Delta, and richer. Each autumn the aerial stems of *Spartina* die, bend down, break, mix into the black muck. Bacteria decompose the leaves, breaking them into small particles, detritus, which the tide spreads across the marsh surface, providing a pasture of food. An astronomer friend of mine saw this instantly when he looked down on the mud: "This place is *trashed* with life."

Pull up the blanket of marsh, give it a shake, and out would tumble coffee-bean snails, *Melampus bidentatus,* little half-inch creatures tinted with brown and green, as well as grasshoppers, beetles, ants, flies, and chinch bugs, which feed on *Spartina*'s tender leaves, and plant hoppers, which suck its juices. Also fiddler crabs and mud crabs, oysters and dense clumps of ribbed mussels, which pave the mud along the creeks where the tide floods regularly. According to one study, this marsh supports more than three and a half million mussels per acre. Out, too, would tumble diamondback terrapins, turtles the size of a small skull, their segmented pentagons fused to form a leathery dome, their reptilian heads spotted like a leopard. The diamondback was once here in great numbers, but its sweet flesh made it a gastronomic delicacy and the target of tireless collectors.

The shake wouldn't loosen such tenacious insiders as the larvae of the common marsh fly, family Chloropidae, which lives in the stems of *Spartina* and eats the plant's tissue. (The adults are so small, only two or three millimeters long, that they are nearly invisible except when swarming.) Nor would it dislodge the larvae of the fierce-biting greenhead fly, whose singular appetites are described by John and Margery Teal in *Life and Death of the Salt Marsh.* "The larvae are maggots, soft, elongate, leathery-skinned, lumpy individuals with a pair of organs for breathing air at one end and a pair of sharp jaws at the other. They wriggle through the mud eating anything they come across, including others of their kind. If a number of *Tabanus* maggots are put together in a dish, the end result is one fat, temporarily contented individual."

Here are some of the thirty or so species of fish that swim the waters of the Great Marsh: the small, glistening fish known as silversides, the four-spined stickleback, anchovy, northern pipefish, two kinds of herring, young striped bass, sea robins, summer flounder, naked gobies, striped mullet and white perch, eel, croaker, menhaden, northern kingfish, and three species of killifish, including the mummichog, a name that comes from a Narraganset word meaning "they go in great numbers."

The sun has reappeared above the cloud reef, a second bloom. In this low morning light the marsh looks different than it does under cloud cover or high sun, not a hazy watercolor wash, but a dazzling mosaic of distinctly different greens. The tide is sliding up the marsh slope, slithering into the creeks and spilling over between the blades of grass. The up, down, in, out of the tides makes this place danger-ous—sometimes inundating animals with lethal doses of salt water, sometimes exposing them to a devastating high-and-dry death—but also inconceivably rich. The tides distribute food and flush out waste, encouraging rapid growth and quick decay. Adaptation to this pulse is the contract that all successful marsh creatures have signed with a country half land, half sea. When the ebbing tide bares the flats, hundreds of scraping chitinous legs and claws scribe the mud as fiddler crabs emerge from their burrows to search for bacteria, fungi, minute algae, and fermenting marsh plants. Tiny star-shaped pigment cells dotting the crab's body obey the compounded rhythms of sun and tide. The cells contain granules of dark pigment, which disperse at daytime low tide, giving the crabs the color of the mud-bank and thus protecting them from predators. At night the pigment granules shrink from the cell's reaches and cluster together, the color fades, and the crabs turn the pale ivory-white of moonlight. These changes occur every day at a different hour, synchronized with the tides.

Now, as the salt tide seeps up the mudbank, the fiddlers are wait-ing until the water reaches their knees before they disappear into their deep mud tunnels to wait out the deluge. Though they breathe air with a primitive lung beneath the edge of their shell, they can hole up in their burrows with no oxygen for long periods—for months in cold water—a feat that makes the limit of our own tolerance for organic variation seem narrow indeed. A few moments' loss of oxygen and we rapidly descend into unconsciousness.

Coffee-bean snails, too, are air-breathers, but they go up rather than down when the tide rises. Like ghost crabs and beach fleas, they are members of a race that is learning to live outside the sea. Somehow they anticipate rising tides, creeping up the stalks of grass well before the water arrives. They take a breath of air that will hold them for an hour or so if the crowning sea submerges them.

Spiders and insects such as grasshoppers keep company with the snail, scaling stems to escape the high tide. This habit exposes the climbers to the keen eyes and hungry beaks of birds. The Teals once described the scene of an especially high tide, insects hopping, jumping, and flying onto taller plants until "only the tallest grasses along the creeks mark the meandering channels and these grasses are weighted and bending at the tips, alive with insects. Sparrows and wrens from the marsh, buntings and warblers from the land, gulls and terns from the beach, and swallows, dip, fly, settle, and swim along the twisting lanes of helpless insects and gorge themselves." I've seen swallows swooping over the marsh, snatching insects from midair, then suddenly dodging a marsh hawk's hook and talon in a startling turnabout of predator and prey.

Sunlight to marsh grass to grasshopper to swallow to hawk; these are some of the links that compose the marsh web. Learning a place is like this, glimpsing the individuals, the pinpoint touches of color on the broad canvas, randomly splattered. You pick them out, sort them out, name them, then tumble them back into the landscape, and by reading and more observation, figure out how they fit together. As more spaces are filled in, the image or weave is revealed, the continuous meshing intimacy. It helps to have a native tutor, and a sense of the storyline, the narrative over time. In the marsh, the little rhythms of the day have a way of focusing attention on particular species, the way the slow, small meter of an Emily Dickinson poem brings each syllable into close-up.

Noon, high tide. The marsh is a flat, dazzling mirror anchored by green studs. The high sun has robbed it of the play of shifting light in which it luxuriated this morning, brought it silently to whiteness. It looks uninhabited, and yet I know that each square inch of mud is crowded with twitchers, alive with drama, tragedy, plot and adventure, fierce eating and being eaten.

The mosquitoes have left me alone this morning, but once the sun goes down, I'll hear what D. H. Lawrence called that "small, high, hateful bugle in my ear." Huge swarms of mosquitoes used to range over this region, bands of millions moving in unison, several feet thick and hundreds of feet wide, their frenzied wingbeats producing a single, singing hum. In 1788 an observer at Cape Henlopen wrote:

> The people are afflicted with a eveil, not much unlike, and almost as severe as, some of the plagues of Egypt. I mean the inconceivable swarms of muscatoes and sandflies which infest every place, and equally interrupt the tranquility of the night and the happiness of the day. Their attacks are intolerable upon man as well as beast. The poor cows and horses in order to escape from these tormentors stand whole days in ponds of water with only their heads exposed.

Delaware is home to fifty-three species of mosquitoes—with names like *Aedes excrucians, Coquilletiddia perturbans, A. tormentor,* and *A. vexans*—each adapted to occupy a particular niche. The high marsh salt-meadow hay around here suits *A. sollicitans,* the salt-marsh mosquito. Females of the species lay their eggs in the moist mud of potholes found in and around the tufts of salt hay, which are flooded only infrequently. When spring tides or storm tides or rainfall fill the potholes, the eggs quickly hatch. The larvae rest just under the surface of the pool, breathing through little snorkel-like air tubes and feeding on microscopic organisms. On their way to adulthood they pass through four larval stages and a pupal phase, a metamorphosis that in warm weather can take less than ten days. When the adults emerge, they mate over the marsh. Then the females set out to search for a blood meal.

In the early 1930s a man could make a dollar a day digging ditches for the Delaware Mosquito Control Commission. The answer to the problem of the salt-marsh mosquito, the state believed, lay in disrupting the insect's life cycle by draining off the small shallow ponds of water that served as breeding pools. With this in mind, managers placed a grid of dots over maps of Delaware's marshes and then connected the dots with a ruler. These straight lines would become ditches hand-dug, twenty inches wide, twenty inches deep, one hundred and fifty feet apart, which would drain all marshes, high and low, whether or not they were suitable breeding grounds for mosquitoes. To help with the project, the federal government assigned four companies from the Civilian Conservation Corps, eight hundred men. One company set up camp in Lewes in a big building on Savannah Road topped by a brass and copper weathervane in the shape of a giant mosquito.

The ditch digging was slow, hard work, but the operation was conducted with military efficiency. In four years the Corps had installed eleven and a half million linear feet of ditches across forty-four thousand acres of Delaware, including virtually all of the salt marsh in the southeastern part of the state.

Every time they dug one of those ditches, it was like pulling the plug from a bathtub. The full effects are only now being uncovered. The rookeries of breeding waterfowl and other birds have shrunk or disappeared for want of pools in which to feed. Where the ditching changed water levels, that tall, tassel-fringed reed, *Phragmites australis,* spread across the marsh, crowding out the marsh grasses so essential to the food web. In some places, the drainage ditches opened areas of marsh to more frequent flooding at lower tide levels. Less organic debris accumulated on marsh surfaces, and populations of invertebrates at the base of the marsh food web crashed. Ironically, the small pools that formed behind the mounds of spoil created new breeding grounds for *A. sollicitans.*

The orderly ousting of the low, wet lands along this coast is not a new thing. For hundreds of years, people have considered these worlds miasmic, breeding grounds of choking vapors, of "exhalations [that] produced ague and intermittent fevers in the autumn and plursies in the spring," said an 1838 edition of the *Delaware Register and Farmers' Magazine*. The only good marsh was a drained marsh. Beginning in the seventeenth century, the Dutch—those masters of land drainage in Europe—and their colonial successors ditched and diked the mirey edges of the New World to create farmland and the squared geometry of our coastal towns. In the 1780s Delaware had 480,000 acres of marshes and swamps. In the 1990s only half of that remains.

Late afternoon pivots into dusk. The tide has begun to recede without my noticing, the eddying currents carrying out the rich detritus from decayed *Spartina* that will feed the hordes of tiny planktonic animals that are themselves food for the greater creatures of the bay and sea.

One proposed solution to the destruction of wetlands is mitigation or "no net loss." The idea is this: Anyone who destroys a wetland must create one of similar size somewhere else. Plant some grass, introduce some keystone species, and hope that these serve as a sort of gravitational force that will draw in the myriad elements of the marsh community. But no new marsh can recreate the complex chemistry of mud cooked over millennia, the dying down of *Spartina* in the cool of a thousand autumns, the slow, steady mixing of bacteria and algae. Nor can it guarantee the proper assembly of species, birds, insects, plants, bacteria, each occupying a precise niche and locked in intimate relationships. The created marsh may look like a marsh to the casual eye, the eye of the passerby. Perhaps in some measure it acts like one. But it is not the real thing. Is it enough to make replicas, perfectly intelligible and diminished?

Sunset, low tide. The mosquitoes have finally found me, tipped off by the hot chemical breath of my skin. They are odd sorts of carnivores. "The lady whines, then dines; is slapped and killed," says poet Brad Leithauser, "yet it's her killer's blood that has been spilled." It is true that only the female pursues a blood meal: the male sticks to nectar. Only she has the long, stabbing mouthparts that penetrate skin. These form a flexible tube with serrations that neatly slice my skin tissue and a curved tip that scans for blood just beneath the skin's surface. When the mosquito finds a capillary, she draws the blood up through the tube with two sturdy pumps in her head. At the same time, she sends saliva back down another hollow tube. The saliva, which inhibits the clotting of my blood, causes the irritating itching and swelling. It can also carry disease. When Thomas Nuttall traveled across the country almost two hundred years ago, he took with him a one-celled parasite of the genus *Plasmodium,* which he had picked up from an *Anopheles* mosquito he met in a Delaware swamp. During most of his remaining years, he suffered malarial attacks.

Those wading birds on the ponds below are my partners in torment. Mosquitoes find their bills and eyes, the flesh peeking through their thin head feathers, their long exposed legs. A hunting green heron will let biting mosquitoes cover its legs and head before it will twitch or flutter and lose its prey. Our blood provides the female mosquito with the protein she needs to produce a new generation. She'll suck up to four times her own weight at a single sitting, about a millionth of a gallon, which she stores in her inner abdomen. (A two-bit tour of the insect would have to pause at this organ, unfettered by appendages and therefore able to distend enormously to house blood.) Her swelling gut triggers the secretion of hormones that prompt her eggs to mature. One blood meal provides enough nutrition to produce up to two hundred eggs. Without it, she can lay only a dozen eggs or so. You have to admire the power packed into her humming body. One ten-thousandth of an ounce and a brain only slightly bigger than the period at the end of this sentence. Her wings hum at two hundred to five hundred beats per second and will carry her up to fifty miles from her brood marsh in search of a blood meal. She can lay a new batch of eggs every two weeks, and may lay as many as three or four batches of eggs during her summer of existence.

Aldo Leopold says that the beauty of marshes doesn't scream at you; it has a slow, lyrical welling effect. Likewise, the deterioration beneath its green ranks only gradually discloses itself, and only to the knowing eye. One woman here knows the marsh well, sees it intimately like the house of her childhood, now skewed and malfunctioning, with termite-eaten floorboards, frayed wiring, rotting beams. She fights hard to save it, with some success: Her detractors call her the wicked witch of the wetlands. I've seen her at meetings with officials deciding the fate of one piece of drowned country after another. She knits while she listens, her needles flashing and clicking harder and faster as her rage mounts, and I wonder whether those pale pink sweaters and booties don't contain the names of the bureaucrats and businessmen who would do in our marshlands.

Randy Cole sees it, too, sees the body with skin intact but bones broken. Gone are the great pools of open water that once covered forty acres of the Great Marsh, pools that were nearly always full, replenished twice in twenty-four hours by tidal streams from the great sea, twice left brimming for crowds of rummaging, raucous ducks, their wings striking water again and again before they broke into the air. In recent seasons, Randy has found few breeding birds; the artificial ponds are not working the open water sorcery. The plaster falls from a mural; locusts consume a section of tapestry, taking with it some critical incidents. Consider the ingredients of any tale: Pull one out and the story changes. If John Donne is right, any death diminishes the whole, even the death of an obscure piece of damp ground. It is, in its way, a reservoir of old authority and a link to our own beginnings.

I swat as evening descends. In the low light there is a kind of intense clarity, a last assertion of detail. Then the light withdraws slowly, and the detail wakens, evaporates, bleeds away. The lines of grass dissolve; the hummocks lose their outline, then their form, gradually, almost imperceptibly. There is a graying, a blending, as everything becomes dim, incomprehensible. The first star is out, a white diamond in a sea of night sky.

Robert Finch

Saving the Whales

from *The Presence of Whales*

On Monday morning, September 30, 1991, Kathy Shorr, a friend who works at the Center for Coastal Studies in Provincetown, called to tell me that sixteen pilot whales had just beached themselves on the shore of Cape Cod Bay east of Sesuit Harbor, about a mile from my house. These were the same whales that had tried to beach themselves in Truro the day before, but members of the Cape Cod Stranding Network had managed to push them off before they got in. I do not belong to the Stranding Network, whose members are trained to aid stranded marine animals, so I wasn't expected—actually, might not be allowed—to help; but Kathy asked me if I would watch what was going on and report back to her.

I drove down to the harbor in my pickup truck and found the whales, most of which were clumped on a single stretch of beach, about two hundred yards east of a long rock jetty. Several dozen cetologists and volunteers were already tending to them, while several hundred onlookers crowded behind yellow-tape police barriers staked in the sand. Four of the whales had died, but the rest had been covered with sheets and blankets and were being kept wet with buckets of salt water. The crews had dug shallow pits around them, so that water would seep in. This would help keep them wet and also partially buoyant, so that they would not be suffocated by their own weight.

The whales had first been spotted about 6:00 A.M. by a fisherman on the jetty. It was now about 10:00 A.M., dead low tide, and there would be no chance of refloating them for several hours. I asked a man who seemed to be in charge if anyone from the Center for Coastal Studies was there. He said, "Not yet, but you can help us turn this next whale." He led me over to two whales off by themselves next to the harbor jetty: a young eight-foot whale and a fourteen-foot female, who was thought to be pregnant. She was obviously uncomfortable and very active, thrashing and wedging herself deeper into a puddle. She had already vomited a couple of times, and her torso was cut in several places by the rocks below the sand. The smaller one did not seem to be in very good shape either; it had trouble breathing and remained rather quiet.

This was the first time I had been near live stranded whales, though on several occasions I had seen them dead and watched them being autopsied. I have been ambivalent about the practice of "rescuing" pilot whales. The species has a long history of apparently voluntary strandings on these shores. To the early Cape Codders, these strandings were considered a gift of Providence, supplying them with meat and high-grade whale oil from the rounded "melon" in the front of the whale's head. When a whale herd was spotted coming in, the people around here regularly set out in small boats to "help" the animals ashore. I have a photograph from the 1930s showing several men in my town posing proudly with spearlike flensing knives and standing on the bodies of a couple of dozen stranded pilot whales. The stripped carcasses were buried in the dunes. A few years ago, tides and currents exhumed the whitened skeletons, which tumbled out onto the tidal flats like a xylophone junkyard. Beachcombers picked up some of the vertebrae to use as drink coasters.

For reasons that are not yet clear, pilot whales largely disappeared from local waters after the Depression. But in the mid-1970s they began to show up and strand again. Most strandings occur from September through December. No one knows why these whales strand—though a number of theories have been offered, including mass suicide, the traplike configuration of Cape Cod Bay, and viral brain infections that disrupt the animals' navigational and echolocation systems. Most stranded pilot whales appear healthy, yet even when they are successfully gotten off a beach, more often than not they try to strand somewhere else, as these had.

A lot of time, energy, and money is spent in these rescue efforts, even though there is no clear way of determining their value. Some research scientists seriously doubt that it is a wise use of limited resources, but they are reluctant to say so, since attempts to save the whales give their organizations good publicity, resulting in donations. Others justify the exercise as an opportunity to learn more about the whales' physiology and behavior. For the volunteers, it is certainly interesting and exciting to work with these animals close up; and there is, of course, a kind of guaranteed satisfaction in being part of any group effort working toward a clear, altruistic goal for a limited time.

But the rescue attempts have bothered me not only because it remains unclear whether or not we are actually helping the whales but also because we seem to go at it with the same kind of unexamined certainty with which we used to drive them ashore only a generation or two ago. I find myself suspecting that some of the people who give generously of their time and assets to help whales, spotted owls, or cats could care less about chronic poverty, drug abuse, inner-city violence, Third World hunger—or, for that matter, a neighbor who is alcoholic, depressed, or unemployed. Were we doing something worthwhile here on the beach, or were we just making ourselves feel good while having an undeniably interesting time?

I have harbored these doubts for a while, but this was the first experience I'd had actually working with stranded whales, and it changed my perspective a bit. For whatever reason the whales had stranded, they were obviously in distress. One female had given birth to a stillborn fetus and then had died; I saw the bloody placenta

hanging out of her genital opening. The people who have worked
with them know that, if not seriously injured, the whales do respond
to care—whether or not they are "grateful"—and that given sufficient opportunity they will regroup and swim off, sometimes only
to strand again. In the absence of hard evidence that these efforts are
actually harming the whales, one can argue that it makes sense to err
on the side of compassion.

I spent the next few hours helping to tend our two whales, carrying buckets of water several hundred feet in over the flats, trying
to keep the sheets over them wet, digging out the puddles in which
they lay, and shoveling sand under their heads to prop them up. During this time, each of the twelve surviving whales was measured; a
blood sample was taken from each, and the animals were marked for
future identification by attaching a numbered plastic tag to the trailing edge of the dorsal fin.

I noticed that the whales kept their eyes closed—probably to
keep out sand. They breathed through their blowholes in great puffs
of air and water vapor at uneven intervals. The blowhole is a black,
ribbed, three-inch-wide tube that goes deep into the head cavity.
Each blowhole has a tight-fitting operculum, or cap, that closes between breaths. A few times I got a faceful of whale breath, and, surprisingly, it smelled clean and fresh, like the smell of ozone in the air
after a storm.

It is hard to think of whales as fellow mammals. They seem so artificial and impervious to the touch—cold, wet, slick, and rubbery.
Yet when I was pouring water over the larger whale's tail, I accidentally nicked a fluke lightly with the shovel blade. Bright red blood
began to flow from the cut and pool in the cloudy water around her.
I felt sick. The tail apparently acts as a heat exchanger, so that the
blubber is thin there and the blood close to the surface.

As the tide began to come in, I walked off the beach to go back
to the truck for my waders. In the dunes between the beach and the
harbor was an amazing sight. Over a thousand iridescent blue-green
tree swallows were flocking among the bayberry and goldenrod,

buzzing, perching, then taking off in sudden mass bursts of flight, only to turn around and group again in a kind of constant dynamic cohesiveness, their white bellies flashing, morning light glinting off their shiny backs. It is an old cliché in nature—vibrant, fecund vitality going on indifferently side by side with helpless, pathetic mortality. But I was held there, mesmerized. At such times it seems not that natural and human values are at odds but that nature encompasses our values and goes beyond them, to realms of meaning that we may not be fashioned to comprehend. All we have is our humanity and affinities, and the hope that these may be enough in this world.

During the morning, some staff from the Center for Coastal Studies had arrived, led by Dr. Stormy Mayo. Stormy (he was born on a boat during a coastal storm) is a fifth-generation Provincetown native and the chief cetologist at the center. The tide had turned and was beginning to reach the whales. Stormy and Dan Morast, a cetologist with the International Coalition for Wildlife, decided to move as many of the animals as possible off the beach and into the harbor, so as to be able to maintain them in a calm, deep-water situation, which would give the whales the best chance to reorient themselves and recover before being let go. The move was accomplished by slipping a large plastic stretcher, with holes for the flippers, underneath each whale, then slipping long aluminum poles through the stretcher sides and attaching the stretcher by chains to a large front-end loader, which carried the whale off the flats and over to the boat ramp inside Sesuit Harbor, some five hundred feet from the beach.

This was not as simple as it might sound—especially getting the stretcher under a two-ton whale, which was liable to start thrashing around when it was disturbed—but we managed. The two whales I had been working with were among the first to be taken off the beach. We followed them over, and as the larger whale was lowered into the water, six or seven of us held onto the stretcher to contain her. On the other side of a small pier, another half-dozen workers in wet and dry suits held three of the transported whales upright in a small penning area.

As soon as our whale was in the water, she seemed to sense the other whales nearby and began to get excited, vocalizing with whistles and clicks and trying to get out of the stretcher. All of a sudden, we realized that there was no holding her. She surged forward and dove, swimming beneath a yellow oil-slick boom that had been roped around the penning area. We thought we had lost her, but almost immediately she dove back under the boom and joined the whales in the pen. Pilot whales are extremely social animals, and the strong herding instinct is suspected of having something to do with their mass stranding behavior.

Transporting the whales off the beach continued throughout the afternoon. A parade atmosphere developed as increasing numbers of onlookers lined the route and cheered each passage of the front-end loader with its cradled, dripping cargo. No one knew how long the whales might have to be kept penned. Stormy said it might be all night. For the time being, the people in the water were simply trying to hold the weakened and disoriented whales upright to keep them calm and together, and waiting for decisions. Since I had no wet suit (and in any case wasn't trained in in-water care), I drove back to the house to get a camping stove, some water, pots, coffee, and hot chocolate. When I got back, I went over to the center's van, which had just arrived with more wet suits. David De King, the center's director, asked me, "Do you want to put on a Gumby suit?" Not having the faintest idea what that was, I said, "Sure." A Gumby suit is a bright-orange one-piece foam dry suit with oversize feet, attached mittens, and a hood. Wearing it, one looks and moves remarkably like the gum-eraser character made famous by Eddie Murphy on the old *Saturday Night Live* show.

I staggered down into the water and joined the other suited people and the whales. There were now nine whales in the pen, in three to five feet of water. High water had prevented the front-end loader from getting the last three off the beach, so they had been let go, in the hope that they would make it on their own. Three people were assigned to each whale in the pen, one holding on to each flipper and a third holding on to the tail. By chance, I was assigned to the large female I had cared for on the beach, with two young students from the Massachusetts Maritime Academy, in Buzzards Bay.

By now, the whales seemed to have calmed down considerably. We tried to keep them in a rough circle with their heads together, and we could hear them occasionally vocalizing. Gumby suits are buoyant, made for swimming and floating rather than diving. As the tide continued to rise in the harbor, several of the lighter people were having trouble keeping their balance without weights. Some lost their footing and ended up floating helplessly on their backs, like small children in snowsuits. I had no such trouble, since my left suit-leg had a leak in it, soaking and weighing down my lower half. At intervals, people were asked if they wanted to be spelled, and at one point a woman waded among us feeding us pieces of fudge, as we opened our mouths like nestling birds.

It was now dusk, and Stormy and Dan decided that we would make an attempt to let the whales go. Two of them had been fitted with temporary radio transmitters on their dorsal fins, and all had been fitted with Cyalumes—flexible plastic light sticks—so that they could be tracked out of the harbor after dark. On signal, we released them slowly and stepped back. The whales began to act like a bunch of drunks, bumping into one another, turning over on their stomachs, swimming upside down. Novices like myself were distressed, but apparently this was expected behavior for stranded whales. Stranding skews their balancing mechanisms, much as ours would be if we were hung up by the feet and spun around fast. An initial reorientation period is normal. Some of the whales recovered sooner than others, and it was clear that the former were trying to aid the latter to keep above water. Gradually, they all began to swim normally and to circle together in a clockwise direction. A plastic net hanging from the boom kept them from swimming under it out to sea, and the rest of us stood in the shallow water, pushing them off when they tried to come into shore.

I say "pushing," but it is clear that a whale of that size will do what it wants to. ("Where does a two-ton whale swim?" is the cetacean version of the eight-hundred-pound gorilla joke.) "Guiding them off" would be more accurate. It was then that I began to think of them as horses—large animals that we pretend we can actually control. They moved like a herd of horses in slow motion. They even sounded like horses, with their heavy, throaty bursts of breathing. It was quite a sight: nine large black fusiform shapes with carnival lights attached to their fins, swimming inside a circle of bright-colored human erasers. It really did look like a circus act, and there was a festive and anticipatory sense as Stormy gave the order to move the boom away and let them go.

Just above us, a line of boats had formed across the inner harbor to keep the whales from going farther in. The crews gunned their motors, blew horns, and beat their hulls with oars, and the rest of us shouted and splashed the water in front of us to encourage the whales to head out (precisely the same tactics, though with an opposite end, employed by earlier generations of Cape Codders). At first, they continued to circle, without going beyond where the boom had been. Stormy surmised that they had "learned their containment." Gradually, however, two large males began to lead the others out. We all began to cheer, but after a hundred feet or so the whales became disoriented again and started to swim to the sides of the channel. We regrouped and tried to steer them back to the middle, but they seemed to become more confused and a little panicky.

After a while, it became clear that they were not going to go out of the harbor. It was now totally dark, and the tide was beginning to ebb. I also realized that I had been in cold water for several hours and that my bladder was about to burst. I slogged up onto shore, where I found someone to unzip the top of my suit; then I slogged back out of the glare of the spotlights to relieve myself. When I got back, a decision had been made to close the boom again and let the animals regroup inside the pen. I asked David De King what the thinking was now. He began to explain the options, then stopped and sighed, "Oh, hell! We don't know what we're doing. Nobody's ever had whales contained this way before. We're making it up as we go."

A half hour later, Stormy, Dan, and the other scientists agreed that the whales should be kept overnight and a release tried again at first light. Wet, cold, and tired, I decided I had had enough. Reinforcements had arrived from the Massachusetts Maritime Academy and elsewhere, so I climbed out, shed my thoroughly soaked "dry" suit and handed it to an eager volunteer. When I got back to my pickup, I found that the bed had been commandeered as a general canteen for making coffee, soup, and sandwiches, so I left it there and called my wife to come pick me up. It was now 9:30. A warm bath and a can of Dinty Moore later, I felt very pleased with myself and slept well till 6:00 A.M., when Kathy Shorr showed up at the door to ask if I wanted to come down to see them let the whales go. I did.

For a while, it looked once again as though the whales wouldn't get the idea, but then they began to move purposefully out into the channel and headed toward the open water of Cape Cod Bay. This time we withheld our cheers and walked beside them cautiously, apprehensively, all the way out to the end of the rock jetty. A crew from the center followed them out of the harbor entrance in a Zodiac (a powered rubber raft), and soon both the whales and the raft were out of sight. We walked back, nourishing a tentative sense of finality and accomplishment, but the most anyone would say was "Keep your fingers crossed." Later that morning, the Zodiac radioed in that the three whales that had been let go off the beach the afternoon before had rejoined the pod, and that they were all swimming off into deep water.

In the next three days, the pod stranded three more times, in Yarmouth and Barnstable, the next towns over. Six more died. The volunteers and the staff were exhausted, but they felt they had to keep trying as long as there was a chance for a viable group to survive. The remaining six were pushed off a marsh at Old Wharf Lane in Yarmouthport a day later. After that they were not seen again.

Marcia Bonta

October

from *Appalachian Autumn*

It comes quietly as mist in the night, but it doesn't vanish as the sun rises. It remains, stronger day after day. It spreads, leaf to leaf, branch to branch, tree to tree. It climbs from the valley to the hilltop. Soon it will possess the countryside. . . . We sum it all up in two words: The Color.
Hal Borland, *Twelve Moons of the Year*

OCTOBER 1. I had to be away for the entire day with Bruce and Steve, something I really did not want to do when I'm keeping a full chronicle of the autumn. Then, coming home near dark, Bruce found that our new lock had been smashed and left lying on our gate latch.

We had originally put up the gate at the bottom of the hollow to keep out "midnight dumpers" who had several times deposited household trash, including an old television set, in our stream. In the first year, the gate had been vandalized a number of times until, one day, it was stolen altogether. Some friends had helped us put in a sturdy, steel, vandal-proof gate, but we could not find a vandal-proof lock. The previous lock had been smashed in July, and oddly enough that one was also left on top of the gate latch, like an offering to appease us.

As we drove up the hollow, Bruce recalled that when our friend had talked with the lumberman about buying the property earlier in the summer, the lumberman had mentioned prospective buyers who had looked at the land in July. Since that was about when we found the previously smashed lock, Steve immediately concluded that the lumberman was responsible for both broken locks. But I refused to believe it. Despite our difference of opinion concerning logging, he seemed to be an honorable, law-abiding man. Surely he would not stoop to vandalism: Steve admitted he didn't know him as well as I did, but he stuck to his opinion. Bruce was ambivalent and did not know what to believe.

OCTOBER 2. We pondered the question overnight, discouraged that once again we would have to buy a new lock and supply keys to emergency crews, friends, and utility companies, as we had done so many times over the past five years.

This beautiful autumn morning I sat outside on the veranda drinking coffee and heard what sounded like a bulldozer over on our lumberman-neighbor's land, so I walked down to the fork in our road to see if I could figure out what was happening. I could see nothing as I looked up at Margaret's derelict house, but it sounded as if the bulldozer was going back down the ridge along the access road the lumberman had built.

When I got back to the house, the telephone was ringing. It was Bruce calling from town. He and Steve had encountered the lumberman's son driving up the road, and he admitted he had smashed the lock yesterday so that he could get a logging crew up the road. Steve had been right after all.

Bruce asked me to call the state police and have them send a trooper to meet us at the gate to file a report. Then I drove down the hollow with the smashed lock. The lumberman's son stuck around and admitted to the trooper he had done it—with only three hammer blows, he said, adding that it was amazing how cheaply locks were made today. The whole scene was weird. Bruce said that he was going to put another lock on the gate, but he urged the son to tell his father that he really wanted to resolve the issues between us.

Why didn't his father return calls? Why didn't he respond to letters? The man looked uncomfortable.

"Did your father tell you to smash the lock?" Bruce asked.

"He told me to get through the gate in any way I could," he responded. He also claimed that his father had ordered him and the rest of the crew to stay 200 feet above the road, using the Lower Road as a rough boundary line. Furthermore, he admitted that they had access to their work site along their haul road through the neighbor's property, but using the hollow road was faster and easier.

Bruce asked the trooper if we could press charges—perhaps that would prompt the lumberman to respond to our concerns—and the trooper agreed. Then, to our surprise, the son suddenly stuck out his hand to Bruce and said he hoped there weren't any hard feelings! Bruce obligingly shook his hand, but he repeated to him that he hoped his father would deal with the issues and answer his letters. And so we left it.

But my peace of mind was blown away. After six years of changing their story, what was really going to happen? Once they had offered to sell the land to us; then they wouldn't. Next they said they were only going to remove the trees killed by gypsy moths. That statement was amended to include all trees over twelve inches in diameter. Now will they even stick to the careful, selective cut they had promised so often, I wondered. Will they respect the 200-foot boundary they agreed upon almost two years ago? Will the lumberman ever confirm that agreement with us?

But in my heart I already suspect what will happen. After so many false starts and threats, this time they mean to totally clear out their property. The beautiful hollow will be destroyed and perhaps the road as well. All those wonderful areas I found last winter, particularly the large trees on the wilderness knoll, will be gone in a few weeks. Autumn, it seems, is the season of rapine around here, which makes it difficult to appreciate the beauty.

Suddenly, autumn has become a time of intense sorrow for me. The brilliant leaf colors seem to symbolize the final flare before the inevitable end—a bright flame, consuming itself like a candle, leaving nothing but a burnt-out, trashed, and dying earth.

To escape the scream of chain saws and skidders, I walked this afternoon to my usual refuge—the Far Field Road. Gray squirrels fed as I sat and watched, soothing my spirits as they went about their business, unperturbed by my presence. Walking back on the Far Field Trail, I saw an ovenbird fly across in front of me and land on a log where it skulked along on its long, elegant, pink legs in usual ovenbird fashion.

Then, as I descended First Field through the locust grove, I heard a high-pitched "cree-cree-cree-cree." An osprey circled above me, a fish clasped in its talons, both fish and osprey facing in the same direction. The raptor made several passes over the field before it flew to a tree branch on Sapsucker Ridge where it stood and looked around silently while I sat down in the locust grove and watched it through my binoculars. Its white head and black eye stripe gleamed in the sunlight, and it looked almost as if a black hood extended down the back of its neck. Whenever a pileated woodpecker called, the osprey glanced around alertly, but otherwise it sat there quietly, looking off into the distance and completely ignoring the fish in its talons.

I felt a hushed charm as I kept it company, but after half an hour I finally broke the spell by trying to see how close I could get to the osprey before it flew. As I walked nearer, it began calling again. Leaning forward, it gave me an excellent view of its snowy underparts. At last it flew directly overhead, still holding the brown fish, probably a trout from the river at the base of our mountain. Then it was off over Laurel Ridge, gone from view in a few seconds, having given me my closest and longest encounter ever with an osprey.

OCTOBER 3. The first "snowbirds" returned today, fluttering down on our driveway and flashing their white and gray tail feathers. Otherwise known as dark-eyed juncos (*Junco hyemalis*), they spend the spring and summer farther north in the cool forests of Canada and

Alaska or in the high Appalachians as far south as northern Georgia. Although they prefer to court and raise their families in hemlock-studded ravines in northern and western Pennsylvania, I have never found any in our hemlock-lined hollow during the spring and summer months. For that reason, I think of them as winter birds along with American tree sparrows, pine siskins, and evening grosbeaks.

Their color pattern is often described as "leaden skies above, snow below," referring to their dark gray heads and backs and white bellies, a striking combination that dulls into touches of brown in both the juveniles and females. But all dark-eyed juncos possess distinctive white outer tail feathers. Juncos are feeder birds, although they usually scratch on the ground beneath instead of landing on my hanging feeder. Since they prefer brushy edge habitats for winter feeding, they spend much of their time in the grape tangle below our back porch, less than six feet away from the seed that spills from the feeder.

Those first arrivals probably wintered here last year, and their presence will attract more migrants. By early December a whole flock of dark-eyed juncos, with a fixed foraging range, will be assembled on our grounds for the winter. So I can be almost certain that the birds at my feeder at the same ones from day to day.

The flock will not always travel together, but it will respect the boundary lines of other foraging flocks. Researchers have found that all members of a single flock do recognize each other and have a definite, quite simple pecking order. The kingpin is A, who is dominant over B and all others, while B is dominant over C and all others, and so on down the alphabet. Dominant birds peck at or chase the subordinates. They may also stretch out their bodies, close their bills, and bob their heads up and down, actions that anyone watching a bird feeder can observe.

The subordinate birds are those that always fly off quickly when other juncos, presumably the dominant ones, come in for food. Sometimes they do fight, either by running at a rival on the ground or by flying up into the air, face to face. Apparently, sex does not determine the pecking order; females have often been observed driving males from feeders.

Back in 1957, Winifred S. Sabine of Ithaca, New York, reported in *The Auk,* journal of the American Ornithologists' Union, that after their last feeding foray of the day, dark-eyed juncos always left in a regular pattern. Each bird would finish eating, pause for a moment or two, then join the rest of the flock in an arbor vitae bush forty feet away. When all were assembled they flew off together in the same direction toward their common night roost—in dense evergreens, thickets, or brush piles.

For years our feeder juncos preferred a thick barberry hedge, between the shed and guesthouse, which twittered with disturbed birds whenever we passed at dusk. There were many old bird nests to sleep in and impenetrable thorns to keep predators out, so they had a safe spot to drowse away the long, cold nights. Then, the small juniper bush we planted in the herb garden, less than ten feet away from the feeder, shot up to ten feet and became the juncos' new night roost. They never fly in there just once every evening, however. Instead, they go in and out, adjusting and readjusting their positions until the bush is fairly bursting with juncos. Watching them from the hall window a foot away provides great entertainment.

The juncos that do not come to our feeder but do spend the winter on the mountain, and there can be several hundred of them, head for the Norway spruce grove at the top of First Field. One winter day near dusk I sat quietly in the midst of several large trees. Juncos zipped in one by one, more and more as the light faded. Many circled above my head. Others retreated just before slamming into me and then sat on nearby branches to scold. Judging from the feces dotting the limbs around me, I was sitting close to a favorite roosting spot. Finally, I stood up and walked away so they could settle onto their rightful branches before dark. Juncos, like many people, are creatures of habit, and to disturb them is to endanger their survival. Once the colors of autumn have faded and all the migrant birds have gone, dark-eyed juncos come into their own. To hear their twitters and trills, to watch them scratch beneath the feeder, to see them on a snowy morning is to appreciate their indomitable spirits.

OCTOBER 4. The skidder was screaming away shortly after 8:00 A.M., the chain saws providing a growling undertone, while the crash of enormous trees reverberated from ridgetop to ridgetop, as if the falling trees were a few yards away. Weary and depressed, I fled to the Far Field to sit with my back against a huge wild black cherry tree and enjoy the peace.

I heard behind me a running animal and assumed it was another gray squirrel, but I remained motionless, hoping it would come near. The animal passed within a foot of me, still running hard, reached the edge of the field, veered left, ran as far as the beginning of a locust grove, turned around for a few seconds in my direction, and then trotted off into the tall weeds of the Far Field. It was, to my utter shock and startlement, a gray fox! I could have reached out and grabbed it had I thought it was anything other than chasing squirrels. Once again this peaceful haven, far from the sounds of lumbering, offered me sudden joy as an antidote for my gloomy thoughts.

The autumn color is glorious this year. Deep gold spicebushes are covered with shiny red berries. The blueberry shrubs on the power-line right-of-way have turned a deep reddish purple. The black gum trees glow in shades of pink, rose, red, and reddish purple, creating an understory haze of color along Laurel Ridge.

Although poets praise the autumnal beauty of New England's sugar maples, no one, so far as I can determine, has similarly immortalized the color of Pennsylvania's black gum trees. Yet despite their plain oval leaves, black gums decked out in Burgundy red are as brilliant as sugar maples. However, they reach their peak nearly a month before most trees color.

Scientists, who are always asking why, have known for years that certain trees, shrubs, and vines take on vibrant hues a full month be-

fore the majority of the woody plants withdraw the green chlorophyll from their leaves. And they can easily explain how color change
occurs in all deciduous growth.

But they have been unable to agree on why some plants change
color weeks before others, flooding their leaves with the enzyme that
breaks down chlorophyll and transports certain chemicals, such as
nitrogen and magnesium, out of the leaves before they drop. This
process unveils the red, orange, yellow, and brown pigments that
have been in the leaves all along and gives our Appalachian forests
their worldwide reputation for flaming color.

Black gum, also known as sour gum, black tupelo, and pepper-
idge, favors swampy woods, hence its lyrical scientific name—*Nyssa
sylvatica,* meaning "water nymph of the forest." But according to
William Carey Grimm's *The Trees of Pennsylvania,* black gum trees are
also common on dry mountain ridges, burned-over forests, and
abandoned fields. Because their heartwood rots early, they are primarily understory trees with an average height of thirty to forty feet.

Here on our dry Appalachian mountaintop, occasional black gum
leaves turn red in late August, and by early September the understory is aflame with them. Hidden beneath their flamboyantly colored leaves are small clusters of half-inch long, bluish black fruits.
Two other understory species that color early are flowering dogwood
and sassafras. Flowering dogwood has leaves that are primarily purplish red and showy clusters of red fruit, while sassafras has yellow
and red leaves and dark blue, shiny fruits, each of which grows on a
club-shaped, bright red stalk.

At the same time, Virginia creeper, sporting flat-topped clusters
of bluish black fruits, entwines both dead and living trees with ropes
of scarlet, and wild grapevines, bearing compact clumps of purplish
berries, smother our thickets in molten gold. The spicebushes lining
our stream are covered with bright yellow leaves and clusters of red
fruits, and the poison ivy that grows in our old corral has leaves ranging in color from yellow and orange to red and produces creamy
white, small, berrylike clusters of fruit. The occasional staghorn su-

mac shrubs at the edge of First Field also turn color early, displaying a deep red to match their five- to eight-inch-long, erect, conical fruit clusters.

Several years ago, Edmund W. Stiles, a biologist at Rutgers University, offered a plausible explanation of early leaf coloring. He had been studying wild fruits and their relationship to birds as consumers and seed dispersers and had discovered that in the summer, when birds lay eggs, grow new feathers, and raise their families, they seem to prefer eating high protein insects. During those times, small fruits such as blueberries, blackberries, and cherries that are high in sugars and other carbohydrates are a second food choice.

But with the onset of migration in late summer, birds begin looking for foods that are high in lipids, or fats, presumably to fuel their long flights. At the same time, many of the plants bearing fat-rich fruits turn color. Furthermore, seasonal bird migrators do include such major fruit-eating species as American robins, cedar waxwings, eastern bluebirds, veeries, brown thrashers, gray catbirds, and hermit, Swainson's, gray-cheeked, and wood thrushes.

Stiles points out that migrating birds are moving through new territory and are not familiar with food sources available along the way. So he hypothesizes that the contrast of colored leaves against a mostly still green forest signals the presence of food to the birds. Hence he has coined a new term for plants that turn color early and coincidentally also have ripe fruit. He calls them "foliar fruit flags." Not surprisingly, the prominent members of this group in the Pennsylvania Appalachians are black gum, flowering dogwood, sassafras, spicebush, Virginia creeper, poison ivy, sumac, and wild grape.

Are those plants signaling to fruit-eating bird migrators the presence of food? Because they have fruits with seeds that need to be dispersed by birds, it seems a likely explanation.

Moreover, the fruit of spicebush, flowering dogwood, black gum, and sassafras are uniformly high in lipids, so the birds are doing themselves a favor by rapidly consuming them. The birds also perform a service for those plants, because fruits high in lipids rot quickly. For that reason they need to be eaten relatively soon and then passed through the birds' digestive systems while the seeds are still viable.

Many foliar fruit flag plants have another characteristic in common. With the exception of sumac and flowering dogwood, their berries are inconspicious and hidden by leaves. So without their colored leaves, the birds might not see the fruit. In addition, the fruiting vines, Stiles maintains, are especially difficult to spot when they are green and twining along trunks and tree branches or vining on the ground in the weeds and grasses. But when the vines turn color, they are strikingly beautiful and easy to see.

So, if Stiles is right, bird migration, plant dispersal, and early leaf color are linked together, demonstrating once again that in nature everything is connected to everything else, in intricate and often little-understood ways, producing a finely tuned system that has continued to evolve over the millennia. To destroy even one link may be disastrous to an entire system. Probably it is only incidental that such processes as leaf color, early or late, also present a feast for humans' eyes and a boost to their spirits.

OCTOBER 5. A flock of American robins came into the yard this morning, and the eastern bluebirds were back and calling, having raised their two families in our bluebird box and then disappeared for a month or so. Since they do this every year, I never worry about them, knowing that they will return, often with friends, to grace the latter days of autumn with their color.

It was warm enough to have our Saturday breakfast on the front porch, and little birds called from the treetops still hidden by leaves. But later, the slightest breeze set the black walnut leaves whirling through the air like a shower of golden confetti. Already the black walnuts in the front yard are naked while the backyard trees are still half-clothed but shedding fast—the last to leaf out in the spring, the first to lose their leaves in the fall, they are more often leafless than leaved in a year.

Since the lumberman and his forester had repeatedly invited us to inspect their work, Bruce and I decided to walk over and take a look. They have bulldozed their way far along the ridgetop and have cut magnificent, huge, 150-year-old red oak trees all the way. Two new roads have been built straight down the steep mountainside, one connected to the Upper Road, the other aiming for the end of the Upper Road where the wonderful knoll of huge trees is—my wilderness grove discovery of last winter. The roads were deep in dry soil, and my boots were as dusty as if I had been walking in the Peruvian desert. The ridge was hot and open now to the burning sun. Much of the ridge road was rocky, the earth quickly scraped away from the soil-thin mountaintop. So many years to build a little soil up there; a few minutes with a bulldozer to destroy it.

Mosquitoes, more than I had seen all summer, rose in clouds from the freshly churned-up dirt. Altogether, what has been done so far is a lesson in devastation. Our one hope is that they may cut only the largest trees and let the rest alone. But the destruction to the soil and to the smaller shrubs, trees, and creatures underneath the bulldozer and skidder is incredibly wasteful. If we have torrential rains, a good portion of what little soil there is will wash away down the mountainside.

So much scarring of the natural world for profit, so little beauty left to nourish the spirit, not only here but throughout the world. Is that why people have less and less spirituality and more and more worship of materialism in their lives no matter what their formal ties to religion are?

By afternoon, back on our own property, the day glowed, activating birds into song and causing butterflies to beat against the windows—the kind of gleaming day more often dreamed of than experienced. I put our morning horror show behind me and faced into the warm wind, streaming with falling leaves. A male American kestrel sat on the telephone wire directly above the bluebird box. He looked small and polite and shy as he peered around—a quiet, seemingly unpredatory creature as serene as the afternoon. The fields sizzled and popped with grasshoppers, crickets, and katydids. Patches of late goldenrod still gleamed and attracted the dozens and dozens of migrating monarchs fluttering over the mountaintop.

I stood on top of Laurel Ridge and watched them as they came out of the northeast, up and over the powerline right-of-way and down into our goldenrod-covered First Field to make a short nectaring stop before heading purposefully south. Because monarch butterflies originated in a warmer climate, they cannot tolerate any long periods of cold weather. Instead of adapting to the cold, they flee from it like so many of our birds do.

A monarch butterfly begins its life as a minute, pearly egg laid by a female on a freshly emerging leaf or flower bud of one of the 108 species of milkweed growing in North America. Milkweed is its larval food as a caterpillar, and each larva requires a large number of leaves to complete its development. To reduce the competition, as soon as a caterpillar hatches, it immediately eats any other eggs it finds on its milkweed. Then it feeds on the milkweed until it pupates. In a short time it makes its final transition into an adult. This whole process from egg to adult takes between three and five weeks, depending on the temperature, and produces up to three and possibly four generations of monarch butterflies by the end of summer.

But, by then, a change has occurred. The last generation of monarchs in mid-August is so influenced by the decreased day length and colder night temperatures that their neuroendocrine systems produce a juvenile hormone. This hormone represses the mating urge in the male and egg production in the female, a state known as reproductive diapause, a period of reproductive dormancy. Not only do the adult ovaries and testes of the butterflies remain immature, but the butterflies are not interested in sex or milkweeds, and the process of aging is greatly slowed down. Instead of using their energies to produce another generation, they begin to feed heavily on the nectar of fall composite flowers. In addition, they join in social nectaring assemblages during the day and form temporary clusters at night. One August I observed a few small clusters hanging from our black walnut trees, but during migration, which usually begins in mid-September, I see only solitary butterflies.

Like migrating birds, monarchs also need lipids (fats) to give them energy not only before but during their migration. They obtain them through drinking flower nectar which they convert and store in a specialized fat body, an abdominal organ similar to our liver. As they near their wintering ground, they store even more lipids, since wild-flowers at those wintering sites deteriorate and can't provide enough nectar for the butterflies.

Since 1930 scientists had known that monarchs migrate and, in fact, large clusters of western North American monarchs spend their winters clinging to favorite trees in about forty California sites along the coastline from north of San Francisco to south of Los Angeles, the most famous being in Pacific Grove. A few smaller assemblages had also been discovered in Florida, presumably a portion of the monarchs from the northeastern United States and Canada. Where, though, did the majority of the eastern monarch butterflies winter?

Fred A. Urquhart of Scarborough College in Toronto was determined to find out. In 1952 he formed the Insect Migration Association, and interested people tagged monarchs by the thousands. From those that were later recovered, they learned that almost all male monarchs die on their way back north in the spring and that monarchs do not fly at night. But their most interesting discovery was that most eastern monarchs migrate from the Northeast to the Southwest, converging on Texas. However, the butterflies could be seen flying farther south, convincing Urquhart that their destination was somewhere in central Mexico.

In 1973 he advertised in a Mexico City newspaper, asking for help in locating the overwintering home of the eastern monarch butterflies. Ken Brugger, an American living in Mexico, responded. In his van, accompanied by his new Mexican bride, he crisscrossed central Mexico for two winters, talking to herders who kept cattle in the Sierra Madre. At last, on January 9, 1975, responding to a local rumor, he discovered *millions* of monarch butterflies on a twenty-acre site in the mountains. They were clinging to Oyamel fir trees that grow at an elevation of 9,000 feet. As one naturalist later wrote, "The clusters . . . sculptured the Mexican highlands into pulsating cathedrals of tiny stained glass windows."

Fred Urquhart was elated. With the help of Brugger, he had finally found the major wintering grounds of the eastern monarch butterflies. For some of those butterflies it is a twenty-four-hundred-mile migration, and when they reach central Mexico, they cling to trees in a semidormant state for most of the winter. This conserves their body heat, since temperatures in the area range from below to just above freezing. To see them then is a wondrous sight. Lincoln Brower, a scientist who has been studying monarch butterflies for many years, described it as "a wall of butterflies. Great draperies hung over the branches, turning them into giant feather dusters, and the trunks were softly wrapped with tightly packed rows of thousands of monarchs clinging to each other and to the bark."

In February, when the temperature begins to rise, the mating and egg production hormones kick in again, and at least some of the butterflies mate at their wintering grounds. They leave the overwintering sites from the middle to the end of March, flying rapidly northeast into the southern United States and continuing courtship and mating along the migration routes and after they arrive in the southern states. According to Brower, the spring recolonization of eastern North America by monarch butterflies is a two-step process. First the overwintering butterflies breed in the south and produce a new generation. It is that generation which continues the migration north when it becomes too hot, in mid-June, for another generation to develop successfully there.

This leads to another monarch mystery that has still to be solved. The monarchs that migrate in autumn are not the same ones that returned from the south. How do they find their way? All scientists can say is that the urge to migrate has to be inherited and that the migration itself involves orientational and navigational responses to unknown cues which can lead the butterflies all the way from Maine to approximately twelve small relict Oyamel fir forests in the remote mountains of central Mexico, seventy-five miles west of Mexico City.

Life is not easy on their wintering grounds, however. Two species of birds, the black-headed grosbeak and the black-backed oriole, eat thousands a day during clear and warm weather. But the weather is not always warm and clear. When it drops below freezing, many monarchs die. Fifty percent perish when their body temperature is lowered to 18 degrees Fahrenheit and 100 percent at 5 degrees. Sometimes storms last for days, and at such times the ground is littered with dead and dying butterflies.

But as is true everywhere today, the greatest threats to monarch butterfly survival, both in Mexico and California, are caused by humanity. In Mexico people press further and further into the mountains in search of land to graze their cattle and wood to cut for fuel and profits; in California it is real estate development that threatens the remaining sites, several of which have already been destroyed. Lately, Mexico has moved strongly to protect its sites, led by Mexican conservationists. Similar efforts have been launched in California.

I hope they will succeed. If I never get to Mexico to see them in their overwintering sites, I can at least look forward to a continual feast of monarch butterfly beauty during their summer and early autumn time here on our mountain.

Edward O. Wilson

The Florida Keys Experiment

from *Naturalist*

Where could we find more Krakatuas?

That question dominated my thought for months after Mac-Arthur and I published our first article on island biogeography in 1963. We had conjured a plausible image of the dynamic equilibrium of species, with new colonists balancing the old residents that become extinct, but we could offer very little direct evidence. There are few places in the world where biologists can study the approach to equilibrium on a large scale. Krakatau-sized events, the sterilization of islands the size of Manhattan or larger by volcanic explosions, occur at most once a century. Another hundred years might then be needed, once the smoking tephra cooled down, to observe the full course of recolonization. How might we get data more quickly, say within ten years?

I brooded over the problem, imagined scenarios of many kinds, and finally came up with the solution: a *laboratory* of island biogeography. We needed an archipelago where little Krakatuas could be created at will and their recolonization watched at leisure.

My dream embraced more than the search for new experiments

in biogeography. I was driven by a more general need to return to the field, to enjoy once again the hands-on kinesthetic pleasures of my youth. I wanted to remain an opportunist, moving among, seeing, and touching a myriad of plants and animals. I needed a place to which I could return for the rest of my life and possess as a naturalist and scientist.

It would have to be a different location and context from those previously enjoyed. I couldn't return to New Guinea to launch my endeavor. Work there would take me for months at a time away from Cambridge, where my duties at Harvard held me tightly. I had also begun experimental work on the social behavior of ants that required a well-equipped laboratory. They were proving too successful to abandon. Not least, I had a family now, Renee and our new daughter, Catherine.

How in the world could I explore an island wilderness while staying close to home? And if I found such a place, how could I turn it into a laboratory? There was only one way to solve the problem: *miniaturize* the system! Instead of relying on conventional islands the size of Krakatau, which are hundreds of square kilometers in area and usually have people living on them, why not use tiny ones, at most a few hundred square meters? Of course such places do not support resident populations of mammals, birds, or any other land vertebrates above the size of small lizards. Vertebrate biologists would not call them islands at all, even in a limited ecological sense. Yet they sustain large breeding populations of insects, spiders, and other arthropods. To an ant or spider one-millionth the size of a deer, a single tree is like a whole forest. The lifetime of such a creature can be spent in a microterritory the size of a dinner plate. Once I revised my scale of vision downward this way, I realized that there are thousands of such miniature islands in the United States, sprinkled along the coasts as well as inland in the midst of lakes and streams.

I thought I had the perfect solution. By exploring such places I would satisfy my emotional and intellectual needs. Working with insects, the organisms I knew best, I could conduct biogeographic research on an accelerated schedule. Succeed or fail, I would stay close to Harvard and my family.

In choosing the site of my laboratory, I preferred marine waters over lakes and rivers—strictly an aesthetic choice. I pored over maps of fringing islands all along the Atlantic and Gulf coasts, from Quoddy Head State Park in down-easternmost Maine to the Padre Island National Seashore in southernmost Texas. I also studied charts of the small islands around Puerto Rico, still a relatively quick jet flight away. A decisive winner quickly emerged: the Florida Keys, if combined with the nearby northern islands of Florida Bay and the southwest mainland coast, seemed ideal. I turned to more detailed navigational charts and photographs for a closer look. The islands came in all sizes, from single trees to sizable expanses up to a square kilometer or more. They varied in degrees of isolation from a few meters to hundreds of meters from the nearest neighbor. The forests on them were simple, consisting in most cases entirely of red mangrove trees. And they were available in vast numbers. One sprawling miniature archipelago west of the Everglades bore the suggestive name Ten Thousand Islands. Almost all of them could be reached in a single day, if you started with an early four-hour flight from Boston to Miami, drove a rental car down U.S. 1 to the Keys, and finally took a short boat trip out to the island of choice.

In June 1965 I flew to Miami to enter my new island world. I was accompanied by Renee and Cathy—now twenty months old, walking, talking, and pulling down every movable object. For ten weeks I explored the small bayside mangrove keys from along Stock Island and Sugarloaf north to Key Largo. My spirits soared. I was back where I was meant to be! Each morning I pushed away from a marine dock in a rented fourteen-foot boat with outboard motor and moved out along the channels that had been cut through the mangrove swamps to the open waters of Florida Bay. I visited one islet after another, passing over turtle grass flats in water sometimes clear and sometimes, especially on windy days, milky white from the churned-up bottom marl. Once or twice a day I saw a distant fisherman or a

powerboat moving to deeper water, but into the swampy archipelagoes of my choice few other people ventured. Less than a mile away
U.S. 1, which runs the length of the Keys to their southernmost
point at Key West, was choked by traffic. It was lined by a noisome
thicket of motels, trailer parks, amusement parks, marinas, fishing
tackle shops, and fast-food restaurants. But beyond hearing range of
the rumble and whine of traffic, the swamps and islets were pristine,
a virgin wilderness. Mangrove wood has little commercial value. No
one but a naturalist or escaped convict would choose to traverse the
gluelike mud flats and climb through the tangled prop roots and
trunks of the mangrove trees. So I had it all to myself: one more time,
a world I knew so well, more complex and beautiful than anything
contrived by human enterprise.

I pushed into the interiors of the islets to examine the arthropod
inhabitants. Sometimes the little forests opened at the center into a
slightly raised glade carpeted with aerial roots and algal mats. Sometimes I found myself beneath the massed nests of clamoring herons,
egrets, and white-crowned pigeons. I drifted along from landfall to
landfall, collecting specimens, studying charts, filling my notebook
with impressions. Mine was anything but a world-class voyage, but
I was as content as Darwin on the voyage of H.M.S. *Beagle*. I ate lunch
in the boat while peering over the side at rich marine life along the
edge of the islets. Just beneath the reach of low tide, the mangrove
prop roots were covered by masses of barnacles, sea squirts, anem-
ones, clams, and green and red algae. Schools of mangrove snappers
and young barracuda prowled in and out of the root interstices and
alga-slimed cavities of the mudbanks. Should I have become a marine
biologist? Too late to think about that now. I was at peace. The only
sounds I heard were the call of birds and the slap of waves against
the hull of my boat. An occasional jet droned high above, to remind
me, you'll come back, dreamer, your life depends on those artifacts
you've tried to escape.

I found what I had come for in the mangrove islets. The trees
swarmed with scores of species of small creatures: ants, spiders,

mites, centipedes, bark lice, crickets, moth caterpillars, and other arthropods. Many flourished in breeding populations, prerequisites for the establishment of an experimental biogeography. And from one mangrove clump to the next, the species changed. For ants the pattern was consistent with competitive exclusion. Below a certain island size, the colonization of some species appeared to preclude the establishment of others. I saw an opportunity in the study of these telescoped patterns. Instead of traveling great distances from one Pacific Island to another to study the distribution of birds, an effort requiring months or years, I could, by guiding a fourteen-footer among the islets, analyze the distribution of arthropods in a period of days or weeks.

How, then, might these mangrove dots be turned into little Krakataus? I saw no easy way, and cast about for some alternative approach. I made the following decision: continue with the mangrove studies, but in addition select other islands lacking trees in order to make sterilization easier. I had learned that treeless sandy islands in the nearby Dry Tortugas are occasionally flooded and swept clean of their low scrubby plant growth by hurricanes. If I could monitor them before and after a big storm, I might observe the recolonization process and establish whether it created an equilibrium. Let the Caribbean's stormy weather be the volcano. At least it was worth a try.

I called on William Robertson, official naturalist of the Everglades National Park, to explain my idea. Bill frequently visited the Dry Tortugas to study sooty terns, a far-ranging species that nests on this remotest of Florida's archipelagoes. He agreed that the procedure might work, and invited me to join his research party on the next boat trip out from the docks at the Everglades town of Flamingo to survey the area. Once settled in dungeonlike rooms at Fort Jefferson, the old Federal stronghold and prison on Garden Key, we took a smaller boat out to the other, smaller islands of the Dry Tortugas. I leaped into the surf and scrambled onto each of the little sandy keys in turn, making a record of the sparse vegetation and arthropods. My notebook was soon complete. All I had to do now was wait for a serious hurricane to pass over in order to begin a study of recolonization.

Providentially, from a biologist's possibly perverse point of view, two hurricanes struck the Dry Tortugas during the next ten months. Betsy, on September 8, 1965, threw gusts up to 125 miles per hour at Fort Jefferson. The milder Alma attained gale force winds on June 8, 1966. Between them they wiped the vegetation off the smallest sandy islands, as I had hoped. By that time, however, I had changed my plan and advanced to a bolder scheme. Why be confined to the haphazard distribution of a few remote keys? And why depend on the passing of hurricanes, which normally strike the Dry Tortugas only once or twice every ten years? The method was in any case not fully experimental. It could not be controlled. Instead, I thought, why not select ideally located mangrove keys from among the hundreds near U.S. 1, then fumigate them with pesticides? It should be possible to kill off all the insects and other arthropods. These islets could be chosen to represent different sizes as well as various distances away from the mainland. Other islets, left unfumigated but otherwise studied in identical fashion, might serve as controls.

At this point, the fall of 1965, Daniel Simberloff joined me as a collaborator. The added vision and inspired effort of this second-year graduate student made it possible to turn the mangrove keys into a laboratory. Dan was primed for an effort of this kind. While an undergraduate at Harvard he had majored in mathematics, graduating magna cum laude. He could have moved on easily to a successful career in mathematics or the physical sciences. But after taking Natural Sciences 5, the famous nonmajors course in biology given by George Wald, he decided this branch of science was more to his liking. During his senior year he interviewed Bill Bossert and me and asked: Is graduate study in biology feasible if one has a stout heart but thin undergraduate training in that subject? Indeed it was, we both responded, especially for a mathematician. If you enter population biology now, the new discipline will reward skills in model building and quantitative analysis. All you need to do is add an all-out effort in biological training.

Simberloff began his Ph.D. study under my sponsorship in the fall of 1964. I hesitate to use the usual expression "studied under me," because in the years to follow I learned as much from him as he did from me. We soon became partners.

Dan at least looked as though he could manage field biology. With somewhat hawkish features, a solid muscular body carried in a relaxed slouch, he might have passed for the kind of Ivy League quarterback who studies calculus or Chinese history too conscientiously to be an athletic star. Like many bright students of the day he was also a leftist radical, of the thinker rather than activist subspecies, suspicious of all authority and fierce enough to be a supporter of Eldridge Cleaver for President. This was quite all right with me. In 1965 the civil rights movement still meant idealism and courage tested on the dangerous back roads of Mississippi. The mere mention of Cuba, recently the site of history's only nuclear confrontation, chilled us both; and the war in Vietnam was slowly gathering momentum. The Florida Keys were bracketed by bases at Homestead and Key West, and the whole area hummed with military activity. That summer I saw my first Green Berets, a platoon riding through the streets of Key West in a troop carrier. My admiration for the military and my vaguely centrist political beliefs were yielding somewhat to uneasiness over the direction the country was headed. Soon Dan and I began to share acerbic jokes about Lyndon Johnson. We watched in resentment as helicopters flew overhead, bearing commanding officers from ships to their homes ashore. We perched on the branches of mangrove trees, collecting spiders and crickets, on a nearly invisible budget, trying to learn how ecosystems are assembled. A dozen helicopter rides would have paid for our entire project. But not one citizen in a hundred would have understood what we were trying to do. It was a time of massive imbalance in favor of military security over environmental security. We had no idea how or when the differential might be redressed, nor did we expect ever to see ecology given national priority as a science. We were just thankful for the opportunity provided us by modest funding from the National Science Foundation. And thankful just to be there, in this beautiful natural environment.

By joining the project, Dan took a career risk. Our endeavor had an uncertain future, because no one had previously tried or even conceived anything like it. If we were unable to eliminate the arthropods completely from the islets, we would be in trouble. If we failed to put scientific names on the myriad of species we found on the islands, our data would be far less valuable. If the colonization of the sterilized islands took ten or twenty years or longer to progress significantly, Dan would have to find other work to complete his Ph.D. thesis. Graduate students were expected to finish their degree requirements, including a complete and reasonably well polished research thesis, in no more than six or seven years. Most accepted low-risk projects, those new enough to generate significant results but close enough to preexisting knowledge and proven techniques to be practicable. Simberloff had none of these assurances. In September 1965 he nonetheless departed for the Florida Keys, with the initial task of selecting the experimental islets.

In the months that followed we divided the labor further. While Dan grew lean and acquired a deep tan laboring on the open waters of Florida Bay, I attended to the administration of the project. The details of my own role ranged from the unusual to the bizarre. For an effort of this kind we had first of all to engage the services of a professional exterminator. Fortunately, there was an abundance of companies in Miami. The executives of the first two I called answered with rich southern accents and clearly thought I was either joking or crazy. On the third try I got Steven Tendrich, vice president of National Exterminators, Inc. He had a northern accent, which gave me hope. Could he manage, I asked carefully, to spray clumps of mangrove in the Florida Bay with short-lived insecticides that would remove all the insects? We would ourselves eliminate by hand the tree snails and other larger animals that might be resistant to the chemical. Tendrich did not hesitate. He said yes, maybe he could do a job like that. Sure, give him some time to study the logistics. But even if it looked promising, he warned, he could not manage much in the field until the fall, when the heavy business of summertime Miami slacked off.

Progress in this sector having been achieved, I went with Simberloff to visit Jack Watson, the resident ranger of the National Park Service, to ask his permission to exterminate the whole faunas of islets. Most of the candidate islets were within the boundaries of the Everglades National Park and Great White Heron National Wildlife Refuge, over which he had partial jurisdiction. Obtaining permission to wipe out animal populations on federally protected land may sound like an impossible dream, but it proved relatively easy. Watson gave it without hesitation, asking only that we keep him briefed. Bill Robertson, our principal contact in the Park Service, was also in sympathy with the rationale and plan of the project. He knew that the targeted islets were no more than clumps of red mangrove among hundreds scattered through Florida Bay. They harbored species or races no different from those abounding elsewhere. We assured Watson and Robertson of our intent to protect the vegetation, and our expectation that the trees would be fully recolonized with insects and other arthropods following the "defaunation," as we now called it. The experiment, Simberloff and I argued, might provide information that would help guide future park management policy. Our earnestness proved persuasive, and we never faced opposition from government officials or the public.

Finally, I set out to contact specialists who could identify the species of insects and other arthropods living on the mangrove islets before fumigation and while the recolonization proceeded. This proved the most difficult task of all. There were at most several hundred entomologists in the United States able to identify insects from the Florida Keys. Their study would be complicated by the fact that many of the creatures we expected to find are immigrants from the

West Indies, especially nearby Cuba and the Bahamas. Among our discoveries were to be the first specimens of the tropical spider family Hersiliidae recorded in the eastern United States and several large and striking long-horn beetles previously known only from the Bahamas. In the end we were able to persuade fifty-four specialists to assist us in the classification of our specimens. Most pitched in with enthusiasm. An expert on spiders, Joseph Beatty, went so far as to visit Simberloff in the field to assist with the on-site identification of the colonists.

During the spring of 1966 Simberloff reported in with his recommendation of islets that seemed well placed either for defaunation or to serve as controls. We began surveys prior to spraying by inspecting every square millimeter of trunk and leaf surface, digging into every crevice, prying beneath flakes of dead bark and into hollow twigs and decaying branches. We collected every species of arthropod we found. Later, after the defaunation, Dan took over the heavy duty of regular monitoring. To disturb the colonists as little as possible, he relied on photographs and his own growing familiarity with the mangrove fauna. It was hard and uncomfortable work, demanding the combined skills of insect systematist, roofer, and restaurant health inspector. Simberloff, the city-bred mathematician, did well. He endured the insect bites and lonely hours in the hot sun I had promised him. Once, after his outboard motor failed, he spent the night on one of the islets, managing to escape only when he hailed a passing fisherman the following morning. Exasperated with the gluelike mud through which we had to wade to reach several of our islands, he built a pair of plywood footpads shaped like snowshoes and drilled holes in them to reduce suction when they were lifted. When he tried them out he sank to his knees and had to be pulled out by me and another companion. I called the invention "Simberloffs" afterward. Dan was not noticeably amused.

I joined him at intervals to give assistance. On one memorable occasion—June 7, 1966—Dan met me at the Miami International Airport just as Hurricane Alma was churning up the central Caribbean

in the general direction of Florida. A storm watch had been posted
for Miami and the Keys. When we awoke the next morning the sky
had clouded over, wind was picking up from the south, and a light
rain had began to fall. The eye of the storm was expected to pass up
the west Florida coast and sideswipe Miami. Here, I thought, was a
rare opportunity to watch a hurricane disperse animals out of the
mangrove swamps and across the water. Travel in high winds seemed
a likely means of colonizing the little islands. I suggested that we
stand inside a nearby mangrove swamp during the storm and watch
for animals blown along by high winds. For some reason that escapes
me now, I didn't think much about danger to ourselves. Simberloff
agreed without hesitation. All right, he said, something interesting
might happen. Good enough.

We were both a little crazy in those days. As stronger gusts of
wind and rain blew in, and the streets began to empty of traffic, we
drove to Key Biscayne and hiked into a patch of red mangrove swamp
along the bay shore facing Miami. The eye of the hurricane was now
passing up the west coast on its way toward landfall in northwest
Florida. The gusts on Key Biscayne reached sixty miles an hour, gale
but not hurricane force. I was disappointed. The wind was not
strong enough to tear insects and other small creatures from the
trees. They all stayed hunkered down safely on the branches and
leaves as the rain-soaked winds roared through. We saw not a single
animal blow by. Nor could we find animals struggling in the water at
the edge of the swamp. I said, Well, let's see what would happen if
an animal *were* blown free. Would the storm-tossed waves carry it
out toward a distant shore? I caught an anole lizard and tossed it ten
feet or so out into the water. To my dismay, it popped to the surface,
swam expertly back to the shelter of the trees, and climbed up a
mangrove trunk. Well, I continued, suppose a full hurricane blew an
anole so far away on open water it couldn't get back. Our little experiment shows that it could swim to the nearest islet if it were not
too far away. Dan, rainwater streaming from his hat, allowed that the

notion was plausible. Our excursion was not a complete loss, but in later years we agreed we were lucky that Alma only brushed Miami. Otherwise we ourselves might have been washed to a distant shore, proving our own hypothesis *in extremis*.

A month later, I joined Steve Tendrich and a crew from National Exterminators on a trip into Florida Bay to spray the first two islets, "Experimental 1" and "Experimental 2," E1 and E2 for short. Simberloff was busy at another location preparing additional islets. We loaded a rented barge with equipment and set forth from a marina on Sugarloaf Key. Halfway out we came upon a stalled sports-fishing cruiser. Observing the law of the sea even in this relatively safe stretch of water, we took the captain and his two fisherman guests on board and back to Sugarloaf. Then we headed forth again. This time we reached E1 and sprayed the little island with parathion. The next morning we proceeded to E2. Here we spotted several nurse sharks, one nearly four feet in length, cruising the shallow waters around the islet. Trouble! The workmen refused to get off the barge. But I knew that nurse sharks never attack people unless hooked or seized by the tail and hauled from the water by the occasional reckless fisherman. They live on a diet of shellfish, crustaceans, and other small bottom-dwelling animals. So I volunteered to stand guard waist deep and drive the sharks away with an oar. Impressed by my specious bravery and with their male pride challenged, the crew got into the water and sprayed E2.

Several days later, after I had returned to Cambridge, Simberloff called with mixed news about E1 and E2. He had made a close inspection of the islets and found that the kill of the arthropods living on the surface of the vegetation had been total. But some beetle larvae living deep in the wood of dead branches survived. We realized we had no way of knowing what other creatures might still live in these deeper spaces. So we quickly agreed that spraying with parathion or some other short-lived insecticide was not enough. In order to run a proper experiment, we had to start with islets scourged of all animal life, with no exception. It would be necessary to fumigate the islets with a poisonous gas, one that penetrates every crack and crevice.

I called Steve Tendrich: could National Exterminators fumigate an island? The ever-resourceful Tendrich responded in his usual positive manner: why not? It was common practice in Miami, he said, to cover entire houses with a rubberized nylon tent and fumigate the interior in order to remove all termites and other insect pests, no matter how deeply hidden in the woodwork. To transfer the method to a large object surrounded by water would be tricky, of course. The crew would need to erect a scaffolding around the islet as a frame for the tent. We couldn't just lay the cover on top of the fragile branches. And something else: the dosage of the gas must be set just right, high enough to kill all the animals but low enough to leave the mangrove trees undamaged. To study a ghost island of dead wood and fallen leaves would have no meaning, I agreed. Not least, I had promised the National Park Service that we would preserve the live vegetation.

So it was to be poison gas. But what kind? We considered and quickly discarded hydrogen cyanide. It was too dangerous for the crew to use under these uncertain conditions, over water with possible stiff winds. Even if we could apply it safely, hydrogen cyanide is water-soluble and would probably kill the marine communities around the mangrove prop roots, an unacceptable side effect. Methyl bromide, Tendrich ventured, might fill the bill, if he could get the dosage just right. Tendrich immediately set up trials, using small mangrove trees in the swamps near Miami. Meanwhile Simberloff collected cockroach egg cases from mangrove swamps for Tendrich to test with various dosages. If these highly resistant insect life stages could be killed without damage to the vegetation, methyl bromide might work.

The window between insect kill and tree kill using methyl bromide was narrow, but Tendrich found it. On October 11, 1966, we all gathered for the first trial on an islet in the shallow waters of Harnes Sound, on the mainland side of Key Largo and a relatively short ride down U.S. 1 from Miami. As the men loaded the gear, we saw ospreys and pelicans flying nearby and herons spearing fish in the shade of the mangrove fringes along walls of barnacles and green algal mats stranded by a dropping tide. Somewhere close by, we had been told, was a nest of bald eagles. The men got the scaffolding up and closed the tent around it without mishap. They pumped the prescribed dose of methyl bromide through a flap-covered opening in the side, in the same manner used to fumigate a small house, then pulled the tent away, allowing the gas to dissipate quickly to harmless levels.

The next day we searched the islet thoroughly and found no trace of animal life. Even the deep-boring insects had been killed. Our colonization experiment was under way at last.

Tendrich, however, was not entirely satisfied with the procedure. It had worked all right at Harnes Sound a hundred yards from the highway, but the metal rods used to create the frame were heavy and clumsy and might be very difficult to transport to the more remote and less accessible mud-flat sites. He began to search for alternative techniques of scaffolding. One day as he drove through Miami he spotted a steeplejack working on a tower atop a hotel, and inspiration struck. Steve stopped the car, took an elevator to the hotel roof, and waited for the man to come down. He asked the steeplejack, whose name was Ralph Nevins, whether it might be possible to erect a small tower like that in the middle of a mangrove swamp, then drape a tent over the guy wires. Sure, Nevins replied—another optimist—why not? Would it be very difficult? Don't think so. Tendrich hired him on the spot. And so it was done thereafter. The rest of our islets were fumigated beneath tents wrapped around the guy wires of a tower raised by Ralph Nevins.

Simberloff continued to carry the main burden of monitoring. He was tied for months to a physically demanding routine of travel, search, and identification. When I found time I came down from Cambridge, and we worked together. Within weeks it was apparent that the project was going to be a success. The recolonization by arthropod species was already well under way. Moths, bark lice, and other flying insects appeared early, at first in small numbers but accumulating and reproducing as time passed. Winged ant queens, newly inseminated during their nuptial flights, landed, shed their wings, and started colonies. Spiders came early in abundance; some were wolf spiders the size of silver dollars. How were they crossing the water? Since there had been no major storms, we guessed that they used ballooning. Many kinds of spiders, when crowded or short of food, prepare to emigrate by standing in exposed places or leaves and twigs and letting out threads of silk into the wind. As the strands lengthen, the drag increases, until the spiders have difficulty holding themselves in place. Finally they let go, allowing the wind on the strands to pull them up and away. With luck they come down again on land, and best of all in some place like a distant mangrove island with few other spiders and an abundance of prey. Those that hit water instead soon become fish food.

Toward the end of the year following the defaunations, a pattern in the colonization began to emerge. With so much of our time invested, we now began to worry that a hurricane might strike, perturbing the new faunas and ruining the continuity of the experimental run. Fortunately, none came close to Florida. In fact no major storm struck the area again until Andrew devastated South Miami and the northern keys in 1992. After a while, we relaxed a bit and broadened our attention to include other aspects of local ecology.

Our first major project was to launch a survey of the arthropods of all the mangrove swamps, in order to gain a picture of the pool of all possible emigrants to the experimental islets. I hired Robert Silberglied, a graduate student working in entomology under my direction, to commence a general survey of the surrounding keys. Bob was a gifted naturalist and a polymath taxonomist who could on sight identify species from a wide array of animal groups. The challenge of a complete arthropod survey was made to order for his talents. He worked tirelessly from island to island, building a large reference collection of insects and other arthropods. His impressive potential was destined never to flower into a full career, however. On January 13, 1982, he died with others in the Potomac River crash of an Air Florida airliner on the outskirts of Washington, D.C. A winter storm was in progress, and the accident was later blamed on wing icing. The flight was to have been the first leg of a flight to Panama, where Bob had planned to continue research on tropical ecology.

Our interest in the Florida Keys, as our research moved onward into 1967, also extended to include conservation. Silberglied and Simberloff heard rumors that Lignumvitae Key, a 280-acre island on the bay side close to Lower Matecumbe Key and its transecting segment of U.S. 1, was an unspoiled paradise covered by large hardwood trees. Undisturbed forest other than mangrove was a rarity in the Keys, and worth investigation. Few people had set foot on Lignumvitae to that time. One was Konrad Lorenz, who later opened his influential book *On Aggression* with a description of the coral reef there and on nearby Key Largo.

When Silberglied and Simberloff put ashore, they were met by the caretakers, Russell and Charlotte Niedhauk, an elderly and reclusive couple who lived on the island alone. The Niedhauks were suspicious of all visitors, and rudely chased most away. But when Bob and Dan revealed that they were biologists interested in conservation of the island, they were given a warm welcome. As they walked inland from the caretakers' house, they confirmed the rumor: almost all the land was covered by a mature tropical hardwood forest. They were thrilled to find themselves in a near-primeval habitat that once predominated in the high islands of the Keys but had been almost completely obliterated by the 1960s. Huge mahogany and gumbo-limbo, including the largest individual of the latter species in the United States, towered over wild lime, torchwood, Jamaica dogwood, boxleaf stopper, strangler fig, and the only large stand of holywood lignum vitae in Florida. Sixty-five species of trees and woody shrubs, all tropical and subtropical, composed the woody flora. The fauna was also a remnant of the old Keys. Candy-striped tree snails hung like grapes from the trunks and branches. Large butterflies, including showy dagger wings, purple wings, and swallowtails, darted and floated back and forth above the shaded trails. Bald eagles, at that time nearly extinct in the eastern United States, were occasional visitors, and Bahama bananaquits were seen from time to time. Later, after he had visited the island, Archie Carr, the great expert on Caribbean natural history, reminded me that the Lignumvitae forest was a tropical West Indian lowland forest of a quality no longer found in the West Indies themselves. The chances of finding stands of old mahogany and lignum vitae on the islands were close to zero.

The Niedhauks were almost paranoid about the future of Lignumvitae Key. It was owned, they explained, by a private consortium of wealthy Floridians who were planning to convert it into a community of expensive vacation residences. All the owners cared about, they said and I later confirmed, was a financial killing. Could the visitors help find a way to preserve the island in its natural state? Bob and Dan conveyed this information to me as soon as they returned to their base. Soon afterward, I visited the island and was similarly enchanted, and fearful. I invited Thomas Eisner, my old friend on the Cornell faculty, to join me on a second visit. Together we prepared an article for *Natural History* about Lignumvitae and its plight. While our effort was under way, I spoke at a meeting of the Florida Audubon Society in Miami on the subject, and to my delight an elderly couple living in Coral Gables pledged $100,000 toward the purchase of the island. It was a big first step toward saving Lignumvitae. But we needed more; the owners had set the tentative price at over $2 million. Their spokesman, a septuagenarian Miami dentist, was gleeful that conservationists had entered the bidding. He made it clear that the final price would be raised as high as the owners could make it. He would love to see his beautiful island saved in its natural state, he claimed, but if we did not act soon the land would go to developers. The Lignumvitae ecosystem, in short, had been placed in ransom.

I contacted Thomas Richards, president of The Nature Conservancy, in hopes of pressing the campaign to a successful conclusion. TNC was, as it remains today, famous for its policy of purchasing environmentally important land for preservation in the public domain. After a visit of his own, Richards committed his organization to the effort. He then approached Nathaniel Reed, an influential administrator in Florida's park system, for further assistance. In the end, after long negotiation, a reasonable price was agreed upon. The island was purchased with funds from The Nature Conservancy and the State of Florida, and Lignumvitae Key was turned into a fully protected State Botanical Site. Today visitors walk along trails where tree snails still decorate the gnarled old lignum vitae trees and dagger wings alight among their delicate blue flowers and petard-shaped yellow fruits. The public can in perpetuity, I trust, witness the Florida Keys as they were in prehistory.

Meanwhile, our experimental project continued to move swiftly forward. By the fall of 1967, a year after we fumigated the islets, the results were all but conclusive. In a formal article published two years later, Simberloff and I summarized the events of recolonization and the reattainment of equilibria:

> By 250 days after defaunation, the faunas of all the islands except the distant one ("E1") had regained species numbers and composition similar to those of untreated islands even though population densities were abnormally low . . . The colonization curves plus static observation on untreated islands indicate strongly that a dynamic equilibrium number of species exists for any island.*

At least the cruder predictions of the theory of island biogeography had been met. The closest island, as expected, had the largest number of species before fumigation, forty-three to be exact, and it regained approximately that number within the year. The most distant island, E1, had the smallest number, twenty-six, and climbed back

---

* "Experimental Zoogeography of Islands: The Colonization of Empty Islands," *Ecology* 50(2) (1969): 278–295.

close to that after defaunation. The other islands, at intermediate distances, had intermediate numbers before fumigation and also returned to their original levels afterward. Two years later, in 1968, these various levels still held.* The turnover in species was very rapid, also as expected from island biogeographic theory applied to small, swiftly occupied islands. In the course of our studies we added many observations on the dispersal and early colonization of various groups of arthropods, including spiders, mites, ants, earwigs, bark lice, crickets, and many others. Dan completed his Ph.D. thesis in the spring of 1968. It had taken us only three years to create miniature Krakataus, in replicate with controls, and follow their histories to an early form of equilibrium.

In 1971 Simberloff and I received the Mercer Award of the Ecological Society of America for our research, a welcome recognition.

We had risked a new approach to biogeography, a subject still considered outside the mainstream of ecology, and succeeded. From many employment opportunities open to him, Dan accepted an assistant professorship at Florida State University, in order to be within easy distance of field sites. In time he became an ecologist of international stature. He conducted additional experiments with mangrove islets, varying their size and shape. He expanded his activities to include field studies on other ecosystems, and used his mathematical skills to conduct critiques of ecological theory and to develop new approaches in quantitative modeling. In time his university appointed him to the Robert O. Lawton Distinguished Professorship.

I did not return to the Florida Keys, and my dream of converting them into a natural laboratory languished. A new possibility—a different opening to the future—had seized my imagination. I wanted to make sociobiology into a single science, one that ranged from apes to chimpanzees.

---

* "Experimental Zoogeography of Islands: A Two-Year Record of Colonization," *Ecology* 51(5) (1970): 934–937.

Marybeth S. Holleman

Awakening

First publication

During his first days of life I barely uncovered my new son for fear he would get too cold. I kept Jamie swaddled in a blanket, his thin arms and legs held tight against his torso. It took both my husband and me to give him his first bath—one to hold his fragile head and unfold his tiny body, the other to gently pat his skin with water.

How could I then, six weeks after his birth, take him out into a wilderness known for its cold wet weather and fatally freezing waters? When I was only pregnant, a friend assured me babies can adjust to changes much easier than we think. I was the one who might not be ready for a camping trip, she said.

Certain I would want to go, I made plans for a late August trip to Prince William Sound. I did what I could to accommodate my baby. Rather than our 15-foot inflatable boat—small, open, close to the water—we would take a charter. And rather than our two-person tent to keep the rain out and the warmth in, a cabin with a wood stove awaited us.

Still I had doubts. Was I pushing the limits of a baby's adaptability? Of parenthood itself? I suspected I was, and felt not just a little self-ish. Yet I could not keep from going.

Every summer, we make at least one trip to Prince William Sound. These trips are much more than just vacations—for me the sound is the essence of wilderness, a place where I can clear my head of all that is unimportant in my life. Stripped of job titles, possessions, acquaintances, the responsibilities of everyday life, I rediscover my own essence. Thrilled to be a mother, I nevertheless didn't want motherhood to deny me something I held so dear.

On these trips, we always went where we wanted when we wanted. We rarely spent more than a day in any one place, choosing instead to explore coves, islands and passageways. Two summers ago, we headed toward Port Nellie Juan on Prince William Sound's western side, 30 miles by water from Whittier. Wind and rain slowed us down; water sprayed our faces and dripped down our necks; waves made the boat bounce up and slam down with such force that seawater drenched our gear. Still, we reached South Culross Passage just north of Port Nellie Juan that afternoon. After several landings, we found a beach suitable for camping and pitched our tent. For the next four days our sojourns were limited only by the amount of fuel our boat could carry. One hot sunny day was spent climbing a mountain on Culross Island. Another day we explored the coastlines of Eshamy Bay and Crafton Island, returning in the evening under a fog so thick we nearly missed the entrance to Culross Passage.

This time would be different. Two weeks before the trip, I tried to imagine being in a small boat on the sound with my son and had recurring images of him slipping out of my arms and falling into the water. Chills traveled my spine as I remembered the experience of a friend a few years ago. Returning to Seward in his boat, Peter found two cold wet boys shivering on the beach, and a swamped boat and drowned father in the water. The boat he found was like his own; it was like ours.

The morning we arrived in Whittier to meet our charter was sunny but windy. The whitecaps would have made rough going in our boat. I felt relieved to have the charter—until I saw it. The *Sound Runner* was only two feet longer than our boat. It did boast a covered front and more space for gear inside, but it fell far short of the big, comfortable cruiser I had imagined. We also discovered four other passengers would join us. Seven adults plus my baby plus our gear—which included our deflated boat, an outboard, tanks of fuel and gallons of fresh water—seemed a dangerously heavy load.

When I asked the boat's captain, Jerry Sanger, if the boat should carry so much weight, he only said, "Let's wait and see if she gets on step. If not, we'll turn back." As images of Jamie falling into the water crowded into my mind, I considered staying behind. My desire to be out in the sound pushed those images back—but not out of sight. We all piled in and headed down Passage Canal. After several tense minutes, the boat leveled and began gliding across the surface. I settled back against my seat.

I sat on the end of a bench in the bow, just under the open-ended cover, with Jamie bundled up and held tight against my chest in a papoose-like carrier. I strained my back against the jarring ride to keep him comfortable and shielded from the wind. Several times water splashed over the side onto my leg, but as long as it missed Jamie I said nothing. Though we passed through some of my favorite landscapes, I barely looked. Instead I watched the waves hitting the boat and listened to the steady drone of the engine.

The other passengers, four women from Maryland and Boston, were on a day trip to see glaciers and sea otters. "How old is your baby?" one asked me. "Six weeks." "You're brave," she smiled. "Perhaps too brave," I murmured.

Finally the *Sound Runner* veered toward shore and Harrison Lagoon came into view. As we motored closer, I could barely make out the cabin among thick underbrush and spruce. The tide was low, baring a wide rock beach punctuated by sun-bleached stumps. Sanger maneuvered the boat through the narrow lagoon entrance, around a crescent-shaped gravel spit, and up onto a rocky beach on the backside of the cabin. I stepped off the boat and felt land beneath my feet and Jamie sleeping comfortably.

Though the sun shone in a cloudless sky and calm waters replaced whitecaps, we spent the rest of the day making the cabin our temporary home. Half our gear was for the baby—I brought too much, I knew, but had no idea which pieces were unnecessary. We took turns entertaining Jamie and gathering firewood, unpacking sleeping bags and clothes, pulling out cookware and food for dinner. The bare walls and floors of the cabin didn't muffle sound like our house, and several times noises startled Jamie into crying.

That evening we ventured as far as the gravel spit which swung out into the lagoon right beyond the entrance. In slanted sunlight, we watched a small flock of glaucous-winged gulls and two young bald eagles circle and swoop over a stream mouth on the far shore. A pair of grebes dove for food in the middle of the lagoon. One eagle, his black body and pure white head evidence of his adulthood, perched atop a dead spruce on a gravel beach directly across from us. Seeing these animals was like seeing old friends again, ones treasured but rarely visited.

That night, the little wood stove couldn't keep the night air out, and I couldn't sleep for worrying that Jamie would be cold. I brought him into my sleeping bag. Tucked securely under my arm beneath the covers, he was so warm he sweated, but he slept well. I slept fitfully, waking often to change positions without disturbing him, or to make sure he was breathing.

We awoke to another clear sunny day. While Andy put our inflatable boat together, I walked with Jamie down to the beach on the Port Wells side. The scene before me seemed to say, yes, you were right to come back to the sound. Across the water, mountains topped with snow soaked up the morning light. Offshore, several sea otters were diving, floating, and eating. Some were only a few feet offshore, closer than I'd ever been to one. I wanted to sit and watch them, but Jamie cried as soon as we reached the beach. The otters dove for safety, resurfacing much farther out.

When the boat was ready, we headed for Barry Arm to watch glaciers. As we left the cabin, I thought back to our first trip to Prince William Sound. We made the rainy cold trip to Blackstone Bay in a few hours. Along the way, rough seas splashed into the boat; seawater coated me and washed inside one of my rubber boots, numbing my toes. When we reached the head of the bay, my body was stiff. Andy cut the engine, and we drifted in front of Blackstone Glacier, watching a blue sky spread from the icefield down the glacier to our boat. I removed my boots and stretched my legs out on the bow. We spent hours in the boat, basking in the sun and watching ice fall from the glacier's towering face. Ever since that trip, one of my favorite things to do in the sound is to motor as close as we dare to the face of a tidewater glacier, then cut the motor and drift, watching and listening to age-old ice make its way to salt water. Some cracks and groans bring forth falling columns of ice, which in turn create huge swells, wide and deep, that make the world tilt when they reach our boat.

The closer we got to Barry Arm, the stiffer the wind blew. I faced backward in the boat so the wind would not be directly on Jamie, even though he was completely covered. I zipped up my coat around him and felt like I was carrying him in my belly once more. I could not see the approach to the glacier, could not see the icy face become larger and taller, filling up more of the sky. All I could see was our wake through the increasingly dense field of ice floating in dark blue waters.

Andy cut the engine, and I turned to face the glacier. For a few minutes we sat quietly, listening to the ice and watching for some to break free. The sun warmed my wind-chilled body; I began to relax. Then Jamie awoke and began to fuss, whimpering and wiggling in his confining space. He was hungry. I tried for a while to nurse him but had to remove my life vest to do so. Around us, icebergs shifted and cracked. Then one off the side of our boat rolled over, expanding like a surfacing whale, as the wake of a calving berg passed it. Instead of being fascinated by the size of the iceberg, by the light passing through its clear blue caverns, I began to fear one nearer us would roll and flip our boat. I remembered hearing of a kayaker who was tossed into the water by a rolling iceberg; I again imagined Jamie falling into the water. We headed for shore.

The shore was of the finest sand I've seen in Prince William Sound. Most beaches are rocky or pebbled at best. Here the sand's fine texture and glinting black color absorbed the sun's rays and molded to any shape. I leaned up against a rock on the sand, holding my baby close. I could still see about half of Barry Glacier. As Jamie nursed, I saw a huge column of ice break loose and fall, like a lightning bolt, into the water.

On the return trip I watched the glaciers recede. As the icefield tapered off into a few chunks, Andy called my attention to a sea otter toward shore. It was a female, a mother with baby on her belly. For a few minutes we watched. Then, rather than dive and disturb her pup, she paddled off.

Though the sun was still high in the sky when we returned to the cabin, I spent the rest of the day inside with Jamie, napping in the warmth of our sleeping bags. The boat trip had tired us both. Andy left us to follow the coast down to an old gold mine we had both been curious about. I made him promise to take pictures and then drifted off to sleep.

The next morning dawned clear, but a cloud bank in the south assured me it would not last. I walked the beach alone. The sea otters, twice as many as the previous morning, were again close to shore. Flat water, no waves breaking the silence. I could hear the otters eating. Most crunched on crab or sea urchin; one made a tap tap tap as it used a rock to break open the shell of its breakfast. I crouched on the beach and watched them. Only one or two nearest me turned to look in my direction; they paddled away halfheartedly. Then another sound broke through the silence—the sound of Jamie crying. I hurried to the cabin to feed him.

Clouds began to move in, though our cabin was still showered in sunlight. Andy took the boat and explored the rock jetty we passed on the way to Barry Arm. He was gone for hours. Several times I took Jamie and walked the beach. Clouds began to lower and soon a fine mist fell, yet I could still make out the jetty and Andy's boat

tied to the rocks. Him, too, I thought. I wondered what he was finding out there.

On past trips we spent hours walking around tidewater pools,
poking among seaweed. These pools, I've found, take time to see. It
is like entering a dark room and waiting for your eyes to adjust to
the darkness. You must sit still, and sit still some more, and slowly
you will begin to see small creatures—fish, snails, starfish, anem-
one—living out their lives.

On his return, Andy said he spent hours watching a young bald
eagle. The eagle sat on the rocks as the tide came in around him. He
did not move, Andy said, as the water curled up around his feet, then
his body. Finally, when it was up around his neck, he stretched up,
shook out his wet feathers, and flew a few feet. Then he swam back
to dry land, using his great wings as paddles. Andy had thought the
bird was injured, but he was probably still learning to fly well.

I left Andy with Jamie and again walked the beach, from the Port
Wells side around to the spit and the lagoon. Clouds blanketed the
mountaintops, and a soft rain dimpled the water. A raft of sea otters
floated offshore. In the quiet waters of the lagoon, I spotted the harbor seal I'd seen every day since our arrival. The seal moved silently
across water so calm that the mountainside of green, lit by sunlight
beneath clouds, was reflected perfectly in it. Only the seal's wake
rippling the water gave away the reflection's illusion. At the end of
the gravel spit, I stood still and watched the incoming tide cover peb-
bles at my feet. I turned and saw through the fine mist a white spot
on the beach. It was a feather—nearly completely white, with just
a few brown speckles, the feather of a young bald eagle. I brought it
to Jamie.

The next morning, a light rain fell. We were to be picked up that
afternoon, but I was not ready to pack. I bundled Jamie and walked
to the beach. Once again, the harbor seal slid across the lagoon and
gulls and eagles fished in the stream. Once more we walked out to
the gravel spit, then through the smooth curved forms of upended

tree stumps. The sea otters were again close to shore. Some turned to look at us as we approached, but did not move away. Jamie and I watched as one dove, reappeared, and brought food to its mouth. It nibbled a bit, then rolled in the water, cleaning the remains from its belly. Two others, fairly young by the dark fur of their heads, porpoised through the water, chasing each other. One barked at the other, then made a series of flips in the water, its body forming a circle, head to tail. Jamie gurgled softly, then made a little bark of his own.

Barry Lopez

Caring for the Woods

from *Audubon*

My family has been in the Americas for almost five centuries. Marín López, a shipwright on my father's side, was in the Caribbean with Cortés in 1511. My mother's English and German ancestors began farming on the Pennsylvania side of the Delaware River valley in the 1650s. A scion of that group later moved to Virginia (where the Holston River still bears the family name); his progeny moved into the Carolinas and eastern Alabama, where my mother was born on a plantation in 1914. One relative in that clan moved on to New Mexico at the close of the 19th century and then dropped from sight. He is recalled as a man obsessed with killing Indians.

My father's family, originally tobacco farmers in Cuba, eventually came to St. Louis and New York as tobacco merchants, though they maintained close ties with Asturias, their homeland in northern Spain. Neither the Romans nor the Moors, my father is still proud to say, ever conquered Asturias. He traces his lineage there back to Rodrigo Díaz de Vivar—El Cid. In her last years my mother followed her own path back as far, to a baron of Somerset who ratified the Magna Carta at Runnymede.

All these centuries later, the wandering, the buying up, the clearing, the planting, and the harvesting of land in my single branch of the family has come down to a parcel in Oregon: 35 acres of mixed

old-growth forest, rising quickly into the foothills of the Cascade
Mountains from the north bank of the McKenzie River. These woods
harbor Roosevelt elk and mountain lion, suites of riparian and
mixed-forest birds, and an assortment of insects, wildflowers, and
mushrooms that trails off into a thousand species.

I understand the desire to own the land, the dream of material
wealth that brought each of my lines of descent to the Americas. I
respect the determination, the tenacity, and the uses to which the
land-profit was put—formal education, for example. But I've come
to believe, at the age of 49, that sacrificing the biological integrity of
land to abet human progress is a practice my generation must end.
If we do not, I believe the Americas will finally wash into the sea like
Haiti, leaving behind a social nightmare.

My wife, Sandra, and I have lived on the right bank of the river
for 24 years. We want to keep this single wooded slope of land in the
West undeveloped and uncut. We want to pass it on like a well-read
book, not the leavings of someone's meal.

The enormous trees and the river, because of their scale, dominate
what we see here, but the interstices of this landscape are jammed
with life: hummingbirds, spiders, butterflies, cutthroat trout, wild
ginger, skinks, the cascading blossoms of wild rhododendron. In the
1940s some of the larger trees—Douglas-fir, western hemlock, and
western red cedar, four to six feet in diameter—were selectively
logged. The selective logging and a fire that burned a long stretch of
the north bank of the McKenzie in 1855 created a forest with a few
tall, rotting stumps; dense patches of younger Douglas-fir; and several dozen massive, isolated, towering trees, 300 to 400 years old, all
standing among many fewer Pacific yew, chinquapin, bigleaf maple,
red alder, Pacific dogwood, California hazel, and the odd Pacific
madrone.

In 1989 a neighbor who owned this slope put 32 acres of it up for
sale. Timber companies that intended to clear-cut the property were

the most active bidders, and Sandra and I were forced to match money and wits with them. But in 1990 we were able to add these acres to 3 we'd bought in 1976. We then completed a legal arrangement to prevent the land from being either logged or developed after we passed away. Good intention toward an individual stretch of land has now become well-meaning of another kind in my family.

We did not set out to preserve these woods. From the start we felt it a privilege, also a kind of wonder, to live here. Twenty-inch spring chinook spawn on a redd in front of the house in September every year. Wild bleeding heart, yellow violets, white flowers such as trillium and wood sorrel, and the red flowers of coralroot are brilliant in the deep, green woods in April and May. I find bear scat, beaver-clipped willows, and black-tailed deer prints regularly on my walks. On the same night we've listened to northern spotted owls, western screech owls, and northern saw-whet owls call. Spotted skunks and a short-tail weasel have tried to take up residence in the house. On summer nights, when we leave the windows open, bats fly through.

From a certain perspective, this wooded hill with its unnamed creek and marvelous creatures—I nearly stepped on a rubber boa one morning on the way to the toolshed—is still relatively unmanipulated; but I try not to let myself be fooled by the thought. The number of songbirds returning each spring I would guess to be half what it was a decade ago. The number of chinook on the redd, though it fluctuates, has also fallen off in recent years. And I've taken hundreds of dead animals off the road along the river—raccoon, brush rabbit, even Steller's jay and mink. People new to the area are apt to log the few Douglas-firs left on their property, to roll out fresh lawns and plant ornamental trees in their place. Their house cats leave shrews, white-footed mice, and young birds strewn in the woods like so much litter.

Driftnets that snag salmon in the far-off Pacific, industrial logging in Central America that eliminates migratory-bird habitat, speeding trucks and automobiles, attractive prices for timber—all of it directly affects these acres. There is no way to fence it out.

The historical detail that might make vivid what, precisely, occurred in the McKenzie River valley after its location in 1812 by Donald MacKenzie—a trapper and kinsman of the Canadian explorer Alexander MacKenzie—is hard to come by, but the story is similar to those told of a hundred other valleys in the West. Beaver trappers were the first whites to sleep in these woods. (Molala and Kalapuya Indians, from the east and west side of the Cascades respectively, apparently camped along the McKenzie in summer, when salmon were running and openings in the heavily forested mountains were crowded with ripening blue and red huckleberries, soft thimbleberries, strawberries, orange salmonberries, blue and red elderberries, and trailing blackberries.) When the free trappers and the company trappers were gone, gold and silver miners filtered in. Toward the end of the 19th century some homestead settlement followed small-scale logging operations along the river, though steep mountains and dense forests made farming and grazing in the area impractical. Clear-cutting in modern times, with its complicated attendant problems—siltation smothering salmon redds, "predator control" programs directed against black bears—has turned the road between our house and Eugene, 40 miles downriver, into as butchered a landscape as any I know in the Cascades.

In the 1980s, when the price of Douglas-fir reached $300 for 1,000 board feet, some small-property owners succumbed—two or three trees might bring them $2,500. The resulting harvest has grown to look like mange on the hills. Hand in hand with that has come real estate promotion, the hundreds of FOR SALE signs along the road a sort of Muzak.

I am not a cynical man, but watching the quick spread of suburban logging and seeing the same house put up for sale every few years—with a little more landscaping, a higher fence, and another

$30,000 to $40,000 added to the price—pushes me closer to it than anything else I know. A long-term commitment to the place, knowledge of its biological limits, or concern for the valley's fate—these do not appear to be a part of the transactions. The hacking away at natural growth, the incessant prettifying with rosebushes and trimmed hedges, and the imposition of incongruous antebellum architecture look like a scatter of bad marriages—reigning husbands with presentable wives.

If I had answers to these problems, or if I felt exempt in this mess, I would be angry about it more often than I am. As it is, Sandra and I pace ourselves. We work on initiatives to control real estate development and rein in logging along the river. We provide a place for the release of rehabilitated raptors, including spotted owls. We work amicably with the state highway department and the Bonneville Power Administration (BPA), which maintain corridors across the land we occupy. We have had to threaten a lawsuit to curb the recklessness of the highway department with chain saws and heavy equipment, and we have had to insist through an attorney that the BPA not capriciously fall "danger trees" along its power-line right-of-way.

But these agencies, whose land-management philosophies differ so strikingly from our own, have slowly accommodated us. Instead of flooding the roadside with herbicides and flailing at it with oversize brush cutters, the highway department now permits us (and others along the river) to trim back by hand what brush actually threatens motor traffic. And the regional director of the BPA wrote into a recent contract that I could accompany his fallers, to be certain no felled tree was sent crashing needlessly into other trees.

Sandra and I ourselves, of course, have not left the place untouched. In January 1991 two windstorms felled about 30 trees. We logged them out with horses and put the money toward the land payment. I have felled standing dead trees that threatened the house. We compost our kitchen waste, laundry lint, and woodstove ashes in the woods. We're planted gardens and built outbuildings. But it is our habit to disturb these acres very little and to look after them in a way only humans can: by discouraging or preventing the destruction other humans bring. I've asked my neighbors to stop dumping refuse on our place. (They had done it for years because it was only "the woods," a sort of warehouse for timber, deer, and fish, and a dumping ground for whatever one wanted to abandon—cars, bedsprings, fuel drums, mall packaging.) I've asked another neighbor's children not to shoot at birds or chop down trees. I've asked unwitting fishermen not to walk through the salmon redd. And, reluctantly, I've gated and posted the land to keep out wanton hunters and people in four-wheel-drives looking for something to break down or climb over.

We know we cannot fence off the endangered chinook redd without attracting curious passersby. Neither I nor anyone can outlaw the product advertising (or foolish popular history) that contributes to images of men taming a violent West. Neither I nor anyone, I fear, can soon change human sentiment to put lands that are unharvested, unhunted, unroaded, or untenanted on the same footing with lands that are domesticated or industrialized. So the birds and animals, the fish and spiders, the wild orchids and other flowers will not have these shields.

Piece by piece, however, as a citizen and as a writer, I want to contest the obsessions that I believe imperil American landscapes—the view that they are principally sources of material wealth or scenic backdrops for a more important human drama. I want to consider the anomalies that lie at the heart of our incessant desire to do good. And I want to see how to sidestep despair, by placing my faith in something larger than my own ideas.

Sandra and I know we do not own these 35 acres. The Oregon ash trees by the river, in whose limbs I have seen flocks of 100 Audubon's warblers, belong also to the families in Guatemala in whose forests these birds winter. The bereavement I feel at the diminishment of life around me is also a bereavement felt by men and women and children I don't know, living in cities I've never visited. And the exhilaration I experience seeing fresh cougar tracks in mud by a creek is an emotion known to any person in love who hears the one-who-is-loved speak.

There is more mystery to be contemplated, there are more lessons to be absorbed, on these 35 acres than all the people in my lineage going back to Runnymede and medieval Asturias could manage, should the study be pursued another 1,000 years. My generation's task, I believe, is to change the direction of Western civilization in order to make such a regard practicable.

When I rise in the morning I often walk down to the riverbank. If it's summer I'm likely to see mergansers, tree swallows, and osprey. I see first light brightly reflected on alder twigs stripped by beaver. I feel the night movement of cool air downriver and see deerhead orchid and blue gilia blooming in the dark-green salal and horsetail rushes.

I am acutely aware, winter or summer, that these waters have come from farther east in the mountains, that in a few days they will cross the bar at the mouth of the Columbia and become part of the Pacific. The ancient history alone of this river, this animate and elusive business of rain and snow and gravity, gives me hope.

Walking back to the house in this serene frame of mind, I know that to love life, to swear an allegiance to what is alive, is the essence of what I am after. I'm moved to forgive whoever does not find in these acres what I do. I glance into the moving picket of trees and shadow, alert for what I've never noticed before, in a woods I'm trying to take care of—as in its very complicated way it is taking care of me.

Kate Boyes

Confluence

First publication

I hold my time on Long Lake like an amulet. It is a charm worn smooth by frequent recall, hibernating in memories until my need for strength wakes it again. Then, I remember . . .

A disk of ice, formed in my cup during the September night, sounds a faint chime as I drink to the morning sun. I stir the fire and watch the crust of frost on my boots thaw slowly in the thin warmth of last night's last bright coals. But I am too impatient to let the boots, still wet from yesterday's hike, warm through. I pull them on resolutely and gather my fishing gear. Nothing can cool my enthusiasm today, for I am off to explore some high falls near the lake's headwaters.

My camp is on a spit that juts out into the lake about a quarter of a mile. The higher section of the spit is all sand and spruce and cedar, but this distills to a wide, clear strip of gray clay at the lake's edge. I head toward the lake's major feeder stream along this open path, looking back occasionally to watch my tracks fill with seeping water and disappear from the impressionable clay.

A light morning breeze stirs the lake and the patches of water plants along its edge. The rasping of sedge to sedge and the lapping of water against shore whisper "shh, shh, shh." Perhaps other creatures are lulled by this; I seem to be the only one awake. But with days changing so fast, I cannot bear to sleep too long. Autumn began and has almost ended in the short time I've camped here, the whole season passing in one week. Green trees fired to peak color in four days and were denuded by wind in another two. Now the bare branches seem exhausted, resting on the seventh. Nature, working feverishly at this latitude and altitude, has managed to squeeze a season in edgeways.

I see something strange up along the spit, just at the base of a tall cedar. From this distance, it looks like gray stones strewn in a rough circle around a core of white litter. I guess that these are the firepit and trash of hunters here for the opening day of bear season; for a moment I am filled with uneasiness, a feeling I rarely experience in the wild. I hesitate, look out across the lake, and scan the forest. Who was here, so close to my camp?

But when I cautiously approach the site, I find an open cache of empty, bone-white turtle eggs. Lumps of hardened clay surround the cache, still laying where they were scattered in some creature's haste to dig up the eggs. Each edge of the lifeless shells draws in on itself, like a scroll, as if resigned to predation, and the shells are almost translucent now after weeks of exposure to sun and wind and rain. My sadness at this loss of life is tempered with relief, for although the predator's tracks have long since disappeared, there is little chance that the raider was human.

Past the spit, the edging of clay gives way to an intermittent path, part substance and part sloshing, which straggles northward and upward along the stream. Picking my way through willow thickets is even slower than wading through water, so the frequent moves from land to stream lend variety and not vexation to the walk. Besides, I am also here to fish, and I accept that fishers' feet are always wet, our boots forever molding to and on us. And the slow, strenuous going gives me an excuse to stop and sketch the chokecherry trees on the opposite bank while I catch my breath. From this side, the fruit's tenuous connection with the mother tree is so faint that the racemes appear to be held in constant suspense, forever in free fall over the stream.

The warm afternoon sun welcomes me when I untangle myself from the last stand of willows and climb the final rise before the falls. Here the stream widens and slows, as if relaxing from its recent rush over granite cliffs. I can see those cliffs up ahead, but in this quiet spot, the falls' roar is faint, subdued by distance. Michaelmas daisies spangle the stream banks. Emerald moss grows in glacial microstriations on boulders, slicking the sides but making soft mats on top. In the shadier backwashes, the first ice since June shocks the shore with its suggestion of a cooling relationship.

Exploration can wait. I lean my fishing rod against a pine, wade into the water, and scramble up a boulder to relax like the stream. I sit quietly for a while and then doze, sit and doze while high clouds drift overhead and change the expressions on mountain faces. Water foams white over the falls, creating currents that pirouette on stage marks only the stream can see. Tangles of trees elbow each other all the way down to the shore. The sun's warmth soaks into my bones. Even occasional flashes of brown trout against the streambed's bright agate can't tempt me to leave my position as watcher of the day.

Then, on the far shore, a shadow one shade darker than the rest emerges from the trees and grows distinct. Bear. She bear, I think. Sun's fire reflects on fur, glossing the bear with a cinnamon glow. My lingering drowsiness veils the implications of the bear's presence, so her shuffling amble from the forest to the stream and the playful way she rolls rocks over to search for insects seem amusing.

The bear stands when she reaches the water's edge, sniffs, and then moves, half upright, into the stream. As her lower body submerges, her front legs extend on the top skin of water, never seeming to break the tension. I am awed by her transformation from lumbering clown to graceful swimmer, her bulk no handicap in the buoyant water.

She crosses the water without swaying; only the long fur fringing off each forearm on the downstream side indicates the current's strength. All of her strokes are facile, effective, sure. The bear is unperturbed by a force that could drag me under and bobble my body along like a chunk of pumice. She heads in my direction.

She is heading toward me, and now I am awake. My eyesight is not enough to understand the bear: my whole body takes her in; my fingers trace her movement through the water; inside my boots, my feet follow every bear stroke. Thought, flesh, and feeling focus together; my life watches the bear.

As the bear swims toward me, memories and physical sensations flash simultaneously through my mind, the past inseparable from the present. Campfire stories. The bear's delicate head nodding above the water. Park flyer warnings. Corrugate waves splashing on the shore behind me. The newspaper account of a woman mauled, her two arms severed and scattered among the flame leaves of fallen autumn foliage.

At first I am afraid. But I struggle to push away thoughts of panic reactions; swim, run, climb—no use, I know. The bear would win any race I start. And so I let go of control in the presence of this creature, gratefully, like a cloistered novitiate, my loss losing significance in the resulting freedom and peace of mind. My past becomes faint as the remnants of a wind-worried cirrus cloud. To be me, here, now; there is nothing else. Fear is gone. She could open me like a cache of turtle eggs and litter me about, or she could pass by. That is fact, that is all. While I wait for her decision, I touch my truest friends—mountains, water, trees—once more with my eyes.

The bear pauses four feet in front of me and slightly to the right. She lifts her head and seems to puzzle over this odd being on the rock. Her eyesight is not enough to understand me; she rises on her back legs and swings her head slowly from side to side. Her head moves smoothly in a rhythm some stray fragment of instinct allows me to recall, a rhythm so familiar it seems I have felt it before. The motion and the gleam of her eyes fascinate me, but I remember, finally, to look away, my head slightly down. I am no threat, and it is important to both of us that I signal my submission.

The bear drops to four legs and moves forward, still to the right, until she is beside me. I watch her with everything but my eyes, the bone, muscle, and hair on my right side following all her moves. We are close enough to reflect each other's warmth, creating a heat that heightens the scent of cedar smoke in my hair and pine pitch in her damp fur. She stays beside me while the streams of water sheeting from her fur lose their force, become trickles, and then slow further until no sound comes from her direction but the last drops' sporadic dapping of the stream's surface.

Suddenly, she expels a deep breath. The sound surprises me and I gasp. Air which exchanged oxygen in her lungs moments before is borne my way, a pulse of life on the breeze. Her breath is drawn with mine.

I wait for the next sound, but only silence comes from her direction. The lack of sound touches me, absorbs me, carries me out with it across the water, expands, and, in expanding, makes me light. Each cell fills with silent space until I am translucent, my face the visage of this place, my body, lake and sky. I disappear—what harm can there be? Clearly, now is the time to turn to bear.

There is no bear beside me. I look down at the water, so recently ruffled by fur, as if expecting to find her essence swirling there in a small eddy. Only the sky and I mirror back. Still, I look down at the water, watching my face shape-shift in the current, watching two stones, bright and variegated as onyx, glitter back at me like eyes.

By the time I wade to shore, several fading impressions in the clay are the only evidence of the bear's passing. I follow her sign until I find a place, just at the edge of the trees, where she stopped, turned to face my direction, and then continued into the forest. I crouch down and place a palm flat in one of her tracks. We pause in the same place; our paths touch here; we both move on.

And then I realize with surprise that I am singing. It's possible the song began as I shambled over stones on my way back to shore; a small hum may have leaked out while my concentration was on footing. But now the song grows in volume and complexity, and it carries me back down the stream to my camp in the near dark of late afternoon. Whole passages flow out of a well of gladness newly tapped. This day has toned my life.

I hold my time on Long Lake like an amulet. It is a charm washed with the amethyst of an autumn sunset on calm water and softly fogged by the opalescence of cedar smoke rising through still night air. In distress, it quiets me until my life is the silence of owl's flight. Again, it resonates with the heartbeat of a bear and with my own pulse, the bear's gift. And always it takes the shape of a waxing gibbous moon, and glows with bits of light captured from that moon which hung above my camp, reflecting the better half of fullness.

John Haines

Days in the Field

from *Alaska Quarterly Review*

Cut wood. Got birch bark.
Picked berries, blue and cran.
Diary of F. Campbell, September 1948

And then the mist burned away above the yellowing birches; the sun shone on the damp, cold earth and warmed it.

We came out early to the field, shrugging away the morning chill, swinging our arms, easing our fingers of their stiffness. The big red tractor started and moved down the furrows, with the yellow digger rattling behind it; and the tawny, earth-flecked tubers spilled up into the sunlight, damp and cold.

By midmorning we were spread out over the field, bending and picking up the potatoes where they lay drying in the sun. Moving slowly east, then west, with baskets and buckets in hand, filling the brown sacks allotted at intervals along the rows. And the dust soon rose above the earth in the brilliant fall sunlight.

There were women among us, housewives come for the outing. A few young men from the military; a derelict or two, seedy, needing the scanty wages. A woman with a small child, who sat in one place and carefully cleaned her potatoes as friends brought them to her in baskets. And from time to time she fed and tended the child wrapped in a blanket and laid on the dusty earth.

Noon came, and a short break for sandwiches and coffee. There was a little time in which to relax, to sit and talk, to smoke, to walk from group to group, remarking on the average size and fullness of the harvest, the autumn distance in the blue sky above us. And then once more to work, moving downslope to where the red machine ran and rattled and turned up the tubers.

Toward dusk, the pickers cleared the field, straggling away by twos and threes. In the gathering light of dusk a big white van backed slowly along the furrows, while the few of us who remained walked before it and swung the heavy sacks aboard to be hauled downhill to the warehouse at the farm.

From the tailgate of a pickup coffee was poured for us by the lean, untalkative foreman, the last strong ration before dark. The last sunlight poured through the dust, ruddy and strong. There was dust in our hair and clothing, dirt in our fingernails. And we stood and drank, and spoke a few final words of the harvest.

The air grew chill, the redness of the light turned into darkness, and we dispersed to the sound of starting engines, voices drifting away over the darkened, sun-warmed field.

On the evening of the third day I picked up my wages and a sack of potatoes gleaned from the rows left behind by the digger. I stopped in town long enough to buy a few needed groceries, and then in the changed fall darkness windy with blowing leaves, I drove back out the long road to Richardson with eighteen hard-earned dollars in my wallet. I went home to my own potato patch on the hill above the river, to the last run of salmon, and to the waiting woodpile.

Each fall, until it seems that the beginning of such things is lost from view—when the birch leaves had begun to turn and loosen, falling in the wind, and with the earth still warm and dry—it was good to stand there in the furrows overlooking the river, to feel one's shod feet on the earth and, bending to that easy work, see the red and yellow tubers turning up and tumbling away from the dry hills. The dry, cloddy clump of plant came up on the face of the shovel: the frost-burned vines grasped, the roots shaken loose of soil, and the whole dead plant thrown aside. Then one more thrust with the shovel into the overturned earth to be sure that not one potato would be lost.

Now and then came a wet, cold September, when the heavy, turned soil clung to the tubers. We had to wash each of them carefully, and wipe them clean one by one. We spread them out on a clean canvas to dry in a brief day of sunlight before packing them away; otherwise they would have rotted in storage.

One year, after the long moose hunt was over, I picked potatoes from Tryph Taylor's frost-bitten field above Harding Lake. In low ground that fall sixty percent of the crop was frozen, a hard loss from an early freeze that drove deep into the hills before the crop could be dug. But those who had planted on higher ground, who hilled their spuds high and late, fared better.

We left the potatoes to dry in the sun for a while, then sacked them and carried them downhill to the storehouse. We left them there to cure for a week or so, then sorted and cleaned them, and put them away into the cellar bins for the winter. They shared space there with cabbages, rutabagas, beets and carrots. For weeks the dim light of the storehouse, the cool darkness of the cellar, kept the fragrance of drying potatoes, subtle and earthy.

It is morning in mid-July. Peg and I are bending over on a slope above Tenderfoot Creek, picking blueberries. It is the hottest day of the summer, ninety degrees in the sun by midmorning. The heat shimmers on the heavy, damp moss; the mosquitoes, put down by the sun, are quiet. The berries are big and ripe, hanging in clusters with a powdery bloom on their blueness, and the wild smell of them comes rich in the heat as we pick them carefully into our cans. By late morning the sun on our backs becomes oppressive; we quit, and drive back over the hill to Richardson. Not all of our cans are full.

In those lucky, faraway years when blueberries were still abundant at Richardson, the day would come in mid-August when they were ripe on the domes. Campbell and I met at his cabin one bright morning, with baskets and pails, and began the six mile hike to the top of Buckeye. And once there in the clear sunlight, we bent over by the hour and through the long day, filling the pails. The sun on our backs, the view to engage us from time to time, as we looked south toward Delta or north toward the headwaters of the Salcha; or if it was a cloudy day, with a cool wind in our faces, hoping the rain wouldn't catch us. All through the afternoon we moved from bush to bush, ranging the meadow, until all the pails were filled. And then in the late afternoon we hoisted packs to our shoulders with a grunt, and walked home, bowed under the weight in the long light of the late summer sun.

In the years that followed, the blueberry crop gradually diminished in the Richardson area, and there came a summer when none were to be found. Each summer thereafter, in late July and early August, I caught a ride to Delta with my big basket and half a dozen small pails. From the Junction I walked three miles out on the Alaska Highway to an old burn where the berries were abundant. I had that patch to myself; there was no one else around. By late afternoon, after a long day of picking, I had all of my cans filled. I walked back to the Junction where I eventually caught a ride back to Richardson. I got home, late and tired, but with a good load of berries in my pack.

Once the berries were home, the following morning was spent in cleaning them. They were then poured out of the cans and sugared down in gallon jars in the old, sourdough fashion. It was the only way we could keep them without canning or freezing. A layer of sugar in a clean jar, then a layer of berries; another layer of sugar, and so on, alternating berries and sugar until the jar was full. The jar was tapped on the floor to settle the berries deeper in the sugar, and then loosely sealed. We put them away in the coldest place we could find. If it was done right, the berries would keep until frost. Spooned out of the jars later from the heavy, clear syrup, the berries were as fresh, as firm and blue as on the day they were picked.

It was good to walk through the woods in late summer with a basket, gathering mushrooms. Boletus sprang up with the first rains in late July or early August, and in a good year they kept on coming until frost. In the open aspen woods especially, and along the forest roads, clumps of the brown and reddish caps emerged from the thin leaf sod on their pale, netted stems. And scattered through the woods, one came on the spread umbrellas of the over-ripe fungus going soft and rotten.

Walking, awake to the color of things underfoot; a stoop down to look, to pull up the mushroom to see if it was wormy or not. And if the fruit was sound and dry, out came the knife—a quick trimming of dirt from the stem, and over the shoulder they went into the basket with a solid thump. In a good day one felt that gradually settling weight on the shoulders.

Behind Campbell's Richardson cabin there was a particularly favored spot, a patch of aspen woods long since gone to the ravages of a miner's bulldozer, the only place in the country where oyster mushrooms could be found in any abundance. We could never be sure just when they'd be there, early or late. They came up overnight, in late summer or early fall, depending on the dryness of the year, on the late rain and the temperature. They had to be gathered immediately or they soon became infested with flies. For Campbell, as long as he was alive, it was easy; all he had to do was to walk out each morning into the woods behind his cabin and look. After his death, when the weeds and brush had taken over his garden and the old cabin had sunk even deeper into the soil, it was touch and go whether we would find the mushrooms or not. We came when we could, calculating the day and the hour. Often enough, all we found were a few brown clutches of them, flyblown and useless. But sometimes we were lucky, and there would be great silky-grey clumps of them in the small clearings under the aspens. On those lucky days, carefully searching that small patch of woods, we had our baskets filled in a short time.

At home, having cooked and eaten our fill, we turned to that fragrant heap of mushrooms, to clean them of soil, then cut and strip them into pieces and place them on the drying rack above the stove. For days the house was filled with the rich odor of drying mushrooms, until that small room smelled like the house of earth itself.

Each year, in late summer or early fall, I cut hay for the doghouses at a shallow pond not far from Canyon Creek. The native grass stood tawny and dry, cured by the sun, at the edge of the pond. It grew in dense bunches, and was tough and durable stuff. The heavy scythe made my arm ache with the long cutting, but the new hay smelled good where it lay behind me in the cool sunlight, waiting for the fork. When enough had been cut for the day, we piled the old box trailer high with it and drove home slowly, with a weighted canvas over the hay to keep it from blowing out onto the road.

Two such loads at least were needed for the long winter. I kept the hay piled on the ground, covered with canvas if the weather turned wet. When the tomato harvest was over and the vines were cleared from the benches, I forked the dry hay into a loose heap in the greenhouse where it would stay through the winter, free of snow. Now and then I shoved a forkful of it into each of the doghouses, while the dogs frisked and barked and tunneled into the new hay, glad for the clean dry bed.

Sometimes I got it late, when the hay had been partly bent by frost or an early snow. Then I went carefully with the scythe, pulling the hay upright and knocking it free of ice before I cut it. If the hay was too much broken down, I had to cut it by handfuls with a knife or a sickle, going slowly around the pond edge, while breaking underfoot the thin ice where the last water had frozen in the puddles. I laid the bundles of hay on a clean square of canvas, shaking them carefully free of frost and snow. When I stored that late, damp hay, I turned it from time to time, letting it cure slowly in the cold, dry air.

And there was a fall, late and snowy, when chores kept me from getting enough dry hay. One cloudy day in late October, with the temperature well below zero, I went up to the high, dry ridge behind the homestead. I dug in the shallow snow and pulled up what I could of the bent and smothered grass. I cut it, beat it free of snow, and carried a load of it home trussed up in a heavy roll of canvas.

Once more it is that time of year, of white smoke, of morning mist burned away by the sun. The leaves are falling, a nearly soundless patter on the root-matted floor of the forest. The last blueberries are sugared down, the pile of birch cordwood grows bigger in the yard; the pink-and-green-mottled chum salmon are running in the river channel. Against the damp green mosses lies the cold red brilliance of cranberries, like the blood of a perishing summer.

We come to them now for the sheer pleasure in gathering them, for the abundant freshness of them, and for the invoked goodness of past years when we picked them out of necessity, ten gallons or more, to be put down beside the sugared blueberries in the darkest and coldest part of the cellar.

We picked them on a dry day when we could, not while the dew or the rain was on them. But some years the fall came on wet, with day after day of rain and fog. And so we waited, doing our chores otherwise, of wood and bark and fish. That calm, dry day would come; we gathered our baskets and pails and headed uphill to the ridge, or down the road to Canyon Creek, wherever the crop was best that year.

And solitary as the work could be, crouched, kneeling, absorbed in the gathering, just the two of us picking in a shared silence along the road; more rarely the berry-picking became a kind of woodsy convocation. I remember how once at Richardson we longtime neighbors went out one afternoon for cranberries in a little gulch east of the Roadhouse. There were four or five of us spread out into the woods, each to his own part of the patch. And after a while we came back to where we had left the car, to find Billy Melvin, 87 years old, lying on his side in the moss, with his head supported by one hand, picking slowly and contentedly into the pail beside him.

The dry, firm berries kept well in a clean flour sack hung up in a cool place, or in a gallon jar with a loose lid. At Campbell's Lake Camp one fall, for want of a better place to store them, we put the jars of berries down in a shallow hole under a pile of hay to keep until November. They were all we had; no store-bought fruit, only the blue and the cran. They were tart, mealy and dry, and would not spoil. Cooked alone, or with rhubarb, or with occasional apples; eaten cold, half-frozen and sweet, with moose-ribs and potatoes, there was nothing better.

It's true that those gallons of berries, eaten day after day, would sometimes seem monotonous in a long winter, and we wished for something new and exotic like oranges and melons; but they were entirely free for the labor of picking and cleaning. And there was something else that would always be deeply associated with them, not easily defined, but a rich and persistent sense of having taken part in an ancient ritual, in the last rites of the season.

There are leaves floating in the rainbarrel. I brush them away with the dipper before filling the pail. Dry hay is curing in the sun; boxes of green tomatoes are ripening on the porch; about the house and the outbuildings there is the strong smell of curing onions, the half-sweet, half-sour odor of drying mushrooms. Cold meat hangs in the shade, the skinned quarters red and darkening to redder still, the white, sweet fat turning yellow. Flocks of pine grosbeaks are feeding on the late rosehips and berries on the slopes above the river; we hear, ever so faintly, their wintry cries in which there is always a tiny tinkle of ice. And over the Tanana and the Delta the cranes are gathering, the slow, gyring ascent of flock after flock, the rolling cries echoing over the dry sandbars, as they drift slowly south in the diminished light of the country.

So it must have been in Egypt, following on the annual flood, when the renewed soil gave back life to the sun; in Sumer, where two rivers water the arid plain, and in the high, dry maizefields of the Incas. In these sometimes slavish days of creaking pushcarts, of stacked and bewildering corridors, of green electronic figures winking, mysteriously multiplying an already insupportable debt, it is good to remember that earlier bounty; what it was to stoop down and lift something from the earth, dry tuber or damp mushroom; to close one's hand on the brown, crumbling soil, to sink one's fingers deep into the moss and feel the night and the frost that are waiting there; if only for a moment, to feel oneself once more at home on the earth.

Meanwhile, another day is almost gone. The snowline has dropped a little lower on the foothills, the air is perceptibly keener. The remaining rosehips wrinkle and dry on the thorny canes; dogwood sinks to a cold, dwarfed purple in the shade of the woods. There is a steely gray light on the river at evening, a light on these hills that sinks ever deeper through the yellowing birches.

Deborah Tall

Dwelling

Making Peace with Space and Place

from *Orion*

To say we dwell somewhere implies permanence, or at least continuity. But at root it means to pause, to linger or delay. We dwell on
a subject, but eventually give it up. So what does it mean to dwell
somewhere? How long do we have to stay?

A home and its land were once widely understood as belonging
to a family forever. Even today, most people in the world are born
and die within a radius of a few miles. But twenty to thirty percent
of Americans move each year, and the average American moves fourteen times over a lifetime. Permanent residence is at odds with our
notion of property—property as commodity, as route to profit
rather than something attained to keep. To change not just your
home or town, but the region of the country you live in, is understood as a way to change your life, and we aim to do that often. In
fact, to stay in one place for life is usually interpreted as being un-
ambitious, unadventurous—a negation of American values. Moving
up in the world means moving on.

The easy replacement of home ignores its emotional charge for
us, ignores how important familiarity is in the constitution of home.

Frequent dislocation, or the sudden destruction of a known environment, can be fundamentally deranging. It means the loss of personal landmarks—which embody the past—and the disintegration of a communal pattern of identity. People relocated from condemned slums, for instance, often suffer terribly. Home is where we know—and are known—through accumulated experience.

When an entire place or landscape is destroyed, the sense of betrayal and disorientation is acute. Harvey Cox recounts the shattering story of a Holocaust survivor from the Czech village of Lidice which shows such loss in the extreme:

> The Germans had arbitrarily picked this hamlet to be the example of what would happen to other villages. . . . They came into the town, shot all the men over twelve, then shipped the wives to one concentration camp and the children to another. They burned the village completely, destroyed all the trees and foliage and plowed up the ground. Significantly they demanded that on all maps of Czechoslovakia the town of Lidice must be erased. The woman survivor confessed to me that despite the loss of her husband and the extended separation from her children, the most shocking blow of all was to return to the crest of the hill overlooking Lidice at the end of the war—and to find nothing there, not even ruins.

The poetry of John Clare records a similar sense of violation, in his case as a result of the Enclosure Act, which, in the late eighteenth and early nineteenth centuries, vigorously transformed the common open-field system of rural England into private holdings in the name of efficiency. Instead of the long strips and winding trails of the old communal arrangement, small square fields and straight connecting roads were rapidly imposed on the land, virtually erasing its prior boundaries and landmarks. Even streams were diverted to fit the plan. The landscape was reconfigured on a blank map.

Inevitably, such a rapid transformation of landscape had profound personal and social consequences. Previously, a parish had been circular in conception, its village at the center of a ring of three or four large shared fields around which crops and cattle were ro-

tated. That was *Landschaft,* from which the word "landscape" derives. It stood for an ideal of habitation, of people's obligations to
one another and the land. A community had to cooperate and follow
traditional customs in order to survive; there was no place for personal idiosyncrasy or procrastination in such a world. Observes John
Barrell, "This obligatory submission to the ancient and customary
was no doubt part of what made open-field parishes—thus turned
in upon themselves—so mysterious to the improver, and so closed
to the traveller; and the effect of enclosure was of course to destroy
the sense of place which the old topography expressed, as it destroyed the topography itself."

All over Europe, from the Renaissance on, the landscape was increasingly divided as in England. A side effect was the prizing of
"shapeliness" in the land, regarding the landscape as a work of art.
Landschaft had become *landschap* in the hands of Dutch and Italian
painters. Landscape painting reflected the growing visual preference
for a landscape composed of balanced parts, while at the same time
it helped to disseminate that as an ideal. At its most extreme, says
Samuel Monk, "The lover of the picturesque was bent upon discovering not the world as it is, but the world as it might have been had
the Creator been an Italian artist of the seventeenth century."

Though enclosure was largely economic and agricultural in mo-
tive, it of course had aesthetic implications, too. And it made social
distinctions more visible—between rich and poor, between places
for work and leisure. It was in this landscape that the great English
gardens were created—by, as Raymond Williams puts it, "a self-
conscious observer [who] was very specifically the self-conscious
owner" of a pleasing stretch of land. It was in this landscape that private property provided both topographical and social place rather
than one's place being communally defined.

The notion of place in which one owns and cares for a plot of land
still exerts enormous influence on contemporary Americans. The
extent and condition of our property, and our choice of style in
dwelling, create a powerful emblem of our identity and status.

At the same time, though, we are awash in a landscape of mobility that eschews connections to particular plots. We are essentially utilitarian about the land, often lacking environmental conscience. Place has come to mean proximity to highways, shopping, and year-round recreation, rather than natural situation or character. In some ways, that's been liberating. In the hierarchy of landowners, admission to place is hard won and restricted; in the landscape of mobility, new communities—be they townhouse tracts or trailer parks—can crop up on the spot and rapidly assimilate new members. Yet we remain caught between nostalgia for place in its traditional sense and cool detachment. We've been told we live in a global village, which sounds a little like a *Landschaft,* but in truth, the technologically shrunken world has left us without much of a foothold.

Numerous modern writers have applauded the condition of "perpetual exile" as ethically healthy, a necessary severance from the sentimentalities of nationalism, for example. Others, though, prominently Simone Weil, have argued for attachment: "To be rooted is perhaps the most important and least recognized need of the human soul. . . . A human being has roots by virtue of his real, active, and natural participation in the life of a community, which preserves in living shape certain particular treasures of the past and certain particular expectations for the future."

Given how often I've moved, my community is widely scattered. My family and friends are deposited all over the continent. Crucial junctures in our lives take place in hospital hallways or over bad coffee in airports. Sometimes I feel stranded at the center of a fragmented orb, my life divided into a series of experiences and places that can never be brought together—except in the solitude of memory.

In many ways, though, our upbringings prepare us for this solitude. The privacy of the typical American home molds us in an image of separateness, turns us of necessity inward. Nowhere else in the world has isolation been such a common pattern of settlement as in America, especially historically in rural America. As settlers moved out onto the rectangular grids the country was carved into, their farmhouses were almost invariably set toward the middle of the plot, very rarely clustered at the corners near adjoining blocks of land so as to provide proximity to other families. (In Quebec, by contrast, farm plots were made long and narrow so that houses could be set side by side along a road.) No gathering of towns or villages was conceived of in the grand design of the grids; each family went it alone. The itinerant merchant materialized, and the mobile library; social life atrophied.

Such individualism and mobility are at the core of American identity. Admittedly, I am the observer and writer I am in part because of the freedom I have had to wander. Mobility is, for many of us, essential to personal and economic development. "Mobility is always the weapon of the underdog," says Harvey Cox. Yi-Fu Tuan, too, reminds us that rootlessness goes hand in hand with American ideals we tend to admire—social mobility and optimism about the future: "To be tied to place is also to be bound to one's station in life, with little hope of betterment. Space symbolizes hope; place, achievement and stability." A fixed place can obviously be seen as a trap, home to drudgery and hopelessness. "To be rooted is the property of vegetables," scoffs geographer David Sopher. To Sopher's mind, the prevailing "domicentric" bias in our thinking has turned "rootless" into the stigmatizing image of the shifty vagabond and made all wandering peoples suspicious—gypsies, tinkers, the Wandering Jew. When people are seen as lacking loyalty to a place, lacking perhaps even the ability to be loyal to places, it is easy to persecute them, see them as threatening to communal stability. The privileged and unadventurous may rightly fear that mobility threatens established traditions, and so they exaggerate the healthy attachment to place into rigid exclusivity and sentimentality. For the underprivileged or disaffected, though, mobility may represent a lifesaving escape, the eluding of oppressive inherited values and the stranglehold of tradition. For a phase of one's life, at the very least, it is a great relief to be free of the influences and expectations that a home place holds, just as one often needs to escape the clutches of one's family in order to mature. Place requires "encounters and obligations," says James Houston; it means accepting certain limitations. Space, on the other hand, is "the arena of freedom."

As a national ideal carried to an extreme, though, mobility has created the circumstances for widespread fragmentation and damage. The avoidance of ties to a place, ties which take years to build, removes constraints, allows us to be indifferent to our towns and cities, to ignore their plights, to say *but this isn't mine.*

In other traditions, a balance between wandering and staying is aspired to, the understanding that a full life involves both venturing out and returning. In the allegorical world of mythical and religious journeys, the greatest challenge of the journey is to return home, to share the lessons of one's experience, to incorporate the journey into its place of origin. While remaining in a single place can indeed be imprisoning, to wander compulsively makes one a noncitizen. There is a delicate dialectic to play out. "Before any choice," says French geographer Eric Dardel, "there is this place which we have not chosen, where the very foundation of our earthly existence and human condition establishes itself. We can change places, move, but this is still to look for a place, for this we need as a base to set down Being and to realize our possibilities—a *here* from which the world discloses itself, a *there* to which we can go." Or as Richard Hugo puts it, "If you are in Chicago you can go to Rome. If you ain't no place you can't go nowhere."

I come from a people in diaspora who only lightly touch the place on earth they happen to be living. My grandparents fled the pogroms of Russia and Eastern Europe, lost the coherence of their villages, but reestablished it, to some extent, in the immigrant streets of New York. Then their children, my parents, fled the city for an American-dream suburban life, severed from the intimate communities of their childhood. None of the many homes my parents made for me and my sister approached what they had come from—their goal was to get as far from that life, with its poverty and ghetto narrowness, as possible. But to me, the streets outside our increasingly pricey homes looked woefully mass-produced and bare—only something for us to buy into, move on from.

Housing developments still grieve me. Not only interchangeable and ubiquitous, they are an ominously forced form of neighborhood, house colors and landscape often strictly controlled. Even street names have been strangled into intimacy—moving beyond earlier schemes based on a theme (trees, race tracks), newer developments often choose a single name and cram together, say, a Windsor Court with a Windsor Mews, a Windsor Drive, Road, Avenue, Lane, and Place. A friend tells me how visiting his mother, having forgotten what Windsor she was living on, and all the houses an identical rosy beige, he drove around desperately in her car, pressing the garage-door opener, waiting to see which door would open to welcome in her car. It is no wonder that we return from these visits "home" dispirited.

Maybe my persistent yearning for a full-fledged home derives more from my Jewish background than I have allowed. Most American Jews come from irretrievably lost places. We remain half at home here, alert enough to pack in a hurry if need be, the ghost of the Holocaust too close for comfort. To not belong, to imagine constantly an elsewhere, becomes a chronic unease. It does not compel, or perhaps even allow, loyalty to one's present place. That is the resistance I'm trying to overcome. When the landscapes we find ourselves in are not diffused with *our* meanings, our history or community, it is easier to turn inward than to attempt to bridge the gap.

Historically, the physical life of Jews and other peoples in diaspora, in ghettos, was cramped and oppressive, often literally cut off from the cultures that surrounded and ruled them. In compensation, think some, the temporal dimension of Jews' lives—their history—gained disproportionate importance. "Their spatial existence was always a tenuous and painful reminder of their insulation from the surrounding world," says critic Stephen Kern. Identity had to be internalized, maintained free of attachment to its physical setting.

This tendency helped define the thinking and writing of many of this century's artists and intellectuals. Proust is a good example, a writer for whom the meaning of places depends entirely on their personal associations: "The places that we have known belong now only to the little world of space on which we map them for our own convenience. None of them was ever more than a thin slice held between the contiguous impressions that composed our life at that time; remembrance for a particular form is but regret for a particular moment, and houses, roads, avenues, are as fugitive, alas, as the years."

His plaint is close to my own sense of loss, but for Proust, the implications are more extreme. Says Kern: "If there is a single illusion that Proust most wanted to dispel it is that life takes place primarily in space. The spaces in which we live close about us and disappear like the waters of the sea after a ship passes through. To look for the essence of life in space is like trying to look for the path of the ship in the water: it only exists as a memory of the flow of its uninterrupted movement in time. The places where we happen to be are ephemeral and fortuitous settings for our life in time, and to try to recapture them is impossible." Places are ephemeral when they are treated as dispensable, when we are not embraced by their traditions, or when the traditions have drained away. Even for exiled modernist James Joyce, Dublin is what solidly persists when chronological time breaks down in his work and fantasy takes over. Place is the concrete, time the fluid. For most of us in this century, it is the reverse. "Most individuals feel almost naked without their wristwatches," notes Wilbur Zelinsky, "but how many carry compasses, maps, or field glasses . . . ?" We continuously, unconsciously, transform space into time, say a city is four hours away rather than two hundred miles.

E. V. Walter, a sociologist specializing in the study of place, points to Freud as another figure whose temperamental affiliation with time rather than space has had a crucial influence on our thinking. "Freud moved theory of the mind away from grounded experience and helped to build the couch as a vehicle abstracting patient from place. Despite his own existential recognition of the inner need that yearns for place, Freud's psychology never integrated personal identity with the sense of belonging, and the real power of places."

Freud even rejects the rich spatial metaphor he invents in *Civilization and Its Discontents* to explain the mind. There, Freud asks us to imagine the city of Rome with its past entirely visible alongside the present, relics from previous periods occupying the same space as contemporary buildings. But just as we construct such a Rome in our minds, Freud abruptly dismisses the notion—because it's physically impossible. The Rome Freud suggests, though, where Renaissance palaces, ancient walls, temples, and modern office buildings would vie for our attention, is exactly the kind of place the willing visitor creates with tourist manuals and an open mind. In Rome, more than in most other places, it's possible to experience a vivid sense of the continuity of human generations in a single place. Rome is an ideal metaphor, in truth, for the landscape of fantasy and memory.

Freud uses archaeological metaphors freely elsewhere in his writings, describing the "unearthing" of his patients' pasts and the "relics" of their experiences, yet he allies the cacophonous mental experience of places with hysteria. The mnemonic symbols of cities, for instance—monuments and memorials—are seen as comparable to irrepressible memories of traumatic experience: "Every hysteric and neurotic behaves like a Londoner who might pause in deep melancholy before the memorial of Queen Eleanor's funeral, instead of going about his business, or who might shed tears before the monument that recalls the ashes of the metropolis, although it has long since risen again in far greater brilliance. Hysterical patients suffer from reminiscences." Instead of recognizing that the symbols and memories of a place are the way people can integrate themselves with a culture, Freud thinks of them as a curable disease. "It seems almost as if he were advocating an indifference to one's environment," historian Joseph Rykwert says.

Wendell Berry, too, wishes psychotherapy were more conscious about restoring our connection to places—"The lost identity would find itself by recognizing physical landmarks, by connecting itself responsibly to practical circumstances." But that is not, typically, how nowadays we "find" ourselves.

We almost cannot, when the stage sets on which we play out our lives are struck with each act. We are left only the plot. The where of our immediate past is often unrecognizable, our further past unlocatable. Many of us are unable to trace our ancestry beyond a generation or two. Even if we can, we have little idea, often, of *what* we've come from, what places have helped to shape our values and temperaments.

Lacking that connection, as most of us do now, how do we come to feel loyal to a place and choose to dwell there? What makes a location even *feel* like a place at all? In my own life, transplanted to upstate New York, I have been hunting down stories, discovering what's legible and instructive in my landscape. In thirteen years here, I have found festering wounds beneath fine scenery, but I have found as well a palimpsest of lives by which I might patch together a sense of connection. My place's traditions are not my own; I have had to adopt them. But having a sense of place may, by now, require a continual act of imagination.

Contributors

Jennifer Ackerman's articles and essays have appeared in *The New York Times, The Nature Conservancy,* and *National Geographic,* where she works as an editor. Her first book, *Notes from the Shore,* which was devoted to the coastal regions of Delaware, was published by Viking in 1995. Like Jan DeBlieu, who lives and writes in North Carolina (*Hatteras Journal*), Ackerman shows every promise of becoming as strong and lyric a voice for the sea as Rachel Carson.

Rick Bass has authored such celebrated works as *The Deer Pasture, Wild to the Heart, Ninemile Wolves, The Watch, Platte River,* and *In the Loyal Mountains.* He resides in the northwestern mountains of Montana with his wife, Elizabeth, and their two daughters. His essays are often seen in such publications as *Audubon, Outside,* and *Sports Afield.* In recent years he has been actively involved in the effort to designate additional wilderness units in Montana, particularly in his home region in the Yaak River Valley.

Marcia Bonta's first book, *Appalachian Autumn,* was published by the University of Pittsburgh Press in 1995. She and her husband live in the Appalachian Mountains of Pennsylvania.

Kate Boyes resides in Logan, Utah, where she is an editor for the important scholarly journal *Western American Literature.* Her essays have been published widely in literary journals.

President Jimmy Carter served in America's highest elected office from January 1977 through January 1981. One of his most notable achievements was signing into law the landmark Alaska Lands Act in 1980. President Carter's many essays on hunting, fishing, mountain climbing, and hiking were recently published in *An Outdoor Journal: Adventures and Reflections.* He has enjoyed the most active retirement of any American president to date, a busy two decades that have included homebuilding for the poor, furniture-making, peacemaking in regions as remote as Haiti and North Korea, fly-fishing, mountain climbing (Kilimanjaro, various peaks in the Himalayas), and syndicated column writing.

Dan Duane is a doctoral student in American Literature at the University of California, Santa Cruz. The son of a surfer of the 1950s and 1960s, Duane surfs every chance he can get. His book *Caught Inside: A Surfer's Year on the Pacific Coast,* will be published by North Point Press, an imprint of Farrar, Straus & Giroux, in 1997.

Robert Finch teaches English at Middlebury College. He has published three classic books about Cape Cod, namely, *Common Ground: A Naturalist's Cape Cod, Outlands: Journeys to the Outer Edges of Cape Cod,* and *The Primal Place.*

Jan Grover lives and works in Minneapolis, Minnesota, where she also pursues a career in freelance writing. "Cutover" is her first publication.

John Haines—poet, naturalist, and essayist—lived for more than forty years on a homestead along the Tanana River in northern Alaska. His book of essays on that experience, *The Stars, the Snow, the Fire,* is one of the finest memoirs ever written about life in the far north. Haines has taught at a number of universities and holds an honorary doctorate from the University of Alaska. His volume of collected poems, *The Owl in the Mask of the Dreamer,* won the 1993 Western American Writer Award for the best book of poetry.

Linda Hasselstrom is the author of the classic memoir *Land Circle,* which chronicles her life on a South Dakota cattle ranch, as well as the death of her husband from cancer. She comes out of a long line of American authors who have sought the healing force of the Great Plains: Francis Parkman, Theodore Roosevelt, Dan O'Brien. In 1990 she became the first woman to ever win a Western American Writer Award.

Marybeth S. Holleman teaches English at the University of Alaska in Anchorage where she lives with her preschool son. She has published widely in literary journals and periodicals.

James Kilgo is a professor of English at the University of Georgia, Athens. He has authored two critically acclaimed works, *Deep Enough for Ivory-Bills,* and *An Inheritance of Horses,* and is an avid outdoorsman, hiking, hunting, and fishing whenever possible.

Barry Lopez grew up in southern California and New York City and later graduated from the University of Notre Dame in Indiana. He has authored such influential works as *Of Wolves and Men, Arctic Dreams* (winner of the National Book Award), *Crossing Open Ground, Winter Notes, Desert Notes,* and *The Rediscovery of North America.* He lives with his wife, Sandra, an artist, in the Cascade Mountains of Oregon.

Judith Larner Lowry learned about California native plants, the subject of her essay, "Gardening at the Seam," while working at nurseries. She is now the proprietor of Larner Seeds, which specializes in the seeds of California native plants. Lowry is finishing a book on gardening with native plants. She lives in northern California.

Gregory McNamee has lived for many years in Tucson, Arizona. He was for a time the editor of the University of Arizona Press, and now writes professionally full-time. His books include *Gila: The Life and Death of an American River, In the Presence of Wolves,* and *The Sierra Club Book of Deserts: A Literary Journal.*

Gary Nabhan holds a doctorate in ethnobotany from the University of Arizona, Tucson. He has gained an international reputation for his pioneering work in the conservation of desert plant seeds. Among his books is *Gathering the Desert,* which was awarded the John Burroughs Medal for Nature Writing. Nabhan is a former MacArthur fellow.

Adele Ne Jame teaches English at the University of Hawaii, Honolulu, and publishes often in literary journals around the country. In 1995 she was nominated for a Whiting Award in poetry.

Richard Nelson has spent his career as a cultural anthropologist in Alaska, where he has devoted himself to the study and preservation of indigenous peoples. His many seminal works include *Hunters of the Northern Ice, Hunters of the Northern Forest,* and *Make Prayers to the Raven.* In 1991 he published *The Island Within,* which was devoted to an island near his home on the Pacific coast and was awarded the John Burroughs Medal for Nature Writing. In 1995 he was awarded the $50,000 Lannan Literary Award.

David Petersen lives in a cabin with his wife, Carolyn, in the San Juan Mountains of Colorado. His books include *Among the Aspen, Racks, Among the Elk, Big Sky, Fair Land: The Environmental Writings of A. B. Guthrie,* and, most recently, *Ghost Grizzlies*. He is also editor of the journals of Edward Abbey, *Confessions of a Barbarian*, as well as Abbey's collected poems, *Earth Apples*. Petersen is currently editing a collection of hunting essays, *The Hunter's Heart*, to be published by Henry Holt in 1997. His articles are often seen in *Sports Afield, Backpacker*, and other national magazines.

Brenda Peterson—novelist, naturalist, and essayist—makes her home in Seattle, Washington, where she writes about nature and human life in the Pacific Northwest. Her first nature book, *Living by Water*, was warmly received, and her articles are frequently featured in popular periodicals such as *Sierra* and *Outside*. Among her latest books is *Nature and Other Mothers*.

Rosalie Sanara Petrouske lives on the Upper Peninsula of Michigan. Her essay "The Root of the Universe" was published in *Paintbrush: The World of N. Scott Momaday*, a special monograph.

Adrienne Ross lives and works in Seattle, Washington, but spends as much time as she can on the beaches and in the forests of the Pacific Northwest. She is a freelance environmental writer.

Frank Stewart is a distinguished professor of creative writing at the University of Hawaii, Honolulu. He has published several books of poetry, edits the journal *Manoa*, and was a Whiting Award winner in poetry. Stewart maintains a three-acre farm on the big island of Hawaii, where he spends time when not teaching or traveling.

Deborah Tall is an English professor at Hobart and William Smith Colleges, where she edits the poetry journal *Seneca Review*. Tall has published three poetry books and a personal memoir, *The Island of the White Cow*. She is married to the poet David Weiss and lives in Ithaca, New York, with him and their two daughters, Zoe and Clea.

Louise Wagenknecht was born and raised in Idaho, where she has worked as a seasonal firefighter for the Forest Service and Bureau of Land Management for twenty years. She and her husband maintain a small sheep ranch in Idaho. She has a bachelor's degree in English literature and writes periodically on topics of interest—such as firefighting and logging—for *High Country News*. She is working on a book about the environmental and economic upheavals that have transformed the Pacific Northwest in her lifetime.

David Rains Wallace is the author of over a dozen works of natural history, including *The Dark Range, Idle Weeds, The Klamath Knot, Bulow Hammock,* and *The Quetzal and the Macaw. The Klamath Knot* was awarded the John Burroughs Medal for Nature Writing in 1983. Wallace has also authored two novels, *The Turquoise Dragon* and *The Vermilion Parrot.* He and his wife Betsy, an artist, make their home in Berkeley, California.

Terry Tempest Williams has authored four acclaimed nature books: *Pieces of White Shell: A Journey to Navajoland, Coyote's Canyon, Refuge: An Unnatural History of Family and Place,* and *An Unspoken Hunger.* She works as a naturalist for the Utah Museum of Natural History and lives with her husband in the mountains outside Salt Lake City. The essay included here is from her recently published book, *Desert Quartet.*

Edward O. Wilson is Baird Professor of Science at Harvard University. He has devoted his career to the study of nature in tropical regions. His books include *Sociobiology, On Human Nature, Biophilia, The Ants,* and *The Diversity of Life.* Wilson has twice been awarded the Pulitzer Prize for general nonfiction and is widely respected around the world for his leadership on the biodiversity issue.

Periodicals Consulted

Alaska Quarterly Review, Department of English, 3221 Providence Drive, Anchorage, Alaska 99508

American Poetry Review, 1721 Walnut Street, Philadelphia, Pennsylvania 19103

Antaeus, Ecco Press, 26 West 17th Street, New York, New York 10011

The Antioch Review, P.O. Box 148, Yellow Springs, Ohio 45387

Arizona Quarterly, Department of English, University of Arizona, Tucson, Arizona 85721

The Atlantic Monthly, 745 Boylston Street, Boston, Massachusetts 02116

Audubon, 700 Broadway, New York, New York 10003

Backpacker, 33 East Minor Street, Emmaus, Pennsylvania 18098

Chicago Review, 5801 South Kenwood, Chicago, Illinois 60637

Cimarron Review, 205 Morril Hall, Oklahoma State University, Stillwater, Oklahoma 74078

Colorado Review, 360 Eddy Building, Colorado State University, Fort Collins, Colorado 80523

Denver Quarterly, Department of English, University of Denver, Denver, Colorado 80210

Esquire, 1790 Broadway, New York, New York 10019

Florida Review, Department of English, University of Central Florida, Orlando, Florida 32816

The Georgia Review, University of Georgia, Athens, Georgia 30602

The Gettysburg Review, Gettysburg College, Gettysburg, Pennsylvania 17325

Harper's Magazine, 2 Park Avenue, New York, New York 10016

Hawaii Pacific Review, 1060 Bishop Street, Honolulu, Hawaii 96813

Hawaii Review, Department of English, University of Hawaii, 1733 Donaghho Road, Honolulu, Hawaii 96822

Indiana Review, 316 North Jordan Avenue, Indiana University, Bloomington, Indiana 47405

Kansas Quarterly, Department of English, Denison Hall, Kansas State University, Manhattan, Kansas 66506

The Kenyon Review, Kenyon College, Gambier, Ohio 43022

Manoa, Department of English, University of Hawaii, 1733 Donaghho Road, Honolulu, Hawaii 96822

The Massachusetts Review, Memorial Hall, University of Massachusetts, Amherst, Massachusetts 01002

Michigan Quarterly Review, 3032 Rackham Building, University of Michigan, Ann Arbor, Michigan 48109

Minnesota Monthly, 15 South 9th Street, Suite 320, Minneapolis, Minnesota 55402

The Missouri Review, 1507 Hillcrest Hall, University of Missouri, Columbia, Missouri 65211

Nebraska Review, Department of English, University of Nebraska, Omaha, Nebraska 68182

New England Review, Middlebury College, Middlebury, Vermont 05753

New Mexico Humanities Review, Department of English, New Mexico Tech, Socorro, New Mexico 57801

The New Yorker, 20 West 43rd Street, New York, New York 10036

Nimrod, Arts and Humanities Council of Tulsa, 2210 South Main, Tulsa, Oklahoma 74114

The North American Review, University of Northern Iowa, 1227 West 27th Street, Cedar Falls, Iowa 50613

North Atlantic Review, 15 Arbutus Lane, Stony Brook, New York 11790

North Dakota Quarterly, University of North Dakota, Box 8237, Grand Forks, North Dakota 58202

The Ohio Review, Department of English, Ellis Hall, Ohio University, Athens, Ohio 45701

Orion, 136 East 64th Street, New York, New York 10021

Outside, 1165 North Clark Street, Chicago, Illinois 60610

Pacific Discovery, Golden Gate Park, San Francisco, California 94118

The Paris Review, 541 East 72nd Street, New York, New York 10021

Prairie Schooner, Andrews Hall, University of Nebraska, Lincoln, Nebraska 68588

Puerto Del Sol, Department of English, New Mexico State University, Las Cruces, New Mexico 88003

Santa Monica Review, Center for the Humanities at Santa Monica College, 1900 Pico Boulevard, Santa Monica, California 90405

The Sewanee Review, University of the South, Sewanee, Tennessee 37375

Sierra, 730 Polk Street, San Francisco, California 94109

Sonora Review, Department of English, University of Arizona, Tucson, Arizona 85721

South Carolina Review, Department of English, Clemson University, Clemson, South Carolina 29634

South Dakota Review, Box 111, University Exchange, Vermillion, South Dakota 57069

Southern Humanities Review, Department of English, Auburn University, Auburn, Alabama 36830

The Southern Review, Drawer D, University Station, Baton Rouge, Louisiana 70803

Southwest Review, Southern Methodist University, Dallas, Texas 75275

Tampa Review, Box 19F, University of Tampa, 401 West Kennedy Boulevard, Tampa, Florida 33606

The Threepenny Review, P.O. Box 9131, Berkeley, California 94709

The Village Voice Literary Supplement, 842 Broadway, New York, New York 10003

The Virginia Quarterly Review, Department of English, University of Virginia, Charlottesville, Virginia 22903

Wilderness, 900 17th Street N.W., Washington, D.C. 20006

ZYZZYVA, 41 Sutter Street, Suite 1400, San Francisco, California 94104

Permissions

Jennifer Ackerman: "The Great Salt Marsh," from *Notes from the Shore.* Copyright 1995 by Viking Penguin. Reprinted with permission of Viking Penguin, a division of Penguin Books USA Inc.

Rick Bass: "Thunder & Lightning," first appeared in *Sierra.* Copyright 1995 by Rick Bass. Reprinted with permission of the author.

Marcia Bonta: "October," from *Appalachian Autumn.* Copyright 1995 by Marcia Bonta. Reprinted with permission of the University of Pittsburgh Press.

Kate Boyes: "Confluence," from *Weber Studies.* Copyright 1995 by Kate Boyes. Published with permission of the author.

President Jimmy Carter: "The Forty-ninth State, but Not in Fishing," from *Outdoor Journal: Adventures and Reflections.* Copyright 1995 by President Jimmy Carter. Reprinted with permission of the author and the University of Arkansas Press.

Dan Duane: "Sharks," from *Caught Inside: A Surfer's Year on the Pacific Coast,* work in progress. Copyright 1995 by Dan Duane. Published with permission of the author.

Robert Finch: "Saving the Whales," from the anthology *The Nature of Nature.* Copyright 1995 by Robert Finch. Reprinted with permission of the author.

Jan Grover: "Cutover," first publication. Copyright 1995 by Jan Grover. Published with permission of the author.

John Haines: "Days in the Field," from *Alaska Quarterly Journal.* Copyright 1995 by John Haines. Reprinted with permission of the author.

Linda Hasselstrom: "The Song of the Turtle," first publication. Copyright 1995 by Linda Hasselstrom. Published with permission of the author.